The Legacy of Hurricane Mitch

Lessons from Post-Disaster Reconstruction in Honduras

Edited by
Marisa O. Ensor

The University of Arizona Press Tucson

The University of Arizona Press

www.uapress.arizona.edu

Library of Congress Cataloging-in-Publication Data

The legacy of Hurricane Mitch : lessons from post-disaster reconstruction in Honduras / edited by Marisa O. Ensor.
p. cm.
Includes bibliographical references and index.
ISBN 978-0-8165-2784-7 (hardcover : alk. paper) — ISBN 978-0-8165-2785-4 (pbk. : alk. paper)
1. Hurricane Mitch, 1998—Honduras. 2. Hurricane damage—Honduras. 3. Hurricanes—Honduras. 4. Disaster relief—Honduras. 5. Hurricane Mitch, 1998—Economic aspects—Honduras. I. Ensor, Marisa O.
HV6361998 .H866 2009
363.34'922—dc22

2009026159

Publication of this book is made possible in part by the proceeds of a permanent endowment created with the assistance of a Challenge Grant from the National Endowment for the Humanities, a federal agency.

♻
Manufactured in the United States of America on acid-free, archival-quality paper containing a minimum of 30% post-consumer waste and processed chlorine free.

14 13 12 11 10 09 6 5 4 3 2 1

To the great women and men of Honduras, survivors of so many crises, who shared with us their experiences, ideas, and homes—whether a house or a space in a disaster shelter. This work is a tribute to their courage and resilience in the face of formidable odds. May it contribute to the generation of knowledge that can lead to better disaster response and more effective efforts to help people improve their own lives.

Contents

Figures

Tables

Preface

There is a common assumption that, under the right circumstances, disasters may create a "window of opportunity" for fresh starts, new possibilities, and even positive change. Post-Mitch Honduras has not experienced the grand transformation that was hailed in the Stockholm Declaration—a statement issued by a group of experts and donors who met in the Swedish capital to develop guidelines for post-disaster reconstruction in the aftermath of Mitch. Nevertheless, Hurricane Mitch did create the stimulus for a considerable measure of legislative reform, a strengthening of civil society, increased international investment, and other potentially significant political and social changes. It even provided the population with a new way of measuring time. People ask: "*Was that before or after Mitch?*" when they want to establish a frame of reference for some other event. Hurricane Mitch provoked the worst disaster ever experienced in Honduras. Its impact was so massive, so pervasive and all-encompassing, that current conditions in the country can accurately be described as "the legacy of Hurricane Mitch."

For some of us, Hurricane Mitch marked the beginning of an intellectually exciting, and often challenging, process of longitudinal and ongoing field research. Others had been working in Honduras for years prior to the disaster. For all of us, the aftermath of Mitch started a period of intense collaborative work, culminating with the development of this collection. Almost ten years elapsed between the fateful days in late October 1998 when Mitch swept over Central America and the time this volume was completed in 2008. In the interim, the world has witnessed the growing frequency and magnitude of disasters and humanitarian emergencies of all kinds, resulting in enormous loss of livelihood and infrastructure.

In Honduras, recovery from Mitch was made more difficult by the severe droughts that affected the country in 2001 and 2002. In contrast, intense flooding and mudslides caused by Hurricanes Katrina, Stan, Wilma, Beta, and Gamma damaged houses and destroyed infrastructure and crops along the Honduran Atlantic and Pacific coasts in 2005. Many other locations across the globe have been ravaged by disasters in the last few years. Landslides killed hundreds and displaced thousands in the Philippines in 2003 and 2006; survivors of the 2005 earthquake in Pakistan are still under the care of the UN Refugee Agency; and Hurricane Katrina devastated the Gulf Coast of the United States in 2005. That same year, India, Germany, and Switzerland were subject to extreme flooding while extensive bushfires and severe droughts ravaged areas of Spain and Portugal. Indonesia suffered the disastrous effects of a massive tsunami in 2004, a powerful earthquake in 2006, and yet another tsunami the same year. These and other catastrophic events in both developed and developing nations around the world have brought a renewed awareness of the urgent need to provide effective and sustainable solutions to the challenges of post-disaster recovery and reconstruction.

In the last decade, significant developments have taken place in the field of disaster scholarship and practice. The increasing realization of the limits of technocratic approaches that view catastrophes only as natural phenomena has been coupled with the recognition that disasters are not simply chance events. Rather, they result from patterns of vulnerability embedded in natural and sociocultural systems. A well-grounded understanding of the structures of vulnerability is the first step toward meaningful mitigation, and this presupposes a more thorough examination of the root causes of catastrophes, including poverty, inequality, underdevelopment, and environmentally unsound practices. The global trend toward increasingly destructive disasters further underscores the necessity of generating new knowledge, sharing existing information, and building on the lessons learned from field research. However, there are still very few examples of long-term studies of post-disaster reconstruction experiences throughout the world. Currently, most of the information available is contained in internal reports and working papers produced by governmental, nongovernmental, and international relief agencies in the aftermath of each catastrophic event.

This book complements the available literature on post-disaster reconstruction by offering a fieldwork-based, scholarly analysis of the impact of Hurricane Mitch in Honduras and of the role of international, national, and local entities in the subsequent reconstruction processes. The case of post-Mitch Honduras exemplifies the inadequacies of post-disaster recovery efforts that limit themselves to alleviating the symptoms, rather than confronting the root causes, of the social and environmental vulnerabilities that prefigured the disaster. Ten years after the event, the long-term consequences of the recovery efforts implemented in Honduras after Hurricane Mitch remain a largely underresearched topic—but one that, we believe, has potentially great application in other cases of post-disaster reconstruction.

Around the world, vulnerability to disasters is on the rise. Current UN predictions estimate that by 2010 as many as 50 million people will be displaced by disasters and related management policies. We might not be able to stop the "natural" phenomena that trigger catastrophes, but we can and must better equip individuals and communities to mitigate and withstand their impact. It is our hope that this volume will encourage the sharing of lessons learned and contribute to the establishment of effective practices that lead to the increased well-being and resilience of those involved.

The Legacy of Hurricane Mitch

1
Understanding Hurricane Mitch
Complexity, Causality, and the Political Ecology of Disaster

Anthony Oliver-Smith

Hurricane Mitch

When Hurricane Mitch made landfall in eastern Honduras in late October of 1998, in many ways it exemplified a more complex form of disaster that seems to be emerging in the late twentieth and early twenty-first centuries. This complexity is rooted in the increasing diversity of forces, both natural and social, that are creating more frequent and more intense climatological hazards, more environments altered in ways that accentuate hazard impacts, and more populations living in conditions of greater exposure and vulnerability. In terms of complexity and causality, there are clear similarities between, for example, Hurricane Mitch in 1998 and Hurricane Katrina in 2005, although one occurred in a small, poor, and underdeveloped nation and the other in a large, wealthy, and developed nation. In both circumstances an intense natural force encountered a society whose environment, infrastructure, and population had been rendered severely vulnerable by social and economic processes deeply embedded in particular approaches to development. Thus, it was not just a case of people living in harm's way; rather, conditions of vulnerability were created largely through human action on the environment. It is highly likely that we will see far too many more events like Mitch and Katrina as the century advances unless measures are taken to ameliorate the conditions of vulnerability that characterize many regions, both developed and underdeveloped, around the world.

My goal in this opening chapter is to provide a theoretical and conceptual background for the analyses of various aspects of Hurricane Mitch offered by the authors in this volume. That is, it is important that Hurricane Mitch not be passed off as simply a natural disaster that punished the people of Honduras. The studies in this book of the death, devastation, and misery left in Hurricane Mitch's wake challenge that interpretation directly; they seek an understanding of the causes and outcomes of Hurricane Mitch within the social, economic, and environmental history of Honduras as it developed within the international community. In order to grasp the crisis that Mitch presented, the complex sources of pre-disaster vulnerability that prefigured and in many ways caused the catastrophe must be seriously grappled with in order to avoid reproducing those conditions and thereby preparing the ground for the next disaster. In that sense, we need to recognize that disasters involve far more than catastrophic events. They are processes that unfold through time, and their beginnings are deeply embedded in societal history. As such, disasters have historical roots, unfolding presents, and potential futures that proceed according to the forms of reconstruction that are undertaken. Such concerns relate directly to the relationship between humans and nature and to strategies for more sustainable forms of development.

Ethnography and Disasters: A Note on Method

Whether their onset is rapid or slow, disasters and the vulnerability leading to them unfold over time—often considerable amounts of time. Likewise, the socioculturally conditioned responses to disasters transpire both relationally and historically. Disasters have pasts, presents, and futures, which may arise from events, such as earthquakes, that people consider to be sudden or from those, such as droughts or toxic exposures, that occur unperceived over long periods only to be recognized well after their initial manifestations. As eminently social events, disasters and responses to them are worked out via complex interactions and discourses in which the needs and interests of many involved individuals, groups, and organizations are articulated and negotiated over the often extended duration of the catastrophe.

Much important data about disasters can be gathered by synchronic (i.e., strictly contemporaneous) slices based on questionnaires, surveys, and "crash" emergency overviews, but the actual processes by which people and communities respond to risk, threat, vulnerability, impact, and recovery are best understood through on-site ethnographic research. The value of ethnographic research is particularly evident in the process of reconstruction, when people must traverse the difficult path between restoration and change. After destruction, the process of negotiation between what should be reconstituted and what should be replaced generally involves tensions among diverse interest groups and values. Methods that privilege narrative and observation—with researchers present and in dialogue with participants to gather local knowledge and information—are far more appropriate for exploring the process of adjustment and recovery than are synchronic forms of research (Oliver-Smith and Hoffman 2002).

Furthermore, disasters—no matter how large in area—are experienced first at a local level. Even an enormous disaster affecting great areas and legions of people—and resulting from a single climatological, geological, or technological phenomenon—ultimately comes down to a compendium of local but related disasters experienced throughout the region and across the numbers and diversity of affected people. Not all communities experience a disaster in the same way or to the same degree. Each community—indeed, each individual—undergoes a catastrophe in the context of a particular profile of vulnerability. The same disaster agent will show great variation in patterns of destruction as well as in interpretation of cause, effect, and responsibility. Such variation challenges a more global, macro approach, yet understanding the total phenomenon, both physically and socially, remains necessary. As a result, disasters compel us to pair multisite ethnography with quantitative methods capable of higher levels of aggregation (Oliver-Smith and Hoffman 2002; Hilhorst 2003).

The spatial-temporal frameworks of disaster research have been relatively narrow, primarily event and site focused. Perhaps this emphasis on the event and site is understandable, given the nature of many disasters as sudden and often dramatic moments in the lives of communities and regions. The short-term emergency and relief stages have captured the overwhelming majority of the attention from social scientists, owing in large part to the traditional definition of disaster as a mainly sociopsychological phenomenon, where the focus is on the behavior of persons and groups in a specific context of disruption and/or damage. However, more recent perspectives on the historical and structural features of disasters have led to increased attention being paid to such longitudinal issues as displacement, forced migration, and reconstruction. Given this new perspective, research should shift from an exclusive focus on the disaster site to greater attention to the multiple sites where policies and practices are developed and where the outcomes are played out. Longitudinal and multisite ethnographic research requires substantial changes in field methods and poses significant challenges for data acquisition and management.

The information presented in this book is primarily drawn from the work of a group of researchers that formed in the winter and spring of 1998–1999. Beginning as a discussion group of eight to ten people at my home in Gainesville, Florida, eventually five people—four anthropologists and a political scientist—undertook a series of research projects on Hurricane Mitch and its aftermath. Funding from various sources (including the International Hurricane Center at Florida International University and the National Science Foundation) was acquired during the six months following Hurricane Mitch. Research was carried out from the summer of 1999 through 2001 on such topics as pre- and post-disaster nutritional patterns among children affected by Mitch (Stansbury et al. 2001), economic diversification in post-disaster frontier areas (DeVries 2000), changes in governance after Mitch (Fuentes 2003), disaster reconstruction and resettlement (Olivo Díaz López 2002), and alternative approaches to post-disaster reconstruction (Barrios 2004) in various regions of Honduras. All the research projects were fundamentally ethnographic in nature, although other methods (both quantitative and qualitative) were also employed. The subsequent addition of William Loker and Manuel Winograd to the project also reflected this ethnographic focus and methodological diversity. Loker's ethnographic narrative captures elements of the experience of rural people facing threat and destruction, details that would be unavailable through other methods. Manuel Winograd describes a reality of vulnerable conditions and proposes a method to assess them based on quantitative and qualitative data that must be gathered and understood through a long-term, on-site presence.

Disaster in Ecological Perspective

In seeking an ecological perspective on disasters, the focus is on the effectiveness of societal adaptation to the total environment, including the natural, modified, and constructed contexts and processes of which the community is a part. Human communities and their behaviors are not simply located in environments. The interface between society and environment is not one of "external contact between separate domains" (Ingold 1992:51). That is, environments are experienced by people, and from that experience emerge the constructs of their culture and social organization. Thus, the development of a society is also the development of its environment, and the resulting relations emerge from multiple and continual processes of exchange through their porous boundaries. Society and environment are interpenetrating and mutually constitutive of the same world, one that consists of the meanings and actions imputed to the inhabitants' capabilities and the possibilities for action provided by natural, modified, and built environments (Ingold 1992:52).

Disasters do not inhere in societies; they inhere in societal-environmental relations. But societal-environmental relations are not relations between two separate entities but rather between two mutually constitutive entities. Environmental features and processes become socially defined and structured just as social elements acquire environmental identities and expressions. Disasters exemplify this interpenetration of society and nature. Thus, any understanding of disaster must be grounded in a theoretical approach that is capable of encompassing the web of relations that link society (the organization of and relations among individuals and groups), environment (the network of linkages with the physical world in which people live and by which they are constituted), and culture (the values, norms, beliefs, attitudes, and knowledge that pertain to that organization and those relations) (Oliver-Smith 2002, 2004).

For a disaster to occur, a necessary (but not sufficient) condition is the conjuncture of (1) a human population and (2) a potentially destructive agent that is part of the total ecological system—including all natural, modified, and constructed features—occupied by the human population. Societies and destructive agents both extend through time, so together they define disaster as an ongoing phenomenon, not an event that is isolated and temporally demarcated. However, the conjuncture of a human population and a potentially destructive agent do not inevitably produce a disaster. A disaster is made inevitable only by a historically produced pattern of vulnerability, as evidenced by the location, infrastructure, sociopolitical organization, production patterns, and ideology that characterize a society. That is, a society's pattern of vulnerability is an essential element of a disaster. This pattern of vulnerability will condition the behavior of individuals and organizations, throughout a disaster's history, far more profoundly than will the physical force of the destructive agent.

Clearly, the question of time becomes crucial if vulnerability is considered essential to the definition of disaster. Both the event dimension and the process dimension of a disaster are traditionally characterized by (1) the appearance of a threat that generates a warning as the initiation point, (2) a process of development through a number of conditions or stages (impact, post-impact emergency, etc.), and (3) some return to stability/normality through reconstruction. All these stages are experienced differently by varying social groups. Yet I would suggest that the life history of a disaster begins *prior* to the appearance of a specific, event-focused agent. Indeed, in certain circumstances (e.g., location in a flood plain), hazards and disasters become part of the profile of any human system at its first organizational moment in a relatively fixed location or area. From my perspective, then, an ecological approach is the one most capable of encompassing the cause and effect of disasters, their development as social and environmental processes and events, their sociocultural construction, and their implications for the community's overall sociocultural adaptation and evolution (Bates and Pelanda 1994:147).

A general ecological approach to disasters is founded on the view that a human population and its sociocultural system—including all the social, economic, political, and technological systems that people generate in their adaptations (or maladaptations)—are an element within a total natural system. The sociocultural system is the primary means by which a human population adapts to its environment, enabling a community to extract food, water, shelter, energy, and other necessities from that environment and to confront and reduce the uncertainty and vulnerability experienced when a community is forced to interact with environmental conditions and forces that threaten its members (Bates and Pelanda 1994:149). To some extent, the forces and conditions in the natural or modified environments in which disasters occur are adaptational challenges to which the community must (but does not always) adequately respond. Insofar as it is impossible to guard against every threat completely, all systems have some degree of inherent vulnerability.

A Political Ecology of Disaster

However, the danger in thinking about adaptation in general—or about disasters in particular—in terms of general ecology is that the human system is usually formulated as a unitary element, one of many that interact in a pattern of energy flows with other elements in the total system. The human population and its intricate sociocultural system thereby becomes a "black box," devoid of internal characteristics, when it is obviously complex and internally differentiated. This complex internal differentiation, which characterizes all but the earliest levels of sociocultural integration, may distribute the benefits of adaptational effectiveness in widely disparate ways in the short term and also in the long term. From this perspective, the patterns of adaptation that evolve in social systems may be effective generally or they may be effective for those favored by the societal power relations or patterns of production and allocation yet ineffective for those not so favored. The same patterns of adaptation that are reasonably effective in the short run may just as well sow the seeds of future vulnerability and disasters in the long run. Research within contemporary human societies thus requires the combination of an ecological framework with an analytical strategy that can encompass the interaction of environmental features with the nature and effects of each society's patterns of production, allocation, and internal differentiation. This strategy also reflects the fact that societies, as adaptive systems, are controlled by contesting interests; thus some sectors are privileged with enhanced security while others are subjected to systemic risks and hazards.

In essence, what we need is a political ecology of disasters. Political ecology situates an ecologically grounded social scientific perspective within a political economy framework by focusing on the relationships between people, the environment, and the sociopolitical structures that characterize the society. In assessing a community's vulnerability and response to disaster, a political ecology perspective focuses on the dynamic relationships between a human population, its socially generated and politically enforced patterns of production and allocation, and its physical environment. Human–environmental relations are always structured and expressed through social relations that reflect the ideologies and physical arrangements through which a population extracts a living from its surroundings. Political ecology recognizes that the social institutional arrangements by which humans exploit the physical environment in their quest for sustenance and shelter are key elements in the evolution of disasters. Our analysis should focus on those conditions surrounding the (threatened or actual) disaster that condition and shape its evolution—most particularly, the conditions that result in forms of development that make the society vulnerable both to socioeconomically and environmentally generated hazards (Oliver-Smith 2002, 2004).

Understanding Mitch: From Multidimensionality to Mutuality to Complexity

Grasping the totality of Mitch is a daunting task because disasters are such multidimensional phenomena; they affect every aspect of human life, including environmental, social, economic, political, and biological. Disasters exist as complex material events and, at the same time, as a multiplicity of interwoven and often conflicting social constructions. Both materially and socially constructed effects of disasters are channeled and distributed variously within the society in accordance with political, social, and economic practices and institutions.

Disasters are realized in both the material and the social worlds—that is, they affect physical reality and they are experienced and interpreted through social constructions. The multidimensionality to which I refer is a consequence of the complex relationship that binds human societies and their particular environments. Hurricane Mitch, like most disasters, was multidimensional because it was both a physical and a social "event/process." Hurricanes are part of a broad array of "objective" natural and technological phenomena that produce or trigger disasters and create a wide variety of physical impacts. The term "disaster" includes event/processes that range from slow-onset phenomena, such as droughts and toxic exposure, to rapid-onset ones, such as earthquakes and nuclear accidents. Hence there is wide variation in the impacts of natural and technological disasters, ranging from rapid destruction and death (as in the case of hurricanes) to effects that can remain physically undetected for many years (as in the case of toxic exposure).

Again like most disasters, Hurricane Mitch was also both socially constructed and variously experienced by different groups and individuals, who generated multiple interpretations of the event. Thus a single disaster agent varied in intensity and character over time and space, thus fragmenting into different sets of circumstances and (sometimes conflicting) interpretations according to the experience and identity of those affected. Mitch thereby revealed the relationships between global and local natural forces, global and local social arrangements, and cultural values and belief systems. The intensity of a disaster's impact, and the stress of recovery and reconstruction, lay bare the fundamental features of a society and reveal its crucial relationships and core values.

Indeed, disasters like Mitch focus with uncommon intensity the widest possible variety of intersecting and interpenetrating processes and events of social, environmental, cultural, political, physical, and technological natures. As disasters develop and occur, all dimensions of a society's structure and the totality of its relations with the environment become involved. There are few contexts in which social and physical mutualism is so starkly displayed as in a disaster.

It is therefore evident that disasters occur at the intersection of nature and culture and demonstrate, often dramatically, the mutuality of each in the constitution of the other. Disaster research needs to bring nature in from "out there" and to reconceptualize *dual* nature–society relations as *mutual* ones. As Ingold (1992) asserts, environmental history and human history are inseparable: each is implicated in the life of the other, and each contributes to the other's vulnerability and resilience. Disasters are among those phenomena whose analysis requires that we dissolve the barrier between human and ecosystemic activity, transforming a relation of difference into one of mutuality of the natural and social worlds. In Hurricane Mitch we can see the deep implications of socially driven environmental change in the patterns of destruction, loss, and suffering in Honduras.

Because disasters are both events and processes, they also share the temporal and spatial dimensions of the systems with which they interact. Disasters are multiscaled phenomena that occur differentially across temporal, spatial, and hierarchical scales, and each level in each scale has its own properties of self-organization and emergence. We use the term "emergence" to signify that each higher level is more than the mere sum of the lower levels' attributes (Gibson, Ostrom, and Ahn 2000:221). The multidimensionality of disasters makes it challenging to develop relevant theory that can be applied to the ever-expanding complexity that they exhibit. An increase in interactions between natural and technological hazards renders disasters more complex, which in turn makes the practical and the theoretical challenges more complex.

Human beings transform the natural environment through their material practices. They produce ecological conditions and environments that enable survival on a day-to-day basis and may also be conducive to continued social reproduction, thereby inscribing particular systems of social relations in the environment (Harvey 1996:183). On the other hand, human transformations of the environment—particularly if structured by nonlocal forces—may enable day-to-day survival yet seriously erode the long-term viability of the environment as well as the population's adaptation to it. Because human environments are socially constructed, the positive and negative effects of these practices are distributed as a reflection of systems of social relations. Therefore, particular forms of social relations create effects that are specific to them. Social, political, and economic power is inscribed through material practices (agriculture, settlements, transportation) in modified and built environments, and one of the many ways they are refracted back into daily living is in the form of conditions of vulnerability. This "inscription" process will reflect materially the contradictions inherent in both the social system and in the relation between society and its environment (Cronon 1983:13–14; as cited in Harvey 1996:27). Thus, contradictions in social relations are expressed through material practices as contradictions within the environment (Harvey 1996:185). Disasters are perhaps the most graphic expression of those contradictions.

Many disasters today are also closely linked to current conditions of environmental degradation (Varley 1994; Fernández 1996). Social and material practices combine with natural processes and evolve into novel forms of hazards: both potential and actual disasters. Environmental degradation, driven by the quest for profit or by people disadvantaged in that quest, is now linked to accentuated vulnerability to both natural and technological hazards around the world. Much has been written about inappropriate natural resource exploitation as rationalized by Western conceptions of the nature–society relationship. Stonich (1993) traces a chain of causal factors derived from conditions of endemic economic crisis, environmental degradation, and inappropriate development models in the creation of vulnerability in Honduras, and she all but predicts the outcomes of Hurricane Mitch. Yet Jansen, also writing on Honduras, cautions us that "land degradation through present agricultural practices is not simply an effect of poverty, inconsiderate acting or a direct consequence of a modernization process which is orchestrated and imposed upon the Honduran peasantry by external capitalist development" (1998:26).

Environmentalists have criticized the Western economic system for its unwillingness to accept the natural limits of environments, continually exceeding them in a relentless pursuit of economic profit. Political ecologists and economic anthropologists contend that the human–

environment relationship is generated in social relations through the double nexus of production. Environmental destruction is thus seen not as a question of exceeding natural limits but rather as a socially constructed outcome of systems of production and social exploitation (Collins 1992:179). This debate clearly has relevance for furthering our understanding of disasters. Because they emerge from the mutuality of human–environment relations, disasters instruct us in environmental limits and also inform us about specific instances of vulnerable conditions created by human social arrangements related to the production process. A study of disasters can contribute to clarifying the question of environmental versus socially defined limits. A finer-grained understanding of disasters recognizes the mutuality constituted by the dialectical interaction of nature and society. We must recognize, to paraphrase Harvey (1996) again, that the environment is a socially mediated context that people experience both positively and negatively—just as the expression of society itself can be positive or negative environmentally.

Complexity, Causality, and Vulnerability

The complexity of disasters necessarily obliges us to deal with the issue of causality. I do not intend here to plunge this discussion into the depths of philosophical and mathematical discourses on causality. Suffice it to say that causality is a much discussed and much disputed concept whose definitional parameters have been debated since Aristotle. Direct relationships of causality are hard to come by. In the strictest sense of the word, if A causes B then A must always be followed by B. When we say, for example, that smoking causes cancer, what we should really say is that smoking causes an increase in the probability of cancer (Spirtes, Glymour, and Scheines 2000). In other words, we should say that A increases the risk of B. Hilhorst notes that the complexity of disasters confounds attempts to describe them, particularly as regards causality, in terms of a linear time frame. Hilhorst further contends that, because disasters involve the interaction of multiple adaptive social and natural subsystems, they remain acutely unpredictable in their development, if not entirely so in their occurrence. To quote an environmental anthropologist colleague, Tom Abel: "Natural systems are incredibly complex. Even with gargantuan computing power, models that aim for realistic descriptions of complex systems, like hurricane forecasters, have had limited success. Add realistic ecosystems to one of those weather models, add earth systems, add realistic human systems, add symbolic systems, and what you get is a mess" (2003). Sounds like a disaster.

The cautions of Abel and Jansen notwithstanding, we cannot rest with that kind of conclusion in the case of actual disasters and the human suffering that occurs in their midst. If disasters are the result of complex interactions of social and environmental factors across different temporal and spatial dimensions, then the issues of causality and of subsequent remediation ("mitigation," in disaster management terms), reconstruction, and prevention become central. Attribution of causality in disasters was a traditionally straightforward process under the hazards paradigm. The hurricane did it, or the earthquake did it. People unknowingly put themselves in harm's way; the role of society was essentially passive. This perspective was succeeded by a more nuanced notion of disaster and disaster causality as the outcome of societally structured vulnerability impacted by a natural hazard (Hewitt 1983).

There are numerous well-constructed and -reasoned approaches to vulnerability (see, e.g., Wilches-Chaux 1989; Cutter 1996; Delica-Willison and Willison 2004; Wisner et al. 2004; Birkmann 2005). For example, Wisner and colleagues (2004) locate the generation of vulnerability in a linked series of causal factors starting with root causes at the level of system organization and ideology. The model then proceeds to link root causes to a set of dynamic processes that in turn produce unsafe conditions. When combined in space and time with a destructive agent from the natural or technological environment, these causal factors produce a disaster. In that sense, then, disasters are often the outcomes of the ways in which society organizes land-use patterns, settlement policies, population densities, and environmental changes that place people and livelihoods at risk. This more complex understanding of vulnerability enables researchers to conceptualize how social systems generate the conditions that place people—often differentiated along lines of class, race, ethnicity, gender, or age—at different levels of risk from the same hazard and at different levels of suffering from the same event (Wisner et al. 2004). In many ways, an approach based on vulnerability addresses several of the dominant perspectives' deficiencies, as noted by anthropological and geographical critics, by situating the causes of disasters in society and by incorporating specific political-economic and social variables in combination with particular environmental features (see Winograd, chapter 3 in this volume). By the same token, we must also recognize that, even under conditions of acute stress, vulnerable individuals retain their "agency" and can perform extraordinary achievements in coping with disaster and reconstruction (see chapters 4–7 in this volume).

When making causal statements about disasters, the vulnerability perspective explicitly invokes the notion of scale. Thus, vulnerability approaches are useful because they oblige us to think about disasters as systemic phenomena. Complex systems are multiscaled phenomena, and self-organization occurs within each nested scale. The central issue that links scale to causality is whether the factors employed to explain a pattern are located at the same level or at different levels within the pattern being examined. For example, the "downward causation" in the previously cited model of Wisner and colleagues uses variables occurring at one level to explain variables at a lower or later level (Gibson, Ostrom, and Ahn 2000:222).

Vulnerability also involves notions of time. In the progression of vulnerability proposed by Wisner et al. (2004), disasters that result from the interaction of root causes, dynamic pressures, and unsafe conditions evolve over time; each factor produces the next to yield a local condition of risk. There are also different spatial scales, starting with largely global ideological systems with a specific national expression and moving down spatially and hierarchically (as well as through time) to more specific contexts of regional dynamic pressures and to specific local unsafe conditions, many of which have ideological, social, economic, and material manifestations (see Winograd, chapter 3 in this volume). The scale of institutional hierarchies also progress downward to greater specificity. The importance of a scalar perspective is that it facilitates conceptualization of self-organizational properties at varying levels, each with its own dynamic within the overall system. Specificity within an overall pattern—and hence variation and nonlinearity—can all be viewed as part of the system itself.

Vulnerability expresses the multidimensionality of disasters by focusing our attention on the totality of relationships in a given social situation leading to conditions that, in combination with environmental forces, produce a disaster. As is apparent from our discussion of spatial, temporal, and hierarchical scales, the concept of vulnerability itself still constitutes a theoretical challenge because it encompasses such a large bundle of unexplicated linkages between apparently disparate elements or forces. Vulnerability is a highly condensed concept, packing a host of social, economic, and environmental factors into a complex set of relationships that are fused together by a theory of causation. The issue becomes further complicated in the context of increasing globalization of natural and socially based systems and their mutual interaction. Moreover, because the time frames during which these linkages produce effects are highly variable, assigning causation becomes both scientifically and politically challenging. However, I am reminded here of Holling's words on the irony of the lag time between cause and effect in environmental processes. "On the one hand, it provides the buffer for incomplete knowledge, thereby allowing experiment and recovery; but on the other, it also exacts few penalties fast enough on the greedy and the stupid" (Holling 1994:93). Causation is definitely involved here.

Complexity and Reconstruction

The complexity of disasters also affects the process of disaster reconstruction. Disaster management is, according to Hilhorst, one form of a complex adaptive system. Such systems can learn from experience, processing information and adapting according to local principles or intentions. In other words, complex adaptive systems do not merely react; they also attempt to gain some advantage from the circumstances. This capacity renders disaster management and reconstruction substantially more unpredictable than planners and policy makers would like (Hilhorst 2004:55). Following this line of thought, I borrow from my colleague Chris de Wet's work in displacement and resettlement studies to assert that complexity in disaster reconstruction is inherent in "the interrelatedness of a range of factors of different orders: cultural, social, environmental, economic, institutional and political—all of which are taking place in the context of imposed space change and of local level responses and initiatives" (de Wet 2005). Moreover, these changes are taking place simultaneously in an interlinked and mutually influencing process of transformation. Internal changes from the displacement process are also influenced by external sources of political power and by the initiatives of local actors. The post-disaster reconstruction process thus emerges from the complex interaction of all these factors in ways that are not predictable and that do not seem entirely amenable to a strictly linear planning approach.

De Wet suggests that another approach is necessary—a more comprehensive and open-ended approach than one that primarily involves a transfer of economic resources—in order to understand, adapt to, and take advantage of the opportunities presented by the inherent complexity of the process. Some might see this perspective as unduly pessimistic, but in fact the limited degree of control that authorities can exercise over a project may enable the disaster's victims to assume more control. The challenge thus becomes developing a policy that supports a genuinely participatory and open-ended approach to reconstruction planning and decision making (de Wet 2005; Barrios, chapter 7 in this volume).

Addressing the many dimensions involved in the concept of holistic reconstruction is far beyond the scope of this chapter. In short, I feel that what's needed is a reexamination of the role played by the complex of environmental, economic, and social factors discussed here in turning Hurricane Mitch into such a cataclysm (see Ensor and Ensor, chapter 2 in this volume). The fundamental question to be asked is how reconstruction can address the complex of factors that produced this disaster in a way that is sustainable, reduces vulnerability, and enables individual members of the community to survive (see Winograd, chapter 3 in this volume). In other words, Honduras had to reconstruct and recover economically *without* reinstalling the same system that generated the environmental degradation and extreme vulnerability in the first place. Reconstruction becomes a test of the social system's capacity to respond to a clear demonstration that the human and environmental destruction wreaked by Hurricane Mitch was deeply rooted in the social and environmental changes that took place over the previous fifty years.

Reconstruction also became an opportunity to explore the degree to which directed interventions can effectively address the linkage between environmental degradation, the vulnerability of local populations, and socially inscribed patterns of economic practice. The dilemma stemmed from the fact that pre-disaster agricultural policies and production practices were often directly linked to environmental degradation and increased vulnerability but were the principal means of generating income in rural areas (Stonich 1993). The immediate issue to be faced concerned the widespread damage to these production activities, which resulted in massive unemployment in key regions and areas of the economy and seriously affected health, nutrition, and general well-being. This impeded both household and community recovery in many regions.

Reconstruction, to be truly transformative, must address the complex of factors that made Hurricane Mitch the horror that it became. In other words, reconstruction had to recognize and reflect this complexity and, in its policies and practices, address the mutuality between society and nature that resides at the core of any such disaster. A perusal of the relevant documents leaves no question that Hondurans and the international community recognized the complex relationships between environmental, economic, and social factors that led to the devastation of Mitch. However, the outcome of reconstruction plans was a set of policies and practices that addressed (effectively, in some cases) symptoms but did little to address causes, thus ensuring that the exercise would have to be repeated in the future, since causes and symptoms each evolve with attempts to address them.

If we view the death and destruction of Hurricane Mitch as being due in part to economically and socially inscribed practices and to the capital and commodity flows that created and sustained those practices both nationally and internationally, then the capacity of the Honduran system to address the root causes of the disaster is limited. For that matter, under current global economic structures, the capacity of any single society to address such root causes is open to question. Yet it would be a serious error if we attributed to globalization the strength of natural law. Globalization is not gravity, and market logics are not physics (Collins 2003). Neither has the force of natural law, and both are cultural phenomena that admit wide variation in both interpretation and application.

Perhaps our most important task in contemporary disasters is to discover and implement those aspects of reconstruction that can feasibly reduce, within the limits of action permitted by existing structures, both environmental degradation and vulnerability to hazards (see Winograd, chapter 3 in this volume). Post-hurricane Honduras provided an important opportunity for economic forms and practices to be altered toward more sustainable forms of use. By the same token, Mitch created a space in which the balance of political power could be shifted to better reflect local realities and the needs of society (see Fuentes, chapter 5 in this volume). Furthermore, reconstruction after Mitch could have helped to establish the range of possibilities for sustainability as an achievable goal of specific directed policies within the limitations established by current economic practice. However, it remains doubtful that the political and economic structures of the nation could, even with the necessity and the incentive of reconstruction, ever truly come to grips with a set of endemic conditions so deeply embedded (by national and international forces) in their own forms and practices.

The authors of the chapters in this book undertake—in a variety of contexts and from a variety of perspectives—to analyze the historical development of vulnerability in Honduras, the event of Hurricane Mitch itself, and the lengthy process of recovery and reconstruction. Ensor and Ensor (chapter 2) address the impact of Hurricane Mitch in Honduras, describing both the event itself and examining the destruction left in its path in the context of the pre-disaster conditions of vulnerability. Framing their analysis in terms of interactions between features of the natural environment and demographic factors, the authors focus on those elements of the sociopolitical and natural environments of Honduras that produced the extreme forms of vulnerability experienced by its population. Such factors as the highly dependent economy, its unequal distribution of wealth, widespread food insecurity, and severe environmental degradation are examined for the roles they played in the outcomes of Hurricane Mitch.

Manuel Winograd's contribution (chapter 3) focuses on a method for determining the areas of vulnerability in Honduras after Hurricane Mitch and for identifying reconstruction and mitigation options for adapting to and coping with future events. Winograd expertly demonstrates how to move from diagnosis and assessment of disaster impacts toward better methods of coping with and reducing the type of environmental and social vulnerability exposed by Hurricane Mitch in Honduras. Basing this approach on concepts of vulnerability, Winograd recognizes clearly the need to broaden time/space scales in both data gathering and analysis, moving from the merely ad hoc responses and reconstruction actions to the underlying causes such as land use, agricultural practices, watershed management, and urbanization, all to develop systematic learning, anticipation of and planning for threats, reduction of vulnerabilities, defining coping strategies, and increasing resilience. The method that he proposes can be translated from scientific language and time scales to the language and time scales of decision makers at all levels.

William Loker's narrative (chapter 4) of his experience before, during, and after the impact of Mitch gives the reader a direct understanding of the social realities produced by a disaster of Hurricane Mitch's magnitude in a country as vulnerable as Honduras. His narrative offers a view of the courage and resilience of individuals and communities despite the systemic vulnerabilities that challenge them on a daily basis. What comes clearly through his narrative is the role of community as a significant resource that people may draw upon in disasters, quite independently of the actions of the state. Eliciting a "moral economy of disaster," Loker reveals how community members consistently placed the well-being of those harder hit by the hurricane before their own immediate needs. The high levels of local autonomy and resilience in the face of the enormous natural power of the storm and the institutional vulnerability of the state remind us that local people retain agency even in the dire circumstances of a disaster's aftermath.

The political dimensions of disaster are the focus of the contribution by Vilma Fuentes (chapter 5), who explores the opportunities for political change that may emerge in the process of post-disaster reconstruction. Foreign aid, in particular, may become a critical component in developing societies. Fuentes underscores the institutional vulnerability of the Honduran state in confronting the challenges of post-Mitch reconstruction. Her chapter analyzes how foreign aid may play a role in altering the relationship between the state and civil society in the aftermath of disasters. She points out that donors may tie their post-disaster assistance to certain "conditionalities" that must be met by countries requiring post-disaster assistance, thereby furthering acceptance of particular development models and discourses. She analyzes both the discourses and policies of donor nations and agencies in their efforts to alter the relationship between the state and civil society in Honduras, leading in certain cases to greater mobilization and political involvement of civil society and obliging the state to become both more responsive and accountable.

Marisa Ensor (chapter 6) highlights how vulnerability is deeply embedded in the basic social relations of a society, particularly at the level of gender relations. She has incorporated the concept of vulnerability into a feminist disaster research agenda, one based on the premise that gender discrimination accentuates women's vulnerability. She employs the concept of vulnerability to analyze the role that gender plays in shaping the interactions between human groups and the environment as well as the differential constraints and opportunities that men and women face in post-disaster reconstruction. Exploring post-disaster reconstruction as a gendered process, Ensor highlights the role of assistance in the reestablishment of traditional gender relations in the aftermath of Mitch. However, she also notes that post-disaster reconstruction may provide moments in which traditional patterns of gender discrimination may be challenged through the creation of new social and political alignments in civil society. However, the degree to which these opportunities have been realized in the aftermath of Mitch is highly debatable.

The tension between hegemonic knowledge systems and local understanding as a source of social conflict that conditions the outcomes of aid is the subject of Roberto Barrios' exploration (chapter 7) of two housing and community development projects in post-Mitch Honduras. Barrios clearly demonstrates how, three years after the storm, one community suffered from endemic conditions of crisis from the institutional practices of reconstruction authorities that limited residents from carrying out mundane tasks of daily existence, whereas residents of another community engaged in a mediational process that allowed the creation of social and material conditions for disaster recovery. Barrios' analysis highlights the importance of the relationship between power and knowledge in implementing community reconstruction schemes. The project that integrated resident knowledge and perspective in a dialogic process developed far more productive outcomes than the project based on the stereotypes of disaster victims held by reconstruction authorities.

The book's final chapter, co-authored by the core members of the research group that formed immediately after the storm, places the reconstruction effort in Honduras in the context of international and national development strategies that closed the twentieth and opened the twenty-first century. Assessing the reconstruction effort within the frameworks of the Millennium Development Goals and the Central America Free Trade Agreement, the authors find some cause for optimism in the rhetoric and policy but little actual evidence of progress in reducing either vulnerability or poverty in Honduras. Nonetheless, despite the lack of any real transformation through the reconstruction process, they point to evident political and social changes. Finally, the authors emphasize the importance of a research strategy that addresses the systemic vulnerabilities of specific societies if disaster mitigation and reconstruction are to address actual causes and not simply to treat symptoms. The lessons that the authors present in this volume provide precisely the sort of sound data and sensitive analysis that can lead to better policies and improved practice in disaster management.

References

Abel, Thomas. 2003. Personal communication (June 4).

Barrios, Roberto. 2004. "Flying Rooftops and Matchbox Houses: The Politics of Knowledge, Performative Realities, and the Materialization of Crisis in the Reconstruction of Southern Honduras after Hurricane Mitch." PhD dissertation, University of Florida, Gainesville.

Bates, F. L., and C. Pelanda. 1994. "An Ecological Approach to Disasters." In *Disasters, Collective Behavior and Social Organization,* edited by Russell K. Dynes and Kathleen J. Tierney, 145–59. Newark: University of Delaware Press.

Birkmann, J. 2005. "Measuring Vulnerability: Conceptual Frameworks and Basic Fundamentals." In *Measuring Vulnerability and Coping Capacity to Hazards of Natural Origin—Concept and Methods,* edited by J. Birkmann. Tokyo: United Nations University.

Collins, J. 1992. "Marxism Confronts the Environment." In *Understanding Economic Process* (Monographs in Economic Anthropology, no. 10), edited by S. Ortiz and S. Lees. Lanham, MD: University Press of America.

———. 2003. *Threads: Gender, Labor and Power in the Global Apparel Industry.* Chicago: University of Chicago Press.

Cronon, W. 1983. *Changes in the Land: Indians, Colonists, and the Ecology of New England.* New York: Hill & Wang.

Cutter, S. 1996. "Vulnerability to Environmental Hazards." *Progress in Human Geography* 20, no. 4: 529–39.

Delica-Willison, Z., and R. Willison. 2004. "Vulnerability Reduction: A Task for the Vulnerable People Themselves." In *Mapping Vulnerability: Disasters, Development and People,* edited by Greg Bankoff, Georg Frerks, and Dorothea Hilhorst. London: Earthscan.

DeVries, Gregory. 2000. "Post-Hurricane Reconstruction in La Moskitia, Honduras." MA thesis, Center for Latin American Studies, University of Florida, Gainesville.

de Wet, Chris. 2005. "Risk, Complexity and Local Initiative in Involuntary Resettlement Outcomes." In *Improving Outcomes in Involuntary Resettlement,* edited by Chris de Wet. New York: Berghahn.

Fernández, M. A. 1996. *Ciudades en riesgo: Degradación ambiental, riesgos urbanos y desastres.* Bogotá: La Red.

Fuentes, Vilma. 2003. "The Political Effects of Disaster and Foreign Aid: National and Sub-National Governance Change in Honduras after Hurricane Mitch." PhD dissertation, Department of Political Science, University of Florida, Gainesville.

Gibson, Clark C., Elinor Ostrom, and T. K. Ahn. 2000. "The Concept of Scale and the Human Dimensions of Global Change: A Survey." *Ecological Economics* 32: 217–39.

Harvey, D. 1996. *Justice, Nature and the Geography of Difference.* Oxford: Blackwell.

Hewitt, K. 1983. *Interpretations of Calamity.* Winchester: Allen & Unwin.

Hilhorst, Dorothea. 2003. "Responding to Disasters: Diversity of Bureaucrats, Technocrats and Local People." *International Journal of Mass Emergencies and Disasters* 21, no. 1: 37–56.

———. 2004. "Complexity and Diversity: Unlocking Social Domains of Disaster Response." In *Mapping Vulnerability: Disasters, Development and People,* edited by Greg Bankoff, Georg Frerks, and Dorothea Hilhorst, 52–66. London: Earthscan.

Holling, C. S. 1994. "An Ecologist's View of the Malthusian Conflict." In *Population, Economic Development, and the Environment,* edited by K. Lindahl-Kiessling and H. Landberg. New York: Oxford University Press.

Ingold, T. 1992. "Culture and the Perception of the Environment." In *Bush Base: Forest Farm,* edited by E. Croll and D. Parkin. London: Routledge.

Jansen, Kees. 1998. *Political Ecology, Mountain Agriculture and Knowledge in Honduras.* Amsterdam: Thela, 1998.

Oliver-Smith, Anthony. 2002. "Theorizing Disasters: Nature, Power and Culture." In *Catastrophe and Culture: The Anthropology of Disaster,* edited by Susanna Hoffman and Anthony Oliver-Smith, 23–48. Santa Fe, NM: SAR Press.

———. 2004. "Theorizing Vulnerability in a Globalized World: A Political Ecological Perspective." In *Mapping Vulnerability: Disasters, Development and People,* edited by Greg Bankoff, Georg Frerks, and Dorothea Hilhorst, 10–24. London: Earthscan.

Oliver-Smith, Anthony, and Susanna Hoffman. 2002. "Why Anthropologists Should Study Disasters." In *Catastrophe and Culture: The Anthropology of Disaster,* edited by Susanna Hoffman and Anthony Oliver-Smith, 3–22. Santa Fe, NM: SAR Press.

Olivo Díaz López, María Jesús. 2002. "Relocating Morolica: Post-Disaster Reconstruction in Honduras after Hurricane Mitch." PhD dissertation, Department of Anthropology, University of Florida, Gainesville.

Spirtes, Peter, Clark Glymour, and Richard Scheines. 2000. *Causation, Prediction and Search.* Cambridge, MA: MIT Press.

Stansbury, James P., Roberto E. Barrios, Carmen Rojas, Rosa Palencia, and Marco T. Medina. 2001. "After the Hurricane: Child Nutrition in Honduran Reconstruction." *Nutritional Anthropology* 24, no. 1: 3–7.

Stonich, Susan C. 1993. *I Am Destroying the Land: The Political Ecology of Poverty and Environmental Destruction in Honduras.* Boulder, CO: Westview.

Varley, A. 1994. *Disasters, Development and Environment.* London: Wiley.

Wilches-Chaux, Gustavo. 1989. *Desastres, ecologismo, y formación profesional.* Popayán, Colombia: Servicio Nacional de Aprendizaje (SENA).

Wisner, Ben, Piers Blaikie, Terry Cannon, and Ian Davis. 2004. *At Risk: Natural Hazards, People's Vulnerability and Disasters.* New York: Routledge.

2
Hurricane Mitch
Root Causes and Responses to the Disaster

Bradley E. Ensor and Marisa Olivo Ensor

The exceptional size, power, and duration of Hurricane Mitch dramatically exposed Honduras' high level of social and environmental vulnerability and also made post-disaster reconstruction efforts particularly challenging. When Hurricane Mitch devastated the country, most of the population were already living in chronic poverty and facing severe resource constraints (Ensor 2003). "When hazards threaten and disasters occur, they both reveal and become an expression of the complex interactions of physical, biological, and sociocultural systems" (Oliver-Smith and Hoffman 2002:5). This chapter addresses the impact of Hurricane Mitch in Honduras, describes the event itself, and examines the devastation left in its wake in light of the highly vulnerable pre-disaster conditions. The interactions between physical and demographic factors and between historical and contemporary political-economic factors are analyzed next, along with the interrelations between these aspects and the local population. The chapter concludes by examining the responses of the Honduran government and the international community, which were instrumental in assisting the victims and helping the country start the recovery process.

Hurricane Mitch

Although Hurricane Mitch was the most devastating hurricane in Honduran history, destructive events have frequently impacted this country. Intense storms, tropical depressions, and hurricanes are relatively common during the rainy season, which typically begins in May or June and continues to November or December. Even when the hurricanes themselves do not reach the mainland, they bring heavy rains that result in floods that destroy homes, damage agriculture, and lead to increased cases of diseases such as cholera. Prior to Hurricane Mitch, full-blown hurricanes struck Honduras every decade or so, killing thousands of people and leaving even more homeless. Hurricane

Fifi killed an estimated 10,000 Hondurans in 1974 (Humphrey 1997:7). Four hundred people died in floods in November 1993. In November 1996, Tropical Storm Marco struck the north coast and destroyed 4,000 homes (Keller et al. 1997:317). Nevertheless, the exceptional intensity and duration of Mitch contributed to far more devastation than any previous storm.

On the afternoon of Saturday, October 24, 1998, Mitch received its name by evolving into the thirteenth hurricane of the 1998 season. Sustaining winds of 87 miles per hour, the hurricane was 124 miles wide and proceeded to travel north from the coast of Panama (where it had formed), dumping rain on Panama, Costa Rica, and Nicaragua. By the afternoon of Sunday, October 25, Mitch had been upgraded to a Category 4 hurricane and slowly angled northwest with winds of 134 miles per hour. The following day, sustained winds increased to 177 miles per hour with gusts of over 200 miles per hour. Mitch was upgraded to a Category 5 (defined as having wind speeds over 155 miles per hour, a storm surge over 18 feet, and a catastrophic damage scale), and a Hurricane Warning was issued from Limón in Honduras to the Nicaraguan border. During the afternoon of Tuesday, October 27, the hurricane changed direction and spun southwest. The Hurricane Warning was expanded across the Honduran coast to the Guatemalan border (Guiney and Lawrence 1999). Mitch spent a record thirty-three hours at Category 5 status (NCDC 1999). As Mitch turned south, the winds dropped to Category 4 status, causing torrential downpours from water acquired over the ocean during the previous days. Twelve hours after touching the Central American mainland, the winds of Mitch slowed and it dropped to the class of tropical storm. On Friday, October 30, Mitch meandered through central Honduras and made a devastating turn around Tegucigalpa, the capital city. Mitch was downgraded to a tropical depression before entering Guatemala on Saturday, October 31 (Guiney and Lawrence 1999).

Every Central American country was affected by Mitch, but none more severely than Honduras and Nicaragua. Honduras, in particular, bore the brunt of the damage. Mitch-borne precipitation in this country ranged from 6.60 to 36.00 inches, when under normal conditions weekly precipitation ranges from 0.30 to 1.58 inches (CIAT-Laderas 1998). All of Honduras' eighteen territorial departments were affected by Hurricane Mitch. The destruction suffered by the northern departments of Cortés and Colón was primarily caused by the powerful winds, while the lowlands in the east, the Choluteca Valley, and the cities of Comayagüela and Tegucigalpa experienced severe flooding. Hydrological features played an important role in the destruction caused by Hurricane Mitch. When the hurricane hit Honduras between October 29 and November 1, intense rains caused major flooding in lowland areas and river basins. In the north, massive rainfall in the Sula Valley caused the Ulúa and Chamelecón Rivers to join, forming a wall of water 5 miles wide that engulfed the cities of Tela, El Progreso, and San Pedro Sula. In the south, the Choluteca River permanently changed course, taking an old channel across its delta into the Pacific Ocean. In fact, the courses of several rivers were so significantly altered by the massive flooding that the Honduran government had to use satellite imagery to remap them. In the capital, Tegucigalpa, the rains produced devastating landslides on deforested hills and mountainsides (United Nations 2002; Bradshaw 2004:7).

According to official estimates from the National Master Plan for Reconstruction and Transformation issued by the Honduran government, the total number of dead reached 5,657; there were 12,272 people injured, 8,058 unaccounted for, 1.5 million affected, and 441,150 who had to move into one of 1,375 temporary shelters because their houses were lost or severely damaged (PMRTN 1999:4). The main concentration of people in shelters was located in the municipalities of Tegucigalpa, Choluteca, and San Pedro Sula. In all, about 276,000 families were affected by the hurricane and over 600,000 people were evacuated. The poorest communities were hardest hit, particularly those living in marginal areas of the urban centers. Many such communities were swept away by flooding, their houses completely destroyed or severely damaged. It is estimated that 60 percent of the country's infrastructure (roads and bridges) was severely damaged or completely destroyed (UN Inter-Agency 1999:1).

Large parts of most urban areas were buried under mud contaminated with sewage, chemical products such as pesticides and fertilizers, and even decomposing human and animal remains, which represented a serious health hazard apart from preventing the return of the displaced population. Sanitation facilities were destroyed in rural and marginal areas of urban centers, increasing the probability of water contamination, the proliferation of disease vectors, and the contamination of food supplies. The Pan American Health Organization and the Honduran National Water and Sanitation Service (SANAA) reported that 80 percent of the country's 3,800 aqueducts were damaged, sharply reducing the supply of potable water for 2.9 million consumers (as cited in UN Inter-Agency 1999:1).

Data provided by the Honduran Ministry of Health indicate that twenty-three of the thirty hospitals in Honduras suffered total or partial damage to their water supply system. Over a hundred health facilities, including hospitals and rural health centers, were seriously damaged and/or out of operation, resulting in a severe lack of minimum health prevention and care at a time when more than 100,000 Hondurans were suffering from various diseases such as diarrhea, acute respiratory illness, dermatitis, malaria, and conjunctivitis. Although food insecurity and undernutrition in Honduras did not begin with Hurricane Mitch, there has been a continued decline in nutrition indicators since the disaster. Anthropometric measurements taken in various areas of Honduras in the summer of 1999 confirmed that resettled families were still confronting a nutritional crisis nine months after the hurricane struck, with food security being compromised by widespread flooding and crop destruction (Barrios et al. 2000:380).

The impact on the agricultural production and infrastructure was indeed unprecedented, as both fields and irrigation systems were severely damaged. The loss of agricultural production (provisionally estimated at greater than 50 percent) and its impact on food security are currently being assessed by missions of the World Food Program (WFP) and the Food and Agriculture Organization (FAO). The value of agricultural losses have been estimated at approximately USD 800 million. Besides the loss of crops for local consumption, cash crops such as coffee and pineapple were also severely damaged, and there was a nearly complete loss of production and export of bananas, a main earner of hard currency for Honduras. These losses had serious consequences for the country's financial situation, and they also caused hundreds of thousands of Hondurans to suddenly lose their jobs and income. Displaced people needed food aid until their return home, requiring a long and gradual reintegration process. Furthermore, upon their return home, they had to wait until the next harvest for locally produced food to become available as well as for their reintegration into normal economic activities (UN Inter-Agency 1999:10). The livestock sector suffered both from the death of a large number of animals and from the loss of pasture to severe flooding and erosion. The cost of rehabilitating the livestock and dairy sectors was estimated at USD 90 million (FAO 1999).

Damage to the education sector was also staggering. Approximately one fourth of the schools throughout the country were destroyed (some 2,800 classrooms), leaving more than 25,500 primary school children with no place to attend. More than 30,000 children at the secondary school level were unable to continue their studies, and more than 2,000 teachers were displaced from their jobs. Community day-care centers and preschool centers were also destroyed or seriously damaged, leaving 75,000 children without attention (UN Inter-Agency 1999:1–2). Table 2.1 summarizes the damages caused in Honduras by Hurricane Mitch.

Although the intensity and duration of Hurricane Mitch itself were clearly significant factors in the widespread destruction, the storm's devastation was compounded by the highly vulnerable economy, unequal distribution of resources, widespread food insecurity, and severe environmental degradation that characterized Honduras *prior* to the disaster (Stonich 1993; DeVries 2000). These factors are discussed in the following sections.

Political-Economic Factors and Vulnerability

An analysis of the historical and political-economic dimensions that led to the current situation in Honduras contributes to a better understanding of the heightened conditions of vulnerability in the region. Honduras' historical political economy produced widespread underdevelopment, which led to high population vulnerability framed by unequal distribution of resources and food insecurity. This situation has increased in severity since the 1980s.

Williams (1986, 1991) has argued that the recent economic and political crises in Central America overall can be traced to earlier processes that evolved from basic structural inequalities, encroachment upon traditional peasant lands, and the transformation of agricultural labor relations that resulted from an overemphasis on export crops. Liberal economic initiatives implemented by many Central American governments during the nineteenth century to expand the production of export crops, particularly coffee, resulted in the privatization of many communally owned and managed lands. These and other actions to promote exports led to the concentration of property in the hands

Table 2.1 Summary of Damages in Honduras from Hurricane Mitch

Individuals	
Dead	5,657
Injured	12,272
Missing	8,058
Homeless	441,150
Urban Centers	
Cities that suffered severe damage	21
Total number of cities affected	60
Municipalities completely destroyed	1
Municipalities partially destroyed	15
Housing and Public Buildings	
Houses destroyed	66,188
Houses damaged	82,735
Shelters built	1,375
Classrooms destroyed	2,800
Transportation	
Bridges destroyed	189
Primary roads damaged	47
Secondary roads damaged	60
Local roads	200
Penetration roads	224
Communications	
Telephone	17,000 lines lost
Television and newspapers	continued service
Health Infrastructure	
Health centers damaged	123
Health centers destroyed	8
Aqueducts destroyed	1743
Latrines destroyed	53,435
Agriculture and Livestock Production	
Agricultural losses	USD 800 million
Livestock losses	no available estimates

Source: Secretaría de Salud de Honduras (1999).

of a small minority and to the spreading marginalization and impoverishment of the increasingly vulnerable rural population. For many families, diminished access to land led to greater dependence on wages earned as seasonal laborers on large farms (ibid.).

Honduras did not become articulated within the world economic system until the end of the nineteenth century, which saw the externally financed establishment of the banana industry and the reintroduction of mining. Through its involvement with the mining and banana industries beginning in the 1880s, the Honduran government initiated its prevailing role as an ally of foreign—especially U.S.—corporations (White 1977:97–98). Before 1950, Honduras lacked a central bank and the primary medium of exchange was U.S. currency. Shortly after his inauguration in 1949, President Gálvez received a mission from the newly established International Monetary Fund (IMF), which had chosen to work in Honduras precisely because of its chaotic financial system. With the IMF's help, the Gálvez administration created the Central Bank and the National Development Bank in 1950: the former with control over monetary matters and the latter providing credit for specific development projects (ibid.: 95). Shortly thereafter, Honduras became a target for a growing network of agencies concerned with supporting expanded government activities, services, and development. These agencies included the United States Agency for International Development (USAID), many of the United Nations agencies, the Economic Commission for Latin America (ECLA), international labor federations, and overseas aid funds of various religious organizations (ibid.: 94–100).

The presence of small peasant farmers and their families on rented, national, or *ejidal* (community managed) land that could be put into commercial production was an impediment to large-scale capitalist expansion. Beginning in the 1950s, large landowners used a variety of methods to have them evicted. The forced evictions, exorbitant rental fees, and declines in available national and ejido land contributed to decreases in the amount of land to which small farmers had access. These factors, along with the increasing allocation of land from food crop production to export crop production and the significant increases in regional production, concentrated landholdings in the hands of a few wealthy landowners and excluded small holders more than ever before (White 1977). Faced with ever-dwindling access to agricultural land and lacking other economic opportunities, small farmers had to deforest hillsides in order to clear land in their desperate efforts to feed their families. This development further exacerbated the problems of ecological degradation and environmental vulnerability.

With international assistance, the Honduran government functioned as an agent of development by improving access to credit, establishing markets, and constructing the requisite regional infrastructure. A domestic, capitalist agricultural sector emerged in the 1950s and, by the mid-1970s, large foreign agricultural enterprises began investing in the area, competing with regional capitalists for land and labor. From mid-century to the present, diversification and growth of agricultural production for export have characterized the Honduran economy. In the mid-1970s, coffee and bananas were supplemented by sesame and melons and later by a wider variety of "nontraditional" exports, especially cultivated shrimp. For the Honduran government, which was mired in a persistent state of fiscal crisis and tied to foreign interests, repayment of mounting external debt took priority over the conservation of natural resources. Export commodities such as cotton, cattle, sugar, sesame, melons, and shrimp attracted international assistance and investment, thereby increasing foreign exchange earnings—whatever their social and environmental costs (Stonich 1993:64).

Development schemes aimed at alleviating Central America's social and economic problems have historically stressed intensified exploitation of the region's natural resources through increased exports of agricultural commodities and forest products, enhanced agricultural productivity, and expanded industrial fisheries. Since the second half of the twentieth century, the Honduran government has contributed to the stagnation of basic grains—corn, beans, sorghum, and rice—by placing price ceilings on basic staples as a way of maintaining cheap food for the growing urban population (Stonich 1993). Export growth through agricultural diversification remained the cornerstone of development strategies in Central America throughout the post–World War II period. Despite the critical need for improved access to institutional credit for smallholder farmers, a survey by the European Commission estimated that fewer than 10 percent of basic grain farmers received institutional credit (USAID 1990:13). The combination of price ceilings and limited credit contributed to the stagnation of small farm food production, the major supplier for the national market, further exacerbating the problems faced by small farmers. The 1970s saw declines in international commodity prices, soaring costs of oil and technological inputs such as pesticides, the collapse of regional markets, and a growing debt burden, factors that sank the region into a severe economic crisis characterized by a decline in economic growth and by worsening inequalities (ECLAC 1986).

Efforts to further diversify and expand agriculture for export to increase foreign exchange are more comprehensible in light of Honduras' deteriorating economic conditions during the 1980s. Honduras, already one of the poorest countries in Central America, underwent a prolonged recession, followed by virtual economic stagnation, since the onset of the debt crisis in the early 1980s (Green 1995:229). Evidence of the international economic crisis emerged in Honduras in 1981 and intensified throughout the decade. The balance of payments and the national treasury suffered serious imbalances. There were significant constraints in supplying imported goods, and private investment dropped in response to the region's political and social problems and to disturbances in the exchange and monetary systems. This situation was aggravated by the economy's vulnerability to external fluctuations affecting the demand and price of its traditional export products such as bananas and coffee (Stonich 1991).

Enormous amounts of foreign assistance attempted to ameliorate the deteriorating social, economic, and ecological conditions throughout Honduras (CONAMA 1991:46–59). Between 1980 and 1989, the real growth rate of its gross domestic product (GDP) was 2.3 percent per year, which was below the population growth rate of 2.9 percent and so led to concomitant drops in wages and living conditions. Rural households were disproportionately affected in part because of the substantial decline in agricultural prices relative to nonagricultural prices, which also discouraged additional investment in agriculture. By late 1989, the major financial lending institutions—the World Bank, the International Monetary Fund, and the Inter-American Development Bank—placed Honduras on the list of countries that were ineligible for new loans because of overdue payments on earlier credits. The impact of the economic crisis was particularly severe on the poor (Stonich 1993:65).

According to conservative estimates, 60 percent of the Honduran economy was controlled, in the mid-1980s, by U.S. companies. The United States is the principal buyer of Honduran exports, the main supplier of Honduran imports, and the biggest creditor for Honduran external debt (Paz 1986). All countries of the isthmus have been under the direct influence of the United States, but none has been more completely controlled than Honduras by its economic, political, and military relations with the United States. From the beginning of the last century, Honduras' principal economic activities have been dominated, directly or indirectly, by U.S. companies. Motivated by security considerations during World War II, the U.S. government began to provide aid to Honduras in the form of road building and health assistance as well as in military training (White 1977:97–98).

Honduras played a marginal role in U.S. foreign policy until after the Sandinista revolution in 1979, when its strategic position was reevaluated (Stonich 1993:2). In the 1980s, Honduras—once "the sleepy backwater of Central America"—suddenly became the hub of U.S. policy in the region (Benjamin 1989:xviii). With Ronald Reagan's ascendance to the U.S. presidency in January 1981, U.S. military involvement in Central America increased dramatically. The United States funneled huge sums of money and thousands of U.S. troops into Honduras as it conducted provocative maneuvers clearly designed to threaten Nicaragua. Nicaraguan refugee camps in Honduras were used as bases for a U.S.-sponsored, undeclared covert war against the Nicaraguan government, which became known as the Contra War. At the same time, the United States was training the Salvadoran military at Salvadoran refugee camps inside Honduras, near the border with El Salvador (Keller et al. 1997:314–15). In 1988, about 12,000 members of the Nicaraguan Resistance Forces (the Contras) operated from Honduras. In return for allowing the United States to station Contra rebels on its border with Nicaragua, Washington rewarded the Honduran government with large sums of economic assistance, which partially mitigated the impact of the IMF's austerity policies (Green 1995:229). The U.S.-sponsored military buildup in Honduras was so massive that even CIA operatives and U.S. embassy officials cynically began referring to the country as "USS Honduras" or the "Pentagon Republic" (Benjamin 1989:xix).

In response to deteriorating social and economic conditions, U.S. policy makers in the early 1980s once again proposed economic reforms in order to defuse political crisis in the region. The goal of the 1984 "Caribbean Basin Initiative" was to establish regional stability through economic growth stimulated by domestic and foreign investment. Agricultural diversification through the promotion of a new set of nontraditional exports was the foundation of this scheme (USAID 1991). The United States pressured the Honduran military to hold elections in 1981, after eighteen years of military rule. However, the electoral process actually resulted in a strengthening of the Honduran military and a consequent weakening of civilian power. In a meeting between both major candidates and the main Honduran military authorities celebrated before the elections, it was agreed that the armed forces would have full control over security issues, including policies toward El Salvador and Nicaragua, as well as veto power over all cabinet appointments. "The electoral process, rather than curbing the power of the military, allowed the military to act with greater impunity now that it was covered by the façade of a civilian government" (Benjamin 1989:xix).

Until the mid-1980s, Honduras was dominated by the military, which enthusiastically supported U.S. efforts to stem revolutionary movements in the region. In effect, the only flourishing sector of the Honduran economy during that decade was the military. As the politicians and military authorities were getting richer off U.S. economic assistance, the bulk of the population were disastrously affected by the severe economic crisis that characterized the decade (Benjamin 1989:xxi). A U.S. government study published in 1986 reported that more than a million dollars of Congressional funds designated to aid the Contras between November 1985 and January 1986 were instead diverted to the Honduran military (General Accounting Office Report 1986). Finally, in November 1988, the Honduran government refused to sign a new military agreement with the United States and President Azcona declared that the Contras would have to leave Honduras. With the election of Violeta Chamorro as president of Nicaragua in 1990, the Contra War ended and the Contras were finally out of Honduras (Keller et al. 1997:315). Since then, civilian leaders have sought to curb the power of the military, with varying degrees of success. Some army officers have been charged with human rights abuses, but many are still to be prosecuted for violations committed in the 1980s. Pressure for a full structural adjustment[1] program had begun to grow in Honduras since even before the end of the Contra War. As U.S. aid began to tail off in the late 1980s, the government was once again forced to ask the IMF and the World Bank for economic assistance. The Bank approved a USD 50 million Structural Adjustment Loan (SAL) in 1988 but then suspended it when Honduras failed to reach an agreement with the IMF the following year; USAID also froze its program (Green 1995:229).

The economic crisis of the 1980s, during which Central American governments struggled with the burden of servicing external debts in a context of deteriorating terms of trade, extended into the 1990s. In 1989 a new government took office in Honduras, led by the neo-liberal Rafael Callejas. He further promoted the liberalization of trade, devalued the *lempira* (the national currency), began a privatization program, and cleared the backlog of debt arrears. His government signed a second Structural Adjustment Loan with the World Bank, followed in 1992 by a three-year loan from the IMF (Green 1995:229). The severe economic adjustment programs implemented in response to pressure from international donor institutions resulted in declines in real income and social services, especially among the most vulnerable segments of society: the rural and urban poor (Stonich 1993:3).

Social expenditure in all areas was reduced at the same time that falling world market prices of the main Honduran commodities (bananas, coffee, sugar, and cotton) resulted in reduced export earnings. The conditions of relative equality—by Central American standards—that had once set Honduras apart from its neighbors quickly vanished (Benjamin 1989:xxi). The economic polarization between politicians and military authorities on the one hand, and the bulk of the population on the other, was exacerbated during the 1980s and today remains a defining characteristic of Honduran society.

Compounding this curtailment of social expenditures was the prevailing centrality of the Honduran state and its authoritarian propensities, wherein corruption for personal gain remained a strong tendency (Loker 2004:185, 188). As Honduras became more dependent on foreign development aid, typically offered with financiers' goals in mind rather than those of the population, there were more projects that could be siphoned for personal gain by functionaries (ibid.: 188). Vertical stratification was also present in the form of patron-client relations at the local community levels (ibid.: 186): people depended on the assistance of local elites and so could not challenge the prevailing distribution of resources and development schemes.

Honduras confronted the 1990s under extremely difficult circumstances. The country was undergoing the implementation of a stern structural adjustment program. Economic stagnation resulted in Honduras having the fourth-lowest GDP per capita in Latin America—higher only than that of Bolivia, Haiti, and Nicaragua. The population suffered from crippling poverty levels, with 70 percent of the total population and 80 percent of the rural population living below the absolute poverty level. The distribution of income showed an extremely skewed pattern, with the poorest 40 percent receiving 7.3 percent of the total while the richest 10 percent collected 50 percent (CONAMA 1991:46–59). The number of landless peasants is estimated at between 100,000 and 300,000 (Trócaire 2004:11). Official statistics also indicate that the incidence of poverty among rural women increased from 53 percent to 60 percent between 1991 and 1999 (FOSDEH 2002).

In 1993, public hostility to structural adjustment was instrumental in electing Roberto Reina on an anti-neoliberal platform. However, his attempt to increase social spending and to defy international pressure for implementing neoliberal measures was doomed from the start by the country's escalating debt burden, its rising fiscal deficit, and declining levels of U.S. aid. As 1994 wore on, the World Bank and the IMF increased their pressure for more privatization, more cuts in transport subsidies, and increases in sales taxes—which, when implemented, provoked widespread strikes and other protests by the Honduran population (Green 1995:229).

Central American governments continued to emphasize nontraditional agricultural exports and sought ways to diversify their export base to generate larger amounts of foreign exchange (USAID 1991). As nontraditional farming expanded—increasing the already high number of landless farmers in the region—land values increased, squeezing smaller producers of their holdings. Without adequate redistribution measures, nontraditional agro-export promotion led to an even more inequitable distribution of income, further impoverishment of the rural areas, and increased vulnerability of the population in general (Garst and Barry 1990:89–90). As a consequence of all these historical factors, when Hurricane Mitch hit Honduras in 1998 the country ranked last among all Central American countries according to the Human Development Index (HDI), an estimate calculated from multiple indicators of life expectancy, educational attainment, and income (UNDP 1999).

Political Ecological Factors and Vulnerability

Deforestation played a key role in the devastating effects of the intense rains borne by Hurricane Mitch. Evidence suggests that deforestation is linked to soil erosion and that both increase the frequency and intensity of hazards in the long run—for instance, by increasing the chances of landslides and generating local flooding through stream damming (Blaikie et al. 1994:135). The connection between unsustainable natural resource-use practices, environmental degradation, and heightened conditions of vulnerability supports the premise that "natural" disasters such as Hurricane Mitch are fundamentally social in nature.

Environmental degradation in Honduras can be viewed as a product of political, economic, and environmental factors. The political and financial intervention by the United States and other powerful international actors (including the World Bank, the International Monetary Fund, and the Inter-American Development Bank) promoted international agricultural capitalism that strongly affected the environment and the people of Honduras (Stonich 1993:63), ultimately promoting the unsustainable exploitation of the country's resources in the name of economic growth and modernization. As described in the previous section, the reallocation of lands from food production to export crop production, the increased concentration of lands in the hands of fewer wealthy landowners, the dwindling access to agricultural lands for the majority of peasants, and the lack of sufficient employment opportunities all led to high levels of poverty and food insecurity. Many Hondurans were forced to seek livelihoods and residential locations on hillsides and mountainsides, resulting in deforestation that in turn resulted in unstable slopes, landslides, and mudslides in the presence of a natural catalyst like Mitch.

Exacerbating these political-economic factors, Honduras experienced an explosive population growth in the second half of the twentieth century, which amounted to a further ecological hazard through environmental degradation. According to the 1910 census, the annual rate of population growth barely exceeded 1.5 percent. By 1950 it had reached 3 percent. From 1960 to 1990, the population growth rate climbed to 3.3 percent (Merrill 1993). The country's high birth rate has resulted in the Honduran population's doubling about every twenty-five years. The 1950 census counted 1,368,605 inhabitants, almost twice as many as counted by the 1926 census. By 1974 the population had almost doubled once again. In 1992, the population was estimated to be 5,092,776, and it reached 6.4 million in 2001 (Country Studies 2004). Current demographic trends continue to be characterized by rapid population growth. According to the UN Development Programme's 2007–2008 Human Development Report, the population of Honduras reached 6.8 million in 2005 and is projected to reach 8.3 million by 2015 (UNDP 2007).

Honduras has consistently maintained high birth rates through the twentieth century. The crude birth rate (CBR; the annual number of births per 1,000 inhabitants) from the beginning to the mid-point of the century fluctuated between 41.7 and 44.5. From around 1950 to 1975, Honduras had the highest CBR in Latin America. Since the mid-1970s, the CBR has steadied somewhat; in 1990, it stood at 39 births per 1,000 inhabitants (Merrill 1993). The total fertility rate (TFR; the average number of children that a woman bears in her lifetime) had dropped to 7.5 children per woman by the early 1970s; since then, the TFR in Honduras has steadily declined. However, this fertility rate varies considerably according to a woman's residence in rural or urban areas and according to income level. In 1993, for example, rural women had an average of 8.7 children while urban women had an average of 5.3 children. Also, the TFR for all upper- and middle-income women, both rural and urban, was 5.8, whereas the TFR was approximately 8 among lower-income women (ibid.).

A clear link can be established between population growth, declining human health, environmental degradation, and increased vulnerability in Honduras. High rates of population growth and a lack of economic alternatives have forced growing numbers of rural peasants to put unprecedented pressures on natural resources by adopting destructive agricultural practices in their home areas or in the last vestiges of tropical forest. A serious problem is the extremely high rate of deforestation, with soils being lost at the rate of 10,000 hectares per year. At this rate, the country could be completely deforested within twenty years (Keller et al. 1997:316). Similarly, the destruction of coastal resources, including fisheries, and the deterioration of watersheds have also reached acute levels in many areas (DeVries 2000). Unsustainable agricultural activities, overgrazing, deforestation, indiscriminate collection of wood for fuel, and uncontrolled use of pesticides are some of the practices resulting in the ecological crisis that plagues Honduras (USAID 1990; WRI 1992). Communities are placed directly at risk in times of disaster because of the dangerous locations of their farms and settlements. When Hurricane Mitch hit, people who lived and worked near rivers and streams had never before experienced water levels and velocities of such magnitude and were totally unprepared to cope with their impact.

High rates of population growth and the lack of economic alternatives have also forced rural populations to seek survival in Honduras' rapidly expanding urban centers. The World Bank estimates that the average annual rate of urbanization remains at approximately 5.5 percent, the highest in all of Central America (World Bank 1992:264–65). Honduras is the only country in Central America with an urban population distributed between two large centers: Tegucigalpa, the capital, with a population of nearly a million inhabitants (Humphrey 1997:215); and San Pedro Sula, a large urban center in the north, with a population of roughly 465,000 people. In fact, San Pedro Sula is the fastest-growing city in all of Central America (ibid.: 186). Many of these rural immigrants end up in overcrowded squatter shantytowns where problems such as violence, inadequate sanitation facilities, and poorly constructed housing on deforested, unstable slopes place their residents in conditions of extreme social and environmental vulnerability.

Furthermore, deteriorating living conditions in ever-growing urban squatter settlements and shantytown areas with inadequate sanitation facilities have resulted in high rates of diarrheal and parasitic diseases, a leading cause of death and disease in the country (Jacobson 1992). Since land suitable for construction purposes is scarce and expensive, many of these shantytowns have been built on highly unstable hill slopes that are prone to landslides and mudslides during the rainy season. In fact, crowded squatter settlements built on the steep hillsides that surround the center of Tegucigalpa were among the neighborhoods most severely damaged by Hurricane Mitch.

As illustrated in the preceding discussion, the latter part of the twentieth century witnessed enormous transformations in the physical and social environment of Honduras. These changes included dramatic environmental degradation, profound alterations in land use patterns, drastic declines in per capita production of basic grains, inadequate employment opportunities to earn cash to buy food, and a general reduction in nutritional status. Food security is beyond most rural people's means because production of the staples they consume has decreased while their ability to buy food has dwindled (Stonich 1991). These constraints have been compounded by significantly high population growth rates, which are placing enormous pressure on the available natural resources. The increasingly unequal distribution of resources resulting from the expansion of export-oriented agriculture further exacerbates the severe human and environmental problems of the area, leading to increased levels of vulnerability among a large proportion of the inhabitants.

Disaster Responses and Vulnerability

The previous two sections discussed the political-economic and ecological factors that framed the catastrophe provoked by Hurricane Mitch. Additionally, lack of disaster mitigation measures and inadequate post-disaster responses further contributed to the vulnerability of the population. For example, the Concepción Dam on the Choluteca River was already full before the rains started. Its operators feared that it would break and, late at night on October 30, made a "high-flow release of 760 cubic meters a second" (Pearce 2001:1) that engulfed several hamlets. A similar situation was provoked by the failure of the Laguna del Pescado Dam. This natural reservoir on a tributary of the Choluteca River had formed some years before after a landslip blocked the river. The authorities never got around to removing the block. According to reports by the USGS, "a large proportion of the natural dam failed, sending a flood wave down the channel" (ibid.: 2) that caused the level of the river to rise quickly by several meters, flooding much of central Tegucigalpa. Furthermore, Honduras did not have a legal framework for the enforcement of planning and construction standards during the immediate post-Mitch period. In many cases, there was no access to appropriate land for housing, and some populations moved back into locations where previous homes had been destroyed in the disaster and/or had to rely on inappropriate building materials. Not until late 2002, after the Maduro administration took over, were these problems addressed by drafting a construction code and a legal framework for emergencies and spatial planning.

Other factors that shaped the conditions of vulnerability in Honduras included the ineffectiveness, or nonexistence, of warning systems and the government's slow response. The Comisión Permanente de Contingencias (COPECO), Honduras' emergency management agency, received only about USD 200,000 as its annual budget, which limited the acquisition of equipment and the hiring of personnel (Fuentes 2003:125–26). Although they attempted to contact the population by radio, print, and television prior to the hurricane's landfall, COPECO was unable to evacuate or even reach the poorest sectors of society (ibid.: 125). Immediately after the hurricane, Honduran and foreign armed forces tried to respond but their efforts were hampered by lack of information due to poor emergency communication infrastructure (ibid.: 126–27). Unfortunately, government agencies failed to offer adequate disaster assistance after some of the communication and transportation systems had been restored (ibid.: 128). Some of the most basic emergency interventions implemented included search and rescue operations, provision of temporary shelter, sanitation programs such as the disposal of human and animal remains, and the distribution of water, food, blankets, and domestic items. The distribution of potable water, in particular, became a critical issue given the massive water shortage. Similarly, emergency sanitation activities had to be implemented to address the loss of, or damage to, sewerage and drainage systems. Health problems included injuries, gastrointestinal and acute respiratory infections, and dehydration. Leptospirosis (a disease spread through contact with rodent urine), which had been virtually nonexistent in the previous year, reappeared in Honduras after Mitch (Telford et al. 2004:8). Additionally, the destruction and displacement provoked by the hurricane triggered, among displaced families, a serious nutritional crisis that the uneven and difficult process of reconstruction has not been able to correct (Bonnard et al. 2002; David, Moncada, and Ordoñez 2004; Oken, Martinez Stoffel, and Stern 2004). The droughts that affected the country in May and June 2001 further compromised the supply of basic grains—particularly for rural subsistence agriculturalists in the southern, central, and western regions of Honduras, where food insecurity is a serious and persistent problem (Delgado 2001).

President Flores launched an international appeal on November 2, 1998, for assistance (UN Inter-Agency 1999:2–3). The Honduran United Nations system, which has ten specialized agencies with offices in Tegucigalpa, established an emergency coordinating group when Mitch hit, which was one of the first agencies to mobilize its resources to help government services involved in relief and rescue operations after the hurricane (Olivo Díaz López 2002). International aid started to arrive in the country immediately after the hurricane in the form of monetary donations. Additionally, the Mexican military provided immediate rescue and relief assistance. The United States and Spain took an early lead in donating relief supplies. The United Nations' Office for the Coordination of Humanitarian Affairs (OCHA) issued "situation reports" to inform the international community and mobilize assistance. A UN disaster assessment and coordination team helped the resident coordinator and the Honduran government manage international assistance, which included such agencies as the World Health Organization, WFP, FAO, and UNICEF (Olivo Díaz López 2002).

In 1998 the Honduran Congress passed the Law of Administrative Facilitation, which concentrated power in the office of the president and allowed President Flores to create a Special Cabinet for National Reconstruction (Olivo Díaz López 2002). Yet because there were concerns about the government's ability to administer aid, the task of receiving, managing, and distributing foreign assistance was given primarily to the Catholic Church and, to a lesser extent, to some Evangelical churches (Fuentes 2003:130). As Fuentes (chapter 5 in this volume) describes, this more direct delivery of foreign assistance strengthened civil society participation and could contribute to changes in state–society relations.

The Honduran state's poor preparedness for emergency response forced most communities to contact foreign nongovernmental organizations (NGOs) directly for assistance. In one case, the mayor of Morolica—a town in southern Honduras that was so devastated by Mitch-related floods that relocation became the only viable option—had to walk two days (about 200 miles) over mountainous regions to reach Tegucigalpa and request government and foreign assistance (Olivo Díaz López 2002; Ensor 2003). Communities were largely left on their own to organize rescue operations, pool resources, and seek help directly from foreign governments and aid organizations (Fuentes 2003:127). Additionally, the immediate process of coping and stabilization involved personal determination and great displays of solidarity; private and public buildings, hospitals, churches, and hotels opened their doors to the displaced and homeless (Olivo Díaz López 2002). In November 1998, the Inter-American Development Bank (IDB) organized a meeting in Washington, DC, to plan reconstruction and transformation with the governments of the Central American nations hit by Hurricane Mitch, international donors, and civil society representatives. In May 1999, another meeting was held in Stockholm to establish principles for effective implementation of the reconstruction and transformation plans. This later meeting, whose purpose was to develop guidelines for post-disaster reconstruction plans, was attended by representatives of the governments of the region, the IDB, specialist organizations and agencies of the United Nations system, and various NGOs. The so-called Consultative Group proposed the formulation of strategies for decentralization and municipal participation, improving government transparency, reducing social and ecological vulnerability, alleviating poverty, promoting respect for human rights, strengthening democratic institutions, and reducing external debt (Fuentes 2003:143–44; Hunt 2004).

The reconstruction phase was officially declared finalized at a ceremony celebrated in Tegucigalpa to commemorate the third anniversary of Hurricane Mitch. Masses were celebrated and medals were handed out to individuals and organizations for especially valiant service. This was also an occasion for the government, NGOs, and foreign donors to step back and assess the overall effect of their efforts. What followed was the implementation of a series of measures collectively known as the Poverty Reduction Strategy Papers (PRSP) initiatives. The recent emphasis on poverty alleviation in Honduras (as in many developing low-income countries) as part of the Millennium Development Goals strategy is likely to have a significant impact on the long-term vulnerability or resilience of the Honduran population. Yet the capacity of these measures to reduce the levels of social and environmental vulnerability in the country appears to be limited, as they emphasize the same kinds of unsustainable practices that characterized Honduras prior to Mitch (see Ensor and colleagues, chapter 8 in this volume).

Conclusion

A combination of factors—including a history of military rule, dependence on the United States and international financial institutions, structural inequalities, corruption, unsustainable practices of natural resource use, and the impact of disasters—have rendered Honduras one of the least developed countries in Central America. The link between uncontrolled economic growth, environmental degradation, and natural disasters is now widely acknowledged. Ongoing global environmental changes, when coupled with unsustainable development practices, have led to the increased vulnerability of people even as disasters have become more numerous and destructive. "The dominant trends in development, such as the transformation of natural resources into things, consumption patterns, urbanization, overuse of natural resources and use of environmentally harmful technologies, are directly responsible for creating natural disasters" (Bari 1998:125). It has been estimated that 90 percent of environmentally related disasters and 95 percent of disaster-related deaths worldwide occur in developing countries

(Munasinghe and Clarke 1995). This volume illustrates that, in Honduras, there is a clear connection between the political-ecological context, differentials in socially constructed vulnerability, and post-disaster reconstruction efforts.

The scale of the devastation and loss of life resulting from a natural phenomenon such as Hurricane Mitch in Honduras was clearly exacerbated by human-made factors. Before the hurricane, two thirds of the Honduran population were living below the poverty line and about half were living in extreme poverty. As Mitch swept across the Honduran landscape, its exceptional size, power, and duration abruptly and brutally altered the already diminished economic, social, and environmental conditions of the country. The destruction had the greatest impact on the most vulnerable segment of the Honduran population: the poorest people. Moreover, this catastrophe exposed Honduras' high level of national vulnerability, which was due to many factors that included inadequate and inappropriate development schemes; irrational, uncontrolled use and occupation of land; and the location, design, and construction of infrastructure (both public and private) without any consideration given to risk or the environment. Foreign donors played a crucial role in the disaster's immediate aftermath and also in the longer-term programs subsequently established (see Fuentes, chapter 5 in this volume). Ultimately, the success or failure of the post-disaster reconstruction measures implemented in Honduras will be determined by how appropriately the needs of the affected women and men are articulated in the proposed interventions.

Note

1. Structural adjustment "refers to the process by which many developing nations are reshaping their economies to be more free market oriented" (Sparr 1994:1). More specifically, structural adjustment is based on the assumption that an economy will be most efficient and productive if market forces operate and if products and services are neither protected, regulated, nor subsidized by the government. Under this approach, governments are encouraged to abandon the "import substitution" models that characterize state interventionism and move toward laissez-faire capitalism (ibid.: 2). Numerous studies have documented the human and environmental costs of structural adjustment, emphasizing the disproportionate impact that the crises and subsequent adjustment measures have had on the poor, minorities, women, and other vulnerable groups (Spring 1989; Sparr 1994; Green 1995).

References

Bari, Farzana. 1998. "Gender, Disaster and Empowerment: A Case Study from Pakistan." In *Through Women's Eyes: The Gendered Terrain of Disaster,* edited by Elaine Enarson and Betty Hearn Morrow. Westport, CN: Praeger.

Barrios, Roberto E., James P. Stansbury, Rosa Palencia, and Marco T. Medina. 2000. "Nutritional Status of Children under 5 Years of Age in Three Hurricane-Affected Areas of Honduras." *Revista Panamericana de Salud Pública* 8, no. 6: 380–84.

Benjamin, Medea. 1989. *Don't Be Afraid Gringo: A Honduran Woman Speaks from the Heart. The Story of Elvia Alvarado.* New York: Harper & Row.

Blaikie, Piers, Terry Cannon, Ian Davis, and Ben Wisner. 1994. *At Risk: Natural Hazards, People's Vulnerability, and Disasters.* London: Routledge.

Bonnard, Patricia, Patricia Haggerty, Anne Swindale, Giles Bergeron, and James Dempsey. 2002. *Report of the Food Aid and Food Security Assessment: A Review of the Title II Development Food Aid Program.* Food and Nutrition Technical Assistance Project. Washington, DC: Academy for Educational Development.

Bradshaw, Sarah. 2004. *Socio-Economic Impacts of Natural Disasters: A Gender Analysis.* Santiago, Chile: United Nations.

CIAT-Laderas. 1998. "Rain Totals from October 25 to 31, 1998." http://www.intertel.hn/org/ciathill/BIBLIOT/DP35/DEMUAL/DP35.htm.

Comisión Nacional del Medio Ambiente y Desarrollo (CONAMA). 1991. *Honduras Environmental Agenda.* Tegucigalpa, Honduras: Graficentro Editores.

Country Studies Honduras. 2004. *Country Studies/Area Handbook Series.* http://countrystudies.us/honduras/.

David, V., M. Moncada, and F. Ordoñez. 2004. "Private and Public Determinants of Child Nutrition in Nicaragua and Western Honduras." *Economics and Human Biology* 2, no. 3: 457–88.

Delgado, H. 2001. "Lack of Food and Nutritional Security in Central America: Contributing Factors and Social Exclusion." *Revista Panamericana de Salud Pública* 10, no. 6: 419–21.

DeVries, Gregory W. 2000. "Post-Hurricane Reconstruction in La Mosquitia." MS thesis, University of Florida, Gainesville.

Economic Commission for Latin America and the Caribbean (ECLAC). 1986. "Central America: Bases for a Reactivation and Development Policy." CEPAL *Review* 28 (April).

Ensor, Marisa Olivo. 2003. "Disaster Evangelism: Religion as a Catalyst for Change in Post-Mitch Honduras." *International Journal of Mass Emergencies and Disasters* 21: 31–49.

Fondo Social para la Deuda Externa y el Desarrollo de Honduras (FOSDEH). 2002. *Situación actual de la implementación de la estrategia de reducción de la pobreza*. Foro Social de la Deuda Externa y Desarrollo de Honduras, Tegucigalpa, Honduras (July 25).

Food and Agriculture Organization (FAO). 1999. "FAO/WFP Crop and Food Supply Assessment Mission to Honduras." http://www.fao.org/documents/show_cdr.asp?url_file=/docrep/004/x1056e/x1056e00.htm.

Fuentes, Vilma Elisa. 2003. "The Political Effects of Disaster and Foreign Aid: National and Subnational Governance after Hurricane Mitch." PhD dissertation, University of Florida, Gainesville.

Garst, Rachel, and Tom Barry. 1990. *Feeding the Crisis: U.S. Food Aid and Farm Policy in Central America*. Lincoln: University of Nebraska Press.

General Accounting Office Report. 1986. *Humanitarian Assistance to the Nicaraguan Democratic Resistance*. Washington, DC: GPO.

Green, Duncan. 1995. *Silent Revolution: The Rise of Market Economics in Latin America*. New York: Monthly Review Press.

Guiney, John L., and Miles B. Lawrence. 1999. *Preliminary Report: Hurricane Mitch*. 22 October–05 November 1999. National Hurricane Center. www.nhc.noaa.gov/1998mitch.html.

Humphrey, Chris. 1997. *Honduras Handbook*. Chico, CA: Moon Publications.

Hunt, Sarah. 2004. *Honduras: Consultative Group Meeting*. TRÓCAIRE, Tegucigalpa, Honduras.

Jacobson, Jodi L. 1992. "Improving Women's Reproductive Health." In *State of the World: 1992*, edited by Lester Brown. New York: Norton.

Keller, Nancy, Rob Rachowiecki, Barbara Reioux, Carolyn Hubbard, and Tom Bronahan. 1997. *Central America on a Shoestring*. Oakland, CA: Lonely Planet.

Loker, William M. 2004. *Changing Places: Environment, Development and Social Change in Rural Honduras*. Durham, NC: Carolina Academic Press.

Merrill, Tim L. 1993. *Honduras: A Country Study*. Washington, DC: Library of Congress.

Munasinghe, Mohan, and Caroline Clarke. 1995. *Disaster Prevention for Sustainable Development and Policy Issues*. New York: The World Bank and the International Decade for Natural Disaster Reduction (United Nations).

National Climatic Data Center (NCDC). 1999. "Mitch: The Deadliest Atlantic Hurricane since 1780." http://www.ncdc.noaa.gov/oa/reports/mitch/mitch.html.

Oken, E., E. Martinez Stoffel, and L. J. Stern. 2004. "Use of Volunteer Medical Brigades to Assess Growth in Honduras." *Journal of Tropical Pediatrics* 50, no. 4: 203–8.

Oliver-Smith, Anthony, and Susanna M. Hoffman. 2002. "Introduction: Why Anthropologists Should Study Disasters." In *Catastrophe and Culture*, edited by Anthony Oliver-Smith and Susanna M. Hoffman. Santa Fe, NM: SAR Press.

Olivo Díaz López, María-Jesús. 2002. "Relocating Morolica: Vulnerability and Resilience in Post-Mitch Honduras." PhD dissertation, Department of Anthropology, University of Florida, Gainesville.

Paz, Ernesto. 1986. "The Foreign Policy and National Security of Honduras." In *Honduras Confronts Its Future: Contending Perspectives on Critical Issues,* edited by Mark B. Rosenberg and Philip L. Shepherd, 181–210. Boulder, CO: Reinner.

Pearce, Fred. 2001. "Dams and Floods. WWF International Research Paper." http://www.wwf.or.jp/lib/freshwater/DamsAndFloods.pdf.

Plan Maestro de la Reconstrucción y Transformación Nacional (PMRTM). 1999. *Reunión del Grupo Consultivo.* Stockholm, Sweden.

Secretaría de Salud de Honduras. 1999. *Programa de preparativos para desastres.* Tegucigalpa, Honduras.

Sparr, Pamela. 1994. *Mortgaging Women's Lives: Feminist Critiques of Structural Adjustment.* London: Zed.

Spring, Anita. 1989. "Gender and International Development: Engendering Adjustment for the 1990s." *Report of a Commonwealth Group on Women and Structural Adjustment.* Commonwealth Secretariat. Pall Mall, London: Marlborough House.

Stonich, Susan. 1991. "Rural Families and Income from Migration: Honduran Households in the World Economy." *Journal of Latin American Studies* 23, no. 1: 131–61.

———. 1993. *I Am Destroying the Land: The Political Ecology of Poverty and Environmental Destruction in Honduras.* Boulder, CO: Westview.

Telford, John, Margaret Arnold, and Alberto Harth, with ASONOG (Asociación de Organismos No Gubernamentales de Honduras). 2004. "Learning Lessons from Disaster Recovery: The Case of Honduras." Hazard Management Unit, World Bank, Washington, DC.

Trócaire Policy Briefing. 2004. "Are PRSPs Combating Rural Poverty in Honduras and Nicaragua? Lessons for a New Generation of PRSPs." County Kildare, Ireland: Trócaire (August).

United Nations. 2002. "United Nations Partners in the Reconstruction and Transformation of Central America." Second Consultative Group Meeting for the Reconstruction and Transformation of Central America, 25–28 May, 1999." Stockholm, Sweden.

United Nations Development Programme (UNDP). 1999. *Informe sobre desarrollo humano Honduras 1999: El impacto de un huracán.* PNUD.

———. 2007. *Human Development Reports. 2007–2008 Report. 05 Demographic Trend.* http://hdrstats.undp.org/indicators/37.html.

United Nations Inter-Agency. 1999. *Transitional Appeal for Hurricane Mitch (Period December 1998 to May 1999). Resident Coordinator of Operational Activities of the United Nations System.* Tegucigalpa, Honduras.

United States Agency for International Development (USAID). 1990. *Agricultural Sector Strategy Paper.* Tegucigalpa, Honduras: USAID Honduras.

———. 1991. *Economic Assistance Strategy for Central America, 1991 to 2000.* Washington, DC: USAID Honduras.

White, Robert Anthony. 1977. *Structural Factors in Rural Development: The Church and the Peasants in Honduras.* Ithaca, NY: Cornell University Press.

Williams, Robert G. 1986. *Export Agriculture and the Crisis in Central America.* Chapel Hill: University of North Carolina Press.

———. 1991. "Land, Labor and the Crisis in Central America." In *Harvest of Want: Food Security in Central America and Mexico,* edited by Anne Ferguson and Scott Whiteford, 23–44. Boulder, CO: Westview.

World Bank. 1992. *World Development Report.* New York: Oxford University Press.

World Resource Institute (WRI). 1992. *World Resources: 1992–1993.* New York: Oxford University Press.

3
From Natural Events to "Natural" Disasters
Assessing Environmental Vulnerability in Honduras

Manuel Winograd

A Holistic Approach

Recognizing and assessing vulnerabilities is an important first step toward creating communities that are more resilient to disasters. The development of indicators of disaster risk and vulnerability enables decision makers to assess the possible impacts of disasters, and such development is a key element of the strategy proposed by the 2005 World Conference on Disaster Reduction and formalized in the Hyogo Framework for Action 2005–2015. Assessments that integrate the views of all stakeholders and reveal the underlying causes of disaster vulnerability show greater potential for improving the efficiency of disaster management than earlier approaches that focused exclusively on the role of environmental extremes. The complex relationship between environmental hazards and sociocultural and economic vulnerabilities needs to be better understood and to be incorporated in disaster reduction strategies.

Almost a decade after Hurricane Mitch, Central American nations, including Honduras, have made notable progress in their civil protection systems (i.e., improving early warning systems and evacuation strategies when hurricanes approach). However, effective strategies for adapting to the increasing variability, frequency, and intensity of environmental extremes and for coping with the enormous socioeconomic consequences have yet to be fully incorporated in disaster planning and policy making. This chapter presents a methodology, developed in the aftermath of Hurricane Mitch in Honduras, to calculate various vulnerability indexes and to evaluate alternative post-disaster responses, and it illustrates an approach that links research with action toward effective risk reduction.

Introduction: A Holistic Approach

A number of studies have examined the impact of climatic events and disasters on specific countries and regions *after* the event occurred (Trujillo, Ordóñez, and Hernández 2000; Meltzer 2001; Freeman et al. 2002; Van Aalst and Burton 2002; Dilley, Chen, and Deichmann 2005). This type of post-event analysis often fails to fully capture the impact of chronic exposure to catastrophic events in a given area, and it tends to overlook the causal linkages that exist between social, economic, and environmental conditions and structures. In turn, the failure to incorporate vulnerability assessment into disaster management leads to a lack of adequate adaptations and coping strategies, with each new environmental crisis rendering the country or region more vulnerable to the next (Freeman et al. 2002). For example, flooding can affect farmers' agricultural production, cause sedimentation in dams that affects a region's future energy production, and provoke landslides that could damage road and electricity infrastructure. A combination of these factors may consequently reduce access to markets, interrupt national energy distribution, and affect the regional, national, and international prices of some crops. Therefore, a systematic analysis of vulnerability requires that adequate attention be paid to the "architecture" of stresses, responses, and coping strategies at different scales of resources and levels of decision.

Holistic approaches are also essential when considering the relationship between poverty, environmental degradation, and environmental hazards. Unsustainable natural resource management practices (such as deforestation, agriculture on marginal land, or destruction of mangrove forests) are often induced, or at least exacerbated, by poverty. Moreover, environmental degradation is likely to result in additional risks. Some event, which itself would have been relatively harmless had the degradation not taken place, might become the proverbial last straw on the camel's back. The degraded natural systems become less resilient to the impact of environmental extremes, the poor lose what few resources they had, and both human and natural systems are left poorer and more vulnerable to future hazards. The resulting cycle of vulnerability and destruction illustrates the premise that sustainable development requires a holistic view (Van Aalst and Burton 2002).

In light of the dramatic increase in large-scale disasters in recent years, efforts to understand and reduce vulnerability have become increasingly pressing concerns for both developed and developing nations. Although notable advances have been made, much remains to be done in the way of alleviating the long-term economic, social, and ecological impacts of environmental extremes. The situation is complicated by the fact that many of the most disaster-prone nations are heavily dependent on sectors—such as agriculture, livestock production, and the exploitation of coastal and riverine resources—that are highly sensitive to environmentally related disasters. Thus, managing disasters and environmental variability has become a crucial element of policy agendas for sustainable development, particularly in those countries, such as Honduras, that are prone to disaster yet have limited resources to cope with the attendant losses (Charvériat 2000).

The Hyogo Framework for Action 2005–2015, agreed upon during the 2005 World Conference on Disaster Reduction (held in Kobe, Japan), defined the development of indicators for disaster risk and vulnerability as one of the key priorities to help support the transition to a more sustainable world. These indicators are conceived as tools for identifying the most threatened areas and social groups, assessing the potential impact of disasters, and enabling decision makers to formulate appropriate policy management responses. Although much remains to be done in the way of translating theoretical models and concepts into "the full practical use of anticipative vulnerability measurement" (van Ginkel 2006:xxi), innovative methodologies for assessing vulnerability at different levels of society have been developed in recent years (see Birkmann 2006 for a critical review of current methodologies).

Using post-Mitch Honduras as a case study, this chapter presents an adaptive strategy for linking the systematic diagnosis and assessment of disasters to the design and implementation of effective responses for coping with and reducing environmental and socioeconomic vulnerability. This approach requires moving beyond the almost exclusive focus on ad hoc responses that has traditionally characterized post-disaster reconstruction interventions in Honduras. Instead, this chapter proposes a systematic and proactive method of identifying key data to prepare for current and future threats, a method that emphasizes reducing environmental and socioeconomic vulnerability and defining coping strategies to increase resilience. It is argued here that the information generated must be not only politically relevant and technically solid but also socially appropriate in order to be accepted and implemented. Information management must also facilitate the definition of regional strategies, elaboration of national policies, and application of local actions. Rather than simply blaming "climatic uncertainty" for the effects of "natural" disasters, this approach proposes to focus on *planning* for possible impacts, *adapting* to adverse consequences, *preventing* negative effects, and *mitigating* direct and underlying causes (Winograd 2002; Winograd, Fall, and Thomas 2005).

The Project

The results described in this chapter were originally developed in the context of a collaborative project—in the aftermath of Hurricane Mitch—between the Land Use Unit of the International Center for Tropical Agriculture (CIAT),[1] the Disaster Management Facility Unit of the World Bank, and the Government of Honduras.

The primary goals of the project included determining the areas with high degrees of vulnerability to climatic-related natural hazards, prioritizing the different Honduran municipalities in terms of identifying reconstruction and mitigation options after Mitch, and identifying adaptation and coping strategies for possible future events. A methodology for analyzing natural disaster vulnerability was defined, validated, and harmonized with participating stakeholders and national institutions. This methodology was based on the development of different vulnerability indexes (for environmental, population, social, and infrastructure vulnerability) in order to prioritize vulnerable groups, areas, and sectors (see figure 3.1).[2]

At the international and regional levels, the primary users of the data gathered through this project include the World Bank and the Central American Commission on Environment and Development/Mesoamerican Biological Corridor (CCAD/MBC). Both the World Bank and the CCAD/MBC have utilized the information presented in this chapter to evaluate and negotiate mitigation and reconstruction options at regional and national levels and also to explore options for adapting to climate variability and change. At national and local levels, the main beneficiaries are again the World Bank, the government of Honduras, national institutions, and the Association of Municipalities of Honduras (AMHON). National and local stakeholders have used these data to explore and negotiate national priorities on reconstruction, rehabilitation, and adaptation options related to land use, urban planning, and early warning systems.

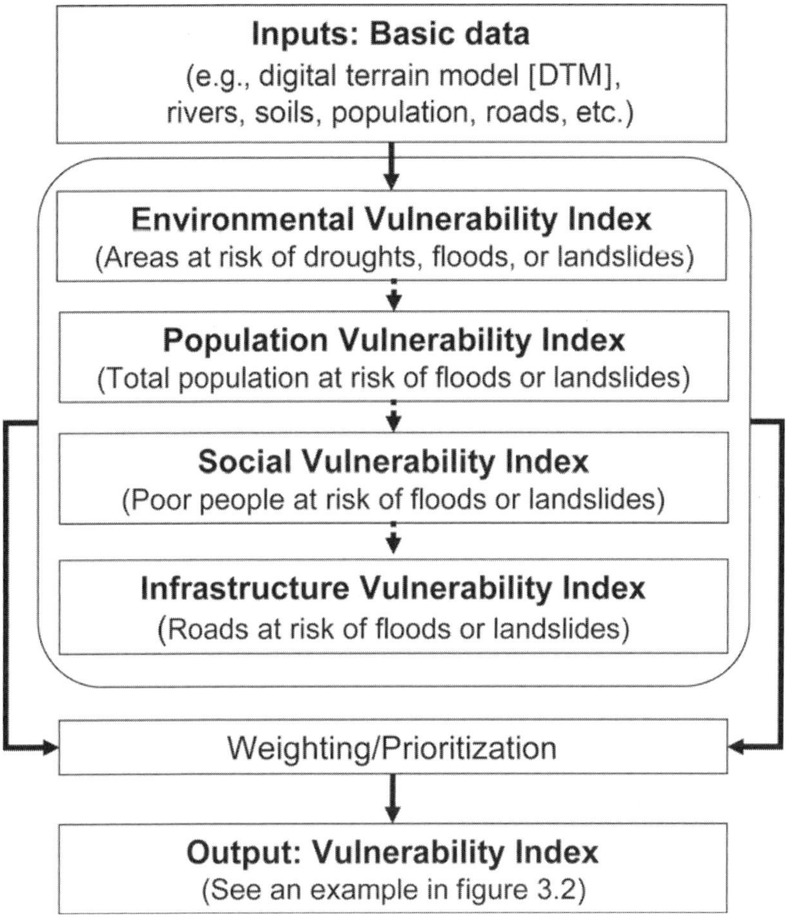

Figure 3.1 Methodology for vulnerability assessment.

Assessing Vulnerability in Honduras

The environmental vulnerability[3] index for Honduras (based on areas vulnerable to drought, landslides, and flooding) indicates that more than 50 percent of the country is at risk of landslides or droughts (60 percent of the land that is used). Additionally, more than 25 percent of Honduran territory is at risk for flooding (50 percent of the land that is used), particularly along the more populated agricultural areas surrounding the axis of San Pedro Sula, Tegucigalpa, and Choluteca.

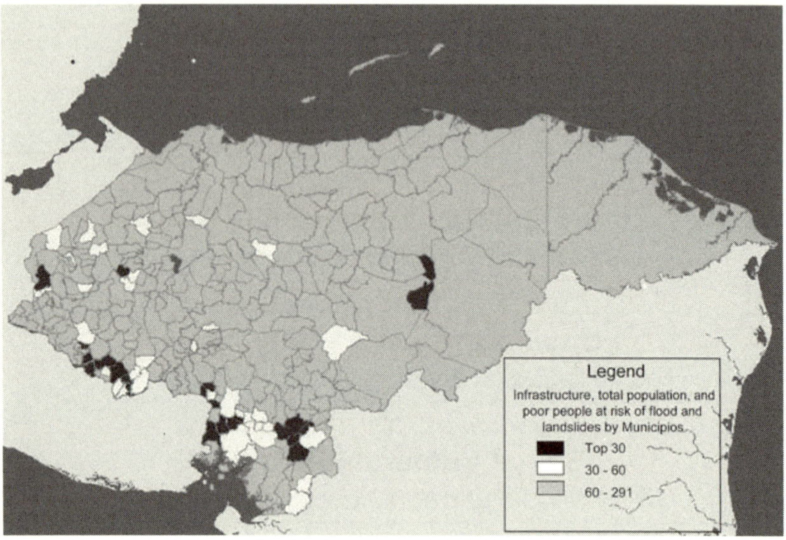

Figure 3.2 Honduran areas prioritized in terms of vulnerability (Winograd et al. 2000).

Figure 3.2 illustrates this situation by integrating the environmental, population, social, and infrastructure vulnerability indexes to obtain a combined vulnerability index that helps identify the most critical priority, or "hotspot," areas (Winograd et al. 2000). Figure 3.2 depicts the location—as determined by the combined vulnerability index—of high-risk areas in the counties of Honduras that must be prioritized in order to identify options for mitigation and adaptation.

Indirect Impacts of Hurricane Mitch

Populations affected by disasters suffer from both immediate direct impacts (e.g., destruction of home and property) and long-term indirect consequences (e.g., loss of accessibility). Official figures tend to reflect the direct impact of disasters and typically ignore indirect ones, yet effectively mitigating the underlying roots of vulnerability (to identify post-disaster reconstruction priorities) requires attention to both. This point can be illustrated by examining the effect of indirect impacts on some of the most impoverished regions of Honduras.

The poor are generally assumed to be among the most vulnerable sector of any population affected by disasters. Considering only the direct impact of Mitch, the Honduran poor do not necessarily appear to have been hit harder than other groups. However, if the indirect effects (e.g., loss of accessibility, defined as travel time required to reach a given location) are also taken into account, then the resulting picture is far more negative. Figure 3.3a shows the areas where more than 10 percent of the accessibility to markets was lost as well as the location of villages with severe and critical levels of poverty. This figure illustrates that the negative consequences affecting some areas, though significant, were primarily indirect and resulted from damage or destruction of the relevant infrastructure. For instance, the difficulty of access between population centers and rural areas is known to have caused serious delays in the arrival of medical aid, food, seeds, and other resources to the isolated populations who needed them most. It is important to note that figure 3.3a shows only those areas of reduced accessibility, not all areas affected by Mitch in any way. This figure was produced by comparing

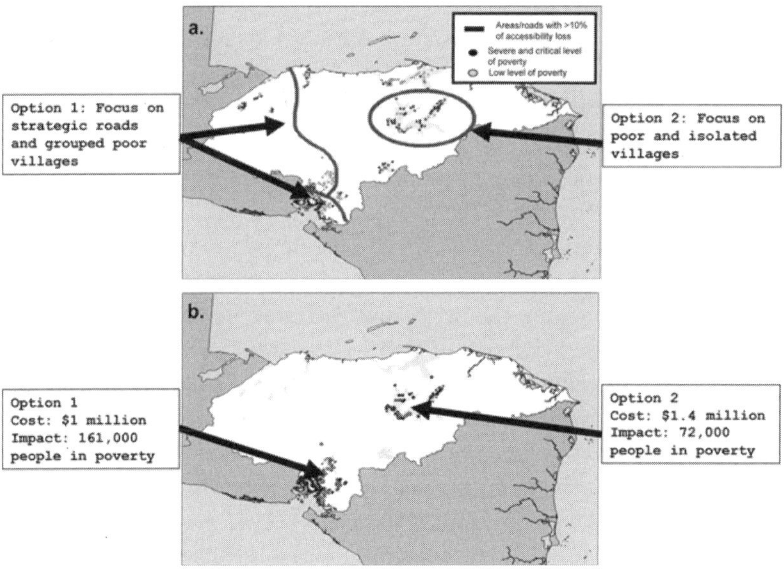

Figure 3.3 Socioeconomic hotspots and reconstruction options in Honduras (Winograd, Farrow, and Nelson 1999).

accessibility before and after Mitch, with losses given as percentages (rather than a value in hours) to capture the perceived loss of accessibility (Winograd, Farrow, and Nelson 1999).

Prioritizing Reconstruction and Mitigating Underlying Causes

A fundamental advantage of disaster management approaches that focus on mitigating the underlying causes of vulnerability is their potential to help identify effective priorities for post-disaster reconstruction. In addition to the data discussed in the previous section, figure 3.3a also shows two potential reconstruction options that would help alleviate the impacts of Mitch on Honduras' poorer population. The first option is oriented toward reconstructing strategic roads in Honduras affected by Mitch and restoring accessibility between the most important cities, ports, and productive resources (with an indirect goal of recovering the accessibility of poor villages). The second option is oriented toward reconstructing the road network that allows access to isolated poor villages. Figure 3.3b shows the costs and benefits of these two options. It is worth observing that the cost is lower, and the number of poor people who benefit is higher, with the first option. Of course, these two options are exploratory and not exclusive. The analysis on which they are based was carried out with the goal of illustrating the importance of using adequate information to explore various planning strategies and to prioritize potential reconstruction options for the most affected sectors (Winograd, Farrow, and Nelson 1999).

Another example of this approach is presented in figure 3.4a, which illustrates that flat areas, where most of the permanent agricultural fields are located, were the areas most affected by the flooding associated with Mitch. Analyses of figures 3.4a and 3.4b further indicate that the floods occurring in the north, center, and south of the country could have been partially due to deforestation and land-use changes in the basin areas where unsustainable agriculture and livestock production practices have become increasingly prevalent. The lack of sufficient ground vegetation cover is also associated with exacerbated erosive processes on mountainsides, which leads to a heightened risk of landslides and mudslides that, if they create temporary blockages of rivers upstream, can then result in sudden water releases and dangerous flash floods downriver. Thus, information on the underlying causes of ob-

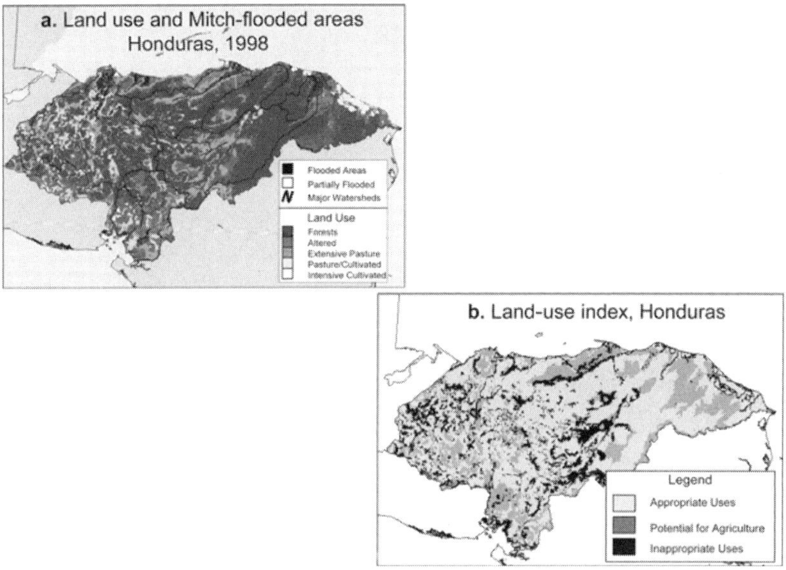

Figure 3.4 Land use and floods after Mitch in Honduras (Winograd et al. 2000).

served effects could be critical in helping to prioritize interventions, determine the financial aid and investments required, identify the people and sectors that would benefit from the proposed intervention, and develop responsive prevention and mitigation planning schedules (Winograd, Farrow, and Nelson 1999).

Evaluation of Adaptation Options

Figure 3.5a shows the environmental vulnerability index at local levels in four communities in the Department of Olancho, Honduras. Figure 3.5b shows the actual predominant production systems and associated land uses, where actual and future vulnerability is high because current land-use practices increase the risk of landslides and flooding. Figure 3.5c shows alternative production systems and land-use options that diminish vulnerability and increase resilience, given that these alternatives *decrease* the risks of landslides, erosion, and flooding.

As illustrated in figure 3.6, mangroves provide a key ecosystem for

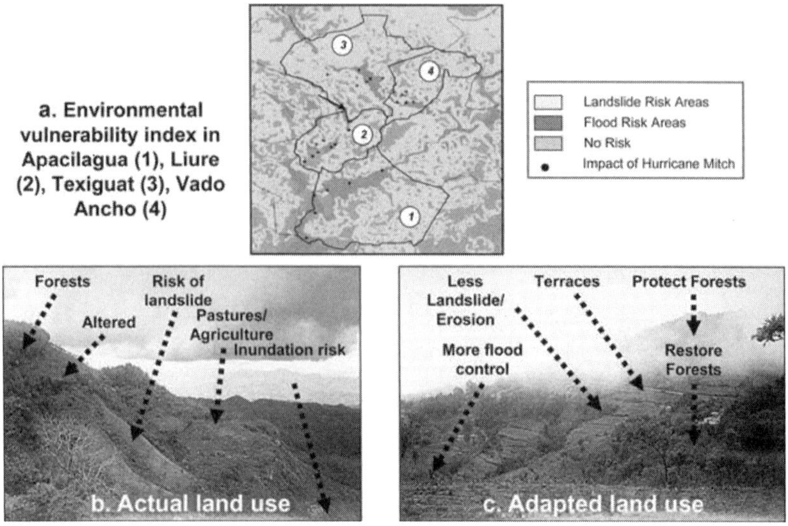

Figure 3.5 Exploration of adaptation options for production systems in Honduras (Winograd, Fall, and Thomas 2005).

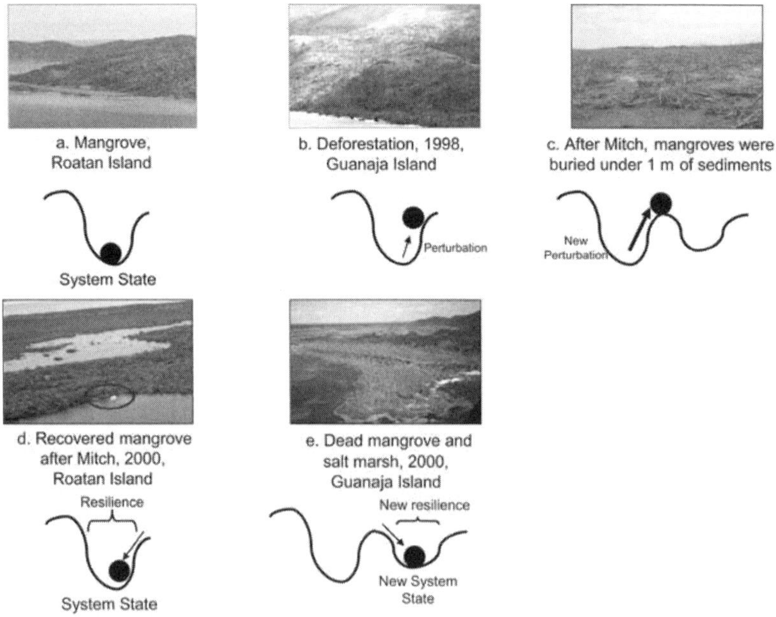

Figure 3.6 Resilience assessment: the case of mangroves in Honduras (Winograd, Fall, and Thomas 2005; photo sources: USGS 2001).

resources (i.e., fisheries, aquaculture, and wood) and environmental functions (protecting coasts from floods and erosion, serving as nurseries for wild fish and birds). On Roatan Island, for instance, the mangroves and forests are well protected and/or well managed (figure 3.6a), resulting in low levels of deforestation in mangroves and upper forests; this has allowed the system to recover from the impact of the hurricane and revert back to a stable state (figure 3.6d) (Winograd 2006).

In contrast, Guanaja Island (figure 3.6b) was poorly managed and experienced high levels of deforestation in mangroves and upper forests. After Mitch, the Guanaja system shown in figure 3.6c was transformed into that shown in figure 3.6e: dead mangroves and salt marshes, and a different ecological system with new functional patterns and associated resources.

With respect to land use and production systems, the analysis of *resilience*—defined by Carpenter et al. (2002) as the capacity of a system to absorb perturbation or stress while maintaining structure and function—shows promising results (figure 3.7). For instance, it is known that when an intense hurricane like Mitch strikes, land-use patterns on hillside areas are likely to change rapidly during the disturbance phase (circle 2 in figures 3.7a and 3.7b). If these strategies involve low capital and mono-crop farming (figure 3.7a), then the low diversity of land-use patterns will likely result in a decrease in resilience and complexity, which explains why the post-disaster reorganization phase is often slow. In many cases, the system will be unable to return to its former equilibrium (circle 3 in figure 3.7a), and key variables such as production diversity and agricultural productivity will almost invariably be altered. A new (re)colonization phase will start, which could result in new land-use patterns and production systems. In contrast, with multi-cropping production systems (figure 3.7b) the diversity of land use increases resilience and complexity, which explains the fast reorganization phase in this case. Thus, the multi-cropping production system can return to its former equilibrium with those key variables unchanged. Overall, analysis of available data suggests that the land-use system prevalent in Honduras appears to be relatively resilient, although not necessarily stable (Kok and Winograd 2002).

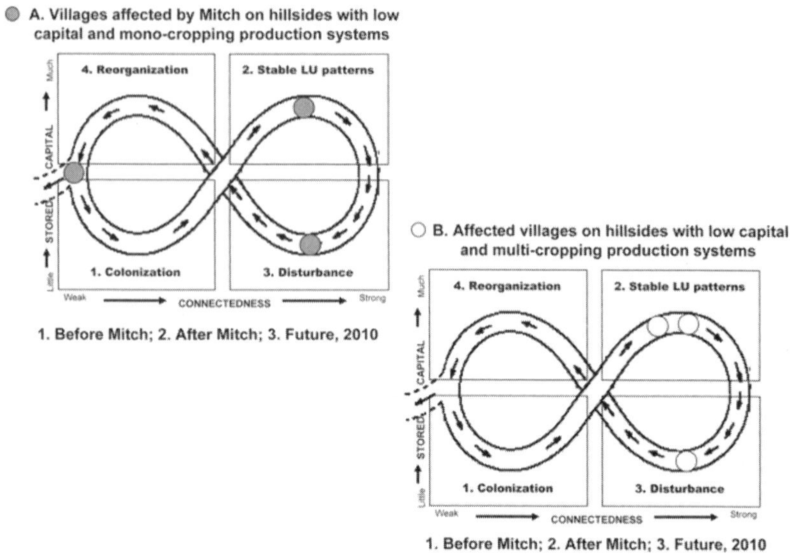

Figure 3.7 Resilience of land use and production systems in Honduras (Kok and Winograd 2002).

From Assessment to Decision Making

Losses from Hurricane Mitch throughout Central America have been estimated at USD 8.8 billion. Multilateral institutions, international agencies, and the governments of various developed countries pledged to donate USD 8.7 billion to the countries of the region (less than USD 3 billion had actually reached those nations by the end of 2004, six years after the disaster). However, research suggests that investments of only USD 0.35 to 0.5 billion for mitigation and adaptation measures (involving land use and early warning systems) would have resulted in losses of USD 3.5 billion being avoided ("Helping the Survivors" 2005).

In post-Mitch Honduras, prevention and adaptation measures have traditionally been perceived as costs rather than as investments in vulnerability reduction. Similarly, policies and interventions have been oriented toward addressing the consequences—rather than preventing the causes—of disasters. Also noteworthy is that fewer than 40 percent of the reconstruction and mitigation projects initiated after Mitch have been located in the most highly affected *municipios* (municipalities). At the same time, a lack of urgency and of appropriate information have contributed to fewer than 10 percent of the reconstruction and mitigation projects addressing highly vulnerable municipios (Winograd et al. 2000; Winograd 2002). Although the dynamics of vulnerability were generally understood, the spatial mapping of static indicators carried out generally failed to represent the importance of some key drivers and issues (e.g., infrastructure and economic access to isolated villages and the effect of uplands deforestation on crops in the lowlands). In fact, many vulnerability assessments conducted in Honduras are still adapted to only short-term evaluation, even though there is a critical need for analyses of long-term risks: the cumulative effects of natural events on vulnerability and on possible synergies and thresholds of climate change (Winograd et al. 2000).

An important requirement in building social and environmental resilience is access to appropriate and up-to-date information that can help reduce uncertainty at all levels of planning and decision making. Indicators must be analyzed in the context of broader frameworks that include vulnerability assessments. Risk mapping should incorporate quantifiable data, including the calculation of indicators that can be compared across such geographical levels as municipalities, regions, and countries; this would enable a more effective prioritization of high-risk populations. On the other hand, such quantitative data are often static and possibly decontextualized. Thus, if quantifiable models are not qualified by a thorough understanding of local political, social, and economic conditions—to include a recognition of both their static and dynamic characteristics—then the value of a risk map will be diminished (Tompkins and Adger 2003; Ziervogel et al. in press). A case in point, with respect to the use of geographic information systems and other technical tools used in disaster management, is the need of what has been termed "socialized pixels." In other words, spatial entities (countries, landscapes, watersheds, ecosystems) must be related to the relevant social actors and users (peoples, households, communities, decision makers) and the causes of vulnerability (livelihoods, landslides, drought, poverty) (Verburg et al. 2004; Winograd 2006).

Another key factor is the establishment and strengthening of local capacities to produce and use information and to identify best practices. Developing real capacity must not be limited to providing institutions, decision makers, and local inhabitants with currently available methods and recommendations. Also needed is additional training on how to implement vulnerability assessments, how to use the information obtained through these methods, and how to improve policy decision making and planning so that the actors and institutions involved are empowered to transform information into action on their own terms. Without good information and knowledge of best practices on the use of vulnerability indicators, it is impossible to foster participation, to manage risk effectively, or to cope with the consequences of dramatic changes. The first essential step is to correct existing practices that misuse data, information, and tools in order to ensure better decisions, facilitate actors' participation at different levels, and enable non-specialists to access and effectively use information.

The case of Honduras clearly illustrates the importance of effective vulnerability assessment in decision making as well as the need to facilitate collaboration among the various stakeholders so that the best strategies for mitigation and adaptation can be identified and implemented. Giving real meaning to data and indicators requires an understanding of stakeholders' needs, a process that involves translating facts into useful data, turning concerns into awareness, and transforming theoretical knowledge into practical action (Winograd, Fall, and Thomas 2005). For government officers and politicians, certainty is desirable, time is often measured in terms of the election cycle, equity is considered a short-term goal, and risk is intolerable. For rural people, on the other hand, uncertainty is inescapable, time is perceived in terms of the next harvesting season, poverty is a constant reality, and risk is integrated into daily life. Given this diversity of perceptions, the challenge for all those seeking to provide effective solutions for the problems caused (or exacerbated) by the impact of disasters entails harmonizing research, decision making, and the priorities of all stakeholders.

Furthermore, the use of information for decision making and planning needs to go beyond simply monitoring the catastrophic effects (on the economy, society, and the environment) of the disaster and planning for the subsequent reconstruction. What is needed instead is a focus on the prevention of the direct and indirect causes in order to mitigate future possible effects (Downing et al. 2003; Ziervogel et al. in press). It is important to note that research on vulnerability needs to assess it not only in terms of exposure to risk but also by considering people's and systems' (in)ability to cope with risks and their impacts. Disaster mitigation must be a developmental strategy. In other words, preventing natural events from becoming disasters requires that policies and actions be proactive rather than reactive. As discussed throughout this volume, a good understanding of social issues is also required. Research shows, for instance, that strong social networks help people recover from the impact of catastrophic events (Christian Aid 2000; Telford et al. 2004). In Honduras, access to social networks increased the number of coping strategies available to hurricane victims in the form of finances (remittances, loans, and donations), resources (food, water, and wood), and help in finding shelter and alternative income sources (Segnestam et al. 2006).

Conclusions

Almost a decade after Hurricane Mitch, the focus of the international community has shifted from efforts to save lives during the impact and immediate emergency phases of disasters, to a broader emphasis on safeguarding livelihoods in the context of increasing incidents of events related to climate change. Similarly, disaster planning and decision making have moved beyond simply monitoring the impact of disasters on the population, the economy, and the environment *after* the catastrophe has already occurred. It is now generally acknowledged that anticipating and better preparing for the consequences of disasters require strategies that address the direct and indirect causes as well as the immediate and long-term responses.

Assessments carried out by the Economic Commission for Latin America and the Caribbean (ECLAC) in Central America conclude that, during the last thirty years, the economic losses due to natural events are equivalent to 2 percent of the region's gross domestic product (GDP) per year (see ECLAC 1999 for such an assessment carried out shortly after Mitch). These studies show that extreme events associated with the ENSO anomaly (La Niña/El Niño phenomenon)—such as storms, droughts, and floods—are expected to increase in the future as a result of climate change. The poor, who tend to live and work in high-risk areas (i.e., slum dwellers on marginal land in urban areas, plantation workers in lowlands, or rural populations on eroded hillsides and vulnerable lowlands and coastal areas where jobs are concentrated) will suffer most as the planet warms and severe climatic events and other natural hazards occur with increased frequency and intensity. The poorer sectors of society are also more likely to lack insurance against losses or access to emergency health care and alternative resources, which makes reducing human vulnerability to extreme events crucially important from a poverty perspective (CIAT-CEPAL-SEI 2002; Segnestam et al. 2006).

In Honduras, the extreme severity of Hurricane Mitch's impact resulted from multiple and interrelated factors (Trujillo, Ordóñez, and Hernández 2000; Segnestam et al. 2006). Ensor and Ensor (chapter 2 in this volume) examine the political, socioeconomic, and environmental factors that prefigured Honduras' conditions of heightened vulnerability at the time of Mitch's impact. The local, state-level, and international responses to the catastrophe—together with the subsequent post-disaster reconstruction strategies discussed throughout this book—will determine the country's capacity to respond to future disaster events.

The material presented in this chapter underscores the need to ensure that the situation on the ground (populations' needs and assets; development and institutional contexts) is linked to the methods and tools used by researchers in a way that reflects the processes taking place in the affected area. Information needs will vary according to the situation, the people involved, and the priorities set by interest groups and decision-makers. Thus, politically relevant, socially acceptable, and technically valid data should be made available to the various stakeholders in order to ensure that assessments are not based solely on partial, anecdotal, or temporary factors. Information on vulnerability, impacts, and adaptation options like those presented in this chapter should be translated from scientific or technical language to materials accessible to decision-makers and actors at all levels. It is also important to link spatial entities (villages, landscapes, watersheds, ecosystems) to social entities (individuals, families, communities, towns) acknowledging both the spatial and temporal dimensions of reality on the ground.

As illustrated in this chapter, priorities regarding disaster preparedness, reconstruction responses, and adaptation options among the different stakeholders may not necessarily coincide. The responsibility for many of the failures in cross-level interactions in post-Mitch Honduras can be found at the national and municipal levels (e.g., lack of early warning systems and poorly integrated natural resources management), but additional factors at the household and community level (e.g., widespread illiteracy, poor community coordination, and inadequate access to disaster information; Segnestam et al. 2006) underscore the need for a more nuanced, multilevel assessment strategy.

Long-term efforts to integrate natural hazard management with broader environmental management were nonexistent in Honduras at the time of Mitch's impact, and almost a decade later they are slowly being implemented at the national level. This contrasts with efforts at the local level, where there has been more emphasis on mitigation and adaptation to prevent hazards from becoming disasters (Meltzer 2001; Olson et al. 2001; Telford et al. 2004; Segnestam et al. 2006; Winograd 2006). Overall, conflicting top-down and bottom-up tendencies are not yet sufficiently integrated in efforts to alleviate vulnerability in Honduras.

The approach discussed in this chapter has the potential to promote increased political and social attention to issues of vulnerability assessment and risk prevention and adaptation, so that they begin to be perceived as investments in the future and not just costs for the present. Systematic disaster risk and vulnerability assessment can help define regional strategies, guide national policies, identify optimal options, and implement interventions at all levels. Disaster management interventions should aim at addressing direct and indirect root causes, planning for possible impacts, adapting to adverse consequences, and alleviating negative effects in order to reduce the vulnerability to future events. This will facilitate replacing reactive ad hoc responses to environmental crises with a better-informed and proactive participation of the affected population.

Ultimately, those seeking to promote sustainable development in disaster-prone regions must not limit themselves to analyzing risks and vulnerabilities. Also required are identifying new methods and approaches that can help affected populations and systems cope with the impact of disasters, advancing ways to foster adaptive capacities and resilience, and promoting policies and preventive measures that address increasing climate change and environmental extremes.

Notes

1. CIAT is one of the fifteen centers that make up the Consultative Group on International Agricultural Research (CGIAR), a strategic alliance of countries, international and regional organizations, and private foundations that

work with national agricultural research systems and civil society organizations including the private sector. The alliance mobilizes agricultural science to reduce poverty, foster human well-being, promote agricultural growth, and protect the environment.

2. For the purposes of this project, *vulnerability* is construed as a function of the risks, dangers, exposure, and adaptation options and coping responses (i.e., Vulnerability = Risk − Responses/Options). *Risk* is defined as the probability and magnitude of the occurrence of danger. *Danger* is the potential threat to humans and their well-being as well as to ecosystems, goods, and services. *Exposure* is the likelihood of suffering impacts and/or losses. *Responses* and *options* are the reactions and adaptive mechanisms used either to prevent or to cope with the impact of a disaster.

3. The *environmental vulnerability index* is based on areas vulnerable to drought, landslides, and flooding. The *population vulnerability index* expresses, by community, the population at risk of flooding plus the population at risk of landslides. The *social vulnerability index* reflects the total population (by community and poverty level) at risk of flooding plus the total population (by "village" and poverty level) at risk of landslides. The *infrastructure vulnerability index* indicates roads at risk of flooding plus roads at risk of landslides plus electricity lines at risk of flooding plus electricity lines at risk of landslides.

References

Birkmann, J. (ed.). 2006. *Measuring Vulnerability to Natural Hazards: Towards Disaster Resilient Societies.* Tokyo: United Nations University Press.

Carpenter, C. S., T. Elmqvist, L. Gunderson, C. S. Holling, and B. Walker. 2002. "Resilience and Sustainable Development: Building Adaptive Capacity in a World of Transformations." *Cambio* 31: 437–40.

Charvériat, C. 2000. *Natural Disasters in Latin America and the Caribbean: An Overview of Risk.* Washington, DC: Inter-American Development Bank.

Christian Aid. 2000. *In Debt to Disaster: What Happened to Honduras after Hurricane Mitch?* London: Christian Aid.

CIAT-CEPAL-SEI in Collaboration with CEPREDENAC and CCAD. 2002. *Cross-Scale Aspects of Vulnerability to Multiple Stresses in Central America.* Unpublished project proposal.

Dilley, M., R. S. Chen, and U. Deichmann. 2005. *Natural Disaster Hotspot: A Global Risk Analysis.* Hazard Management Unit, World Bank, Washington, DC.

Downing, T., A. Patwardhan, R. Klien, E. Mukhala, L. Stephen, M. Winograd, and G. Ziervogel. 2003. *Vulnerability Assessment for Climate Adaptation.* Adaptation Planning Framework, Technical Paper 3. New York: UNDP.

Economic Commission for Latin America and the Caribbean (ECLAC). 1999.

Honduras: Assessment of the Damage Caused by Hurricane Mitch, 1998. Implications for Economic and Social Development and for the Environment. Santiago, Chile: United Nations Economic Commission for Latin America and the Caribbean.

Freeman, P., L. A. Martin, R. Mechler, K. Warner, and P. Hausmann. 2002. *Catastrophes and Development: Integrating Natural Catastrophes into Development Planning.* Working Papers no. 4. Disaster Management Facility Unit, World Bank, Washington, DC.

"Helping the Survivors." 2005. *The Economist* 374, no. 8048 (January 8–14): 27.

Kok, K., and M. Winograd. 2002. "Modelling Land-Use Change for Central America, with Special Reference to the Impact of Hurricane Mitch." *Ecological Modeling* 149: 53–69.

Meltzer, J. 2001. *Assessment of the Political, Economic, and Institutional Contexts for Participatory Rural Development in Post-Mitch Honduras.* Ottawa, Minga Program Initiative, International Development Research Centre, Ottawa, Canada.

Olson, R. S., R. A. Alvarez, B. P. Baird, A. Estrada, V. T. Gawronski, and J. P. Sarmiento Prieto. 2001. *The Storms of '98—Hurricanes Georges and Mitch: Impacts, Institutions Response, and Disaster Politics in Three Countries.* Boulder Natural Hazards Research and Applications Information Center, University of Colorado, Boulder.

Segnestam, L., L. Simonsson, J. Rubiano, and M. Morales. 2006. *Cross-Level Institutional Processes and Vulnerability to Natural Hazards in Honduras.* Stockholm, Sweden: Stockholm Environment Institute.

Telford, J., M. Arnold, A. Harth, and ASONOG. 2004. *Learning Lessons from Disaster Recovery. The Case of Honduras.* Washington, DC: World Bank.

Tompkins, E., and N. Adger. 2003. "Building Resilience to Climate Change through Adaptive Management of Natural Resources." Research Working Paper 27, Tyndall Centre for Climate Change, Norwich, UK.

Trujillo, M., A. Ordóñez, and C. Hernández. 2000. *Risk-Mapping and Local Capacities: Lessons from Mexico and Central America.* Oxford, UK: Oxfam GB.

U.S. Geological Survey (USGS). 2001. http://landslides.usgs.gov/research/other/hurricanemitch/mitch_ppt/.

Van Ginkel, H. 2006. "Foreword." In *Measuring Vulnerability to Natural Hazards: Towards Disaster Resilient Societies,* edited by J. Birkmann, xx–xxii. Tokyo: United Nations University Press.

Verburg, P., A. Veldkamp, L. Willement, K. Overmars, and J. C. Castella. 2004. "Landscape Level Analysis of the Spatial and Temporal Complexity of Land-Use Change." In *Ecosystems and Land Use Change* (Geophysical Monograph Series, vol. 153), edited by R. DeFries, G. Asner, and R. Houghton. Washington, DC: American Geophysical Union.

Winograd, M. 2002. "Natural Disasters in Honduras." TIEMPO 43, no. 2: 11–14.

———. 2006. "Sustainability and Vulnerability Indicators for Decision Making: Assess the Two Sides of the Same Coin." *Colloque: Usages des indicateurs de développement durable,* Montpellier, France (3–4 April).

Winograd, M., B. Fall, and J. P. Thomas. 2005. *Formation de formateurs sur l'évaluation de la vulnérabilité et les stratégies d'adaptation* (Training of trainers on vulnerability and adaptation strategies assessment). Dakar, Senegal: CIAT, ENDA, SEI, UNITAR, C3D Project, ENDA-TM.

Winograd, M., A. Farrow, and A. Nelson. 1999. *Hurricane Mitch: What Happens When Natural Disaster Takes Out Your Transport System?* Washington, DC: World Bank.

Winograd, M., S. Schillinger, A. Farrow, and I. Hernandez. 2000. *Vulnerabilidad frente a desastres naturales en Honduras.* Cali, Colombia: CIAT, http://gisweb.ciat.cgiar.org/Vulnerabilidad/index.htm.

Ziervogel, G., C. Cabot, M. Winograd, L. Segnestam, K. Wilson, and T. Downing. In press. "Vulnerability Assessments and Risk Maps: Do They Help to Protect the Vulnerable? A Case Study of Honduras." In *Approaches to Vulnerability: Food Systems and Environments in Crisis,* edited by Linda Stephen, Tom Downing, and Atiq Rahman. London: Earthscan.

4
A Flood of Impressions
Riding Out Mitch and Its Aftermath

William M. Loker

Throughout this volume, the reader is treated to social scientific analyses of the response of international, national, and local entities (down to the household level) to the disaster that was Hurricane Mitch. The foregoing chapters have provided a social and historical context to understand how the storm affected Honduras in the ways that it did and how Honduras' position in a global political economy of aid structured the institutional response to Mitch. This chapter has a different goal.[1] In it I provide a narrative of the arrival of Mitch and its immediate aftermath, seeking to answer this question: How was Mitch perceived as it hit, and what was the immediate response of one set of "ordinary" Hondurans to the hurricane? The perspective taken here is local: reflecting events and responses in one small corner of the country where I was working—carrying out human ecology research on the impact of a major hydroelectric dam on local communities—when Mitch hit.

As it highlights the coping mechanisms drawn on by isolated and largely poor households in the face of adversity, this chapter presents a kind of "moral economy of disaster" (cf. Scott 1976; Oliver-Smith, chapter 1 in this volume). The chapter offers a hopeful perspective on the construction and maintenance of community as an important resource upon which people draw in disasters, quite independently of actions of the state. Also, as this volume amply demonstrates, events such as Mitch are as much sociocultural as natural phenomena and so provide a lens through which to view societies, revealing the fault lines and mechanisms of cohesion at work.

Finally, in this chapter I show how my own perceptions of Hurricane Mitch varied dramatically from those of the people around me and advance some preliminary ideas to account for these differences. The chapter takes the form of relatively concise commentaries on field notes recorded in the days immediately preceding and following Mitch. There are references to people and places involved in my research and in response to the disaster. The names of places have not been changed.

However, pseudonyms for individuals are used throughout except for the Avila and Bendeck families (who gave permission for their names to be used) and officials of the ENEE, the *Empresa Nacional de Energía Eléctrica* (the Honduran national electric company), who were acting in their official capacities. Text in square brackets represents later additions to the field notes, which are otherwise reproduced verbatim from my notebooks. Monetary values are in *lempiras,* the Honduran national currency (at the time of Mitch, the exchange rate was about thirteen lempiras to the U.S. dollar).

Context and Prelude

My first inklings of Hurricane Mitch came on October 23, 1998, via that slender, invisible thread that is the link to the "outside world" in much of rural Honduras: the radio. I was in the *caserío* (small village) of Palo de Agua (population 125) on one of my periodic forays to interview people in the towns and villages that now find themselves near the shores of the reservoir of the El Cajón dam, Central America's largest hydroelectric dam. From my "home" in Montañuelas (largest town around the lake, with about 800 souls) I would periodically head out to the countryside to talk with people about their lives, their livelihoods, family members who had migrated, and how things had changed since the dam's completion fourteen years earlier, in 1984.

I had just arrived in Palo de Agua from the town of El Mango, on the other side of the lake. There I had stayed with Simón Pérez, checking in with him and members of his family and trying to get a feel for El Mango, a town that I had not visited in two years. I had first visited in 1983 (before the dam was completed) when starting my research in the El Cajón region.

El Mango lies at the end of a road recently opened up by the ENEE, which operates the El Cajón dam, as part of a development project designed to help some of the villages affected by the dam. The road had just been punched through the red clay hills to the east of El Mango, connecting it to the next town. But the road had washed out with the first rains and was now impassable after an unusually rainy October, a month when it had rained hard nearly every day. October marks the end of the rainy season in this part of Honduras, a time when the countryside is usually a muddy mess of swollen rivers and washed-out roads and trails. The rains should have been tapering off, but instead they seemed to be gaining in intensity. Not good for the roads. Not good for the bean crop. Not good if a major hurricane is heading your way—which no one knew at the time. I had an excellent talk with Simón, on tape, about the history of the town and how things had changed with the construction of the dam.

This was good, and it made my trip to El Mango worthwhile. I had spent much of my time in El Mango, when I was not chasing elusive interviews, shelling *achiote* (*Bixa orellana*) on Simón's porch, talking with his ancient mother, and trying to keep my increasingly restive stomach under control. After a couple of days there, I said "adios" to Simón and his family, knowing that I might never see them again. I was met at lake's edge by Enrique, who owned a small, motorized skiff and had agreed to drop me in El Mango and pick me back up at the appointed time. As I boarded the skiff, I passed a group of folks from El Mango waiting by lake's edge for the ENEE boat to come pick them up for one of the increasingly frequent meetings to discuss development plans for the lake and villages. They had been notified that the boat would come by for them at 8 A.M. It was now 10. I would later hear the boat pass by about 1 P.M., when I was on the trail to Palo de Agua. Typical.

What follows is the excerpt from my field notes that marks my first mention of Hurricane Mitch.

> 10/23/98
>
> Palo de Agua
>
> In other news, the radio says a tropical storm is heading for Honduras with heavy winds and rain. Should bring extensive flooding to San Pedro Sula . . . and Tegucigalpa. Should finish off the job of filling up the reservoir, now at > 260 masl [meters above sea level]. It is a Pacific storm [*note:* this is wrong, but I misinterpreted early radio reports; Mitch actually developed in the waters off Venezuela] coming up from Panama. And finally, it is blackfly/xexene season here. Noseeums to contend with in the early A.M. and late P.M. Sigh. I wonder if I will make it to Majadas before the storm hits? My health is better, recovered from the bad burps in El Mango.

Not a very auspicious beginning to the worst disaster to hit Honduras in its recorded history, but then one often does not know the import of events *before* they happen.

Mitch Arrives

I spent two days in Palo de Agua, including attending a meeting of electric company personnel, where they told an increasingly skeptical group of *campesinos* (rural small farmers) of yet another administrative model for the development projects designed to help them recover from the dislocations caused by dam reservoir's flooding of their lands. I then headed up the hill to the twin towns of Mal Paso and Las Majadas—seeking more interviews, touching base with old friends, contacting new folks. The next mention of Mitch in my notes follows.

> 10/26/98
>
> 12:50 P.M. Montañuelas
>
> Back in Montañuelas from Majadas. Walked down the muddy . . . trail from Majadas this A.M. . . . We left with the news of Hurricane Mitch in our ears. Mitch is a category 5 hurricane that is scheduled to skirt the Atlantic/Caribbean coast of Honduras in the next 24 hrs with winds of 150 miles an hour, but is not expected to cross the isthmus. . . . It is predicted to bring heavy rain to the interior of the country. It has been raining here daily the whole month of October. It rained heavily last night, all night, in Majadas. It rained the day before. It has rained and rained and rained. All the trails are a muddy mess. The reservoir has risen considerably in the last two weeks. . . . And this hurricane just might top it off at 285 masl—its maximum level. They are probably wondering at the ENEE if they should let water out of the reservoir now in anticipation of the storm. But all the rivers are swollen and it would probably provoke considerable flooding in San Pedro Sula to release . . . water now. They may also be wondering at El Cajón if the dam can hold 285 masl of water or if it will leak, or—god forbid—fail.

This concern was apt. In fact, the reservoir rose 30 meters (about 100 feet) over a period of ten days as the waters of Hurricane Mitch poured in. It is estimated that more than 9,000 cubic meters of water per second flowed into the reservoir during that time period. Total flood waters from Mitch retained by the time the storm had passed are estimated at 1.5 cubic kilometers (Hawker 2000:23). The often maligned El Cajón dam was, indeed, tested, but it did hold. Had the dam collapsed it would have wiped out scores of towns and cities downstream, including San Pedro Sula, Honduras' second-largest city and home to a burgeoning *maquiladora* (factory garment assembly) industry. Hats off to the Swiss and Italian engineers who built the dam, and to the Hondurans at the ENEE for its effective management.

I vividly remember listening to the radio in Majadas. The Honduran national radio station, HRN, broadcast a feed in English from the (U.S.) National Hurricane Center in Miami. It was incongruous, and scary, listening to the radio in a wattle and daub shack over a breakfast of tortillas and beans and hot, sweet coffee as this disembodied voice with a southern drawl spoke urgently of the magnitude of this storm, the anticipated storm surge, and the need to evacuate all low-lying areas along the coast. At that point no one expected the storm to stall off the Honduran coast and whirl around over the island of Guanaja before taking an abrupt and totally unpredicted turn south over the isthmus, over Honduras—in fact, directly over the El Cajón dam and reservoir.

With my return to Montañuelas, I found myself back "home" in the house of Gumercindo Avila and Concepción Reyes and ten other people: assorted children, grandchildren, and a son-in-law. I'd become something of a fixture around the place, having known the family for more than fifteen years. My stay brought them some much-needed income in payments for room and board, light in the form of a battery-powered lantern, work in the form of field assistance ably provided by Gumercindo, and occasional tins of meat and other strange foods that broke the monotony of a diet based 80 percent on tortillas and beans. From Gumercindo and Conce's I visited most of the households in town: interviewing people, taking oral histories, participating in meetings and conversations on verandas, and otherwise getting a feel for life in this remote rural area of Honduras and for how things had changed with the coming of the dam. Gumercindo and Conce's house was a small and crowded, poor but lively version of the typical rural house: wattle and daub, tin roof, dirt floor, small wood-burning *fogón* (oven) for cooking, and a chronic shortage of everything but children. By this point, Hurricane Mitch was beginning to dominate the airwaves, a major disaster in the making.

10/27/98

8:37 P.M. Montañuelas

Raining hard with gusty winds. The hurricane, Mitch, is stalled off the coast of Honduras. I went out this afternoon and looked around. . . . The effect of the hurricane is pretty impressive given that it is still 100 km from Guanaja and probably 300 km from here. It's causing flooding and landslides in various parts of the country and I am concerned that Montañuelas will either be cut off—the road out is in terrible shape—or that the emergencies in other parts of the country will prevent food and other supplies from reaching here or both. So I went out and bought 10 lb of beans, 16 lb of sugar, 5 lb of potatoes, 4 lb of rice, some eggs, etc. to stock up. There is plenty of maize for tortillas in the house. This could go on for a week the way the storm is behaving. I am also trying to keep organized in case the roof lifts off the house and I have to leave in a hurry. Trees are groaning and the roof is creaking.

10/28/98

3:45 A.M. Montañuelas

It's raining hard and blowing. I can't sleep for worrying about what is going on around me—from the rattling roof to the rising waters, of the creek next to the house . . . and the El Cajón reservoir. As I lie awake I play out various disaster scenarios, from this house going, to the roads and airports (head for Palmerola! [U.S. military base]). When daylight comes, two long hours away, I plan to pack an evacuation pack with my most necessary possessions in case I need to walk out of here to Comayagua [major town, about 80 km away, located on a paved road]. My notes, a set of clothes, camera, GPS, water filter, flashlight, a little food, maps. Hopefully it won't come to that.

3:13 P.M. Montañuelas

Twelve hours later and guess what? It's still raining and blowing. Hurricane Mitch is still off the coast of Honduras, inching closer to landfall as the hours pass. There were actually a few breaks in the rain today. During one, I insisted that we go get firewood up in the hills above town. In the middle of our expedition, the rain returned and we all got soaked. . . . As far as the hurricane goes, we are *far* from out of danger. At around noon today, the eye passed over Guanaja. It is now on a track to take it to Roatán, Utila and on to Tela. But it is moving slowly and erratically, alternatively strengthening and weakening. I still have not packed my evacuation kit.

At this point we were all glued to the radio. Attempts to carry on "business as usual," either for me or for farmers trying to get to their *milpas* (cornfields) to harvest maize or plant beans, was pretty much out of the question. I was rather panicked, though most people in Montañuelas were still relatively nonplussed. What's a little rain? Honduran farmers generally *love* rain, and while too much of a good thing is a bother, it's not a disaster. At least not yet. But pity those poor families who planted milpas along the edge of the reservoir. It had been a good bet in years past, when the reservoir never rose to its theoretical maximum. But this year, some folks would lose their milpas. Most people had vague memories of Hurricane Fifi, which hit Honduras in 1974. Fifi caused a lot of damage along the coast and the Aguán River valley. But there was nothing in anyone's historical memory to prepare them for a hurricane/tropical storm in the mountainous interior of the country. It was, as disaster experts say, "a high-magnitude, low-frequency event"—big, but exceedingly rare. Excellent for catching folks unawares.

10/30/98

10 A.M. Montañuelas

The seriousness of the situation is beginning to sink in to people here and to me, too. Although the high winds have abated, it continues to rain off and on and right now it is pouring. I woke up last night at 2 A.M. and it sounded like someone had turned a high-pressure fire hose on the house. It was gusting and raining hard. The ditch/quebrada that is about 15 mts [meters] north of the house was roaring. . . . Night before last a church under construction collapsed. Last night, one of the walls of Chito Ruiz's house collapsed. Fortunately, it fell outward instead of inward toward the interior of the house; if not, someone might have been killed.

The news from La Libertad [the county seat, about 40 km away] is also bad. The river through town flooded, wiping out a bunch of businesses, including the two gas stations in town. Now there is no fuel. Several bridges between here and La Libertad are also wiped out. Lajas [another nearby town] is incommunicado and of course, Montañuelas is, too. Soon there will be no fuel here to run the corn grinding mills or run the cars. And now the supplies to replenish the *truchas* [small stores] will also not arrive. This is what I anticipated when I went out and purchased all that food, but no doubt it's going fast, feeding four adult males, two females and four children. I have three tins of Spam left and four little *Jamónes Diablos* [deviled hams] which I am hoarding for a "rainy day." Hah! Landslides in La Libertad wiped out a neighborhood of 100 houses. At least 25 are dead. The mayor, Andino, was on the radio today appealing for help.

And of course the news from around the country is also bad. It's raining everywhere and the same problems affecting La Libertad are being felt everywhere, often in a manner more extreme. Places that have never flooded are flooding. Places that are routinely flooded are swamped. In short, the worst disaster since Hurricane Fifi in 1974 and probably worse. More people probably died during Fifi, but property damage is worse this time.

I am once again confined to quarters. I may go out on another firewood expedition, but after getting soaked last time, I am not anxious [to do so].

Last night at 2:30 A.M. when it was pouring and the *quebrada* [brook] roaring, I repacked my evacuation pack. Now I realize I will have to walk to La Libertad, 40 km away, to get out. . . . The rain is forecast to continue for another 48–72 hours. Oh, I almost forgot, the water system is down here, too. A landslide at the water source has buried the intake pipe. So we are now hauling water in buckets.

We tracked the storm's progress on the radio. Every couple of hours, they would give the latitude and longitude of the location of the storm's eye, relayed from U.S. weather satellites. I punched the numbers into my GPS and watched with interest as the storm turned south and passed directly over us before moving southward to Tegucigalpa and Choluteca and into the Pacific. From there it rebounded, hit Guatemala, and brushed by Florida. Quite a run.

In the next set of field notes there is brief mention of trees planted. These were part of the ENEE's development project, a reforestation effort (described more fully in Loker 2004). Many of the trees were planted along the edge of the reservoir and, as indicated, were lost to the rising waters.

10/31/98

10:51 A.M. Montañuelas

The rain continues, off and on, with varying levels of intensity. The storm has moved south of us now, toward Tegucigalpa. . . . It's now just a tropical mess, not even a tropical storm. I went out yesterday to El Encinal [nearby small village] and here's what I found. A large tree blocks the road. . . . At the rise of the hill to Encinal, there is a smallish landslide that has left deep mud on the road. A little ways up the road on the downhill side is another slide about 20 × 100 mts that took out part of a milpa and *frijolar* [bean field]. . . . I . . . checked in with Betillo. I had wanted to interview him since meeting him in his milpa . . . back in June. I found him now watching the news on a grainy, battery-powered black-and-white television. He seemed somewhat shell-shocked by the goings on, but left the tube to talk hurricane. He showed me his wind-flattened *postrera de maíz* [second crop of maize] and we both marveled at how fast the lake was rising. He pointed out men in the distance *tapiscando maíz* [harvesting maize] in the rain while the lake rose to claim milpas planted on . . . lands . . . that had not flooded for years. Celso has lost his milpa, drowned in the lake. Isidro lost a postrera just entering into *elote* [green corn]. Trino lost part of his frijolar to a landslide.

We went back inside and talked about the disaster happening all around us. It's hard to talk milpa under the circumstances. He thinks a lot of frijolares will be lost, too, to plant disease and excess moisture. We also agreed that the price of maize might well rise from its currently depressed levels of 100–160 lempiras per *carga* [a carga equals about 200 pounds] due to crop losses in other parts of the country. As mentioned, with a few exceptions, most of the milpas here are in OK condition. Betillo lost a lot of one milpa to a "small *huracán*" [windstorm] back in September and now a postrera to a real hurricane.

After Betillo's I went back to Adrian's, who had returned from his walk to the Rio Yunque. He said it's raging (no surprise!) and that milpas are under water. He also observed that many of the trees planted are also under water, which I confirmed the day before during my trip to the *vivero* [tree nursery]. (The reality is that the lake has risen A LOT since my walk to the *vivero.* If 20 percent of trees were under water then, 80–90 percent are underwater now.) . . . At several points lately I have mentioned how the storm has messed up my work. I do recognize, though, that it presents an opportunity to see how people react to the disaster. It's like the old saying about lemons: If life gives you lemons, make lemonade. If life gives you disaster, study disaster aid. I also recognize that my research must take a back seat to the humanitarian crisis unfolding here.

Re: disasters, on the radio last night, it was reported that the road repair company Brazos de Honduras had lost 25 million lempiras in road equipment in La Libertad, in a land slide that also destroyed

100 homes and caused an undetermined number of deaths. The loss of the equipment means further delays in road repair, longer isolation here, since equipment to fix the road is lost.

Things are starting to get scarce here in the stores, too, as I anticipated. The diesel to run the corn mill is about out—only one or two days' supply. There is no kerosene in town. Hence there will soon be no refrigeration, either. The road is out . . . Gloria hopes to send a mule to Lajas to bring diesel.

Montañuelas has really not suffered any catastrophic damage. Most of the problems here are more a matter of inconvenience rather than major disasters. At least until someone has a major medical emergency and needs to get out of here in a hurry. But because Montañuelas produces basic grains and there are hens, eggs, cattle and a few pigs around, hopefully hunger will not be a problem. There is an acute shortage of money to buy things but I don't think any shop owner would have the courage to deny someone food in a time of crisis. They'd have to sell on credit until the stuff ran out. Then it's a diet of tortillas and? There are few beans around as they are all planted. I think the *ganaderos* [cattlemen] are going to have to kill a few cows to get the town through this crisis. Hopefully that will be enough. There is also talk of sending a boat down to the dam to buy supplies at Santa Cruz, if there is anything to be had there. Hopefully it will occur to the ENEE to check up on these communities, find out about their needs and send disaster assistance. The community here has maize, but little else at this point—or at some point in the not so distant future.

8:08 P.M.

I made the rounds today talking with a few influential people in town about the need to coordinate efforts to deal with the present and future crisis in Montañuelas and surrounding communities. First I had a long talk with Gumercindo about how I saw things playing out here: gradual shortage in the stores as they run out of goods and are not resupplied. Eventually—in 3 or 4 days—generalized scarcity and panic buying by the few with money. The road to La Libertad will not be repaired for many days (weeks?) and the same process will occur in Lajas; might take a little while longer, but it will happen. Therefore, a need to coordinate efforts to get the community through the next few weeks.

> Gumercindo agreed, so we set out to drum up support for the idea. . . . [The mayor] was out trying to rescue maize from a flooding milpa. I talked at length to his wife . . . a shopkeeper in town. She agreed with the basic scenario. She has/had the last sack of sugar in town and said she noticed a lot of people coming to the store who are not regular customers and buying 2, 3, 4 pounds of sugar, not the usual 1 or ½ pound. (Of course, I bought 16 pounds of sugar 4 days ago; I was the first to start panic buying!) . . . I then went to look for Gumercindo. He was at Fernando's house talking to Fernando, Victor and Fernando's sons. I worked the conversation around to the need to get to the dam somehow and work with the ENEE and Army to get a transport system in place to supply the town and surrounding communities. They agreed with my scenario and said they would support such a plan. How to get to the dam? Tomás Guevara has a motor boat—if it did not sink in the rapid rise of the lake! And he usually comes to church in Montañuelas on Sunday. He lives across the lake in Manacal. There is also Enrique in Agua Blanca—we could row over and seek his help. And finally there is the five-hour walk/mule ride to Terreritos, with a 90-minute rowboat ride across the lake to the ENEE. While one group goes to the dam, others should take mules to Lajas. Others should work on rehabilitating the road to Lajas. All this needs to be worked out in a semi-orderly way tomorrow at the *Patronato* [Town Council] meeting. . . . We'll see what happens. Tomorrow will be critical. Will the boat owner show up? Will the Patronato act effectively? Will the community respond? I hope the answer is "yes" to all of those questions.

The preceding entries are notable on two counts. One, they chronicle the accumulation of small but significant impacts on household food production. How households are differentially affected by disasters is largely lost in the large-scale national or international responses to these events. Often, differential vulnerability is linked to social class, which influences not only the stocks of financial and social resources upon which people can draw but also the location (in terms of hazardous zones) of inhabitants. Secondly, it draws our attention to the perception of events as structured by historical memory and social situatedness. People in the area had minimal exposure to broad disaster; recall that a similar event was unknown in historical memory. Previous hurricane damage in Honduras was limited to the Caribbean littoral and did not extend to the country's interior. Recognizing the magnitude of events was facilitated by national media (radio) representations of the disaster. Still, local institutions were slow to respond.

At this point, the narrative shifts to the aftermath of the storm and efforts to cope with the disaster.

After the Flood: Around the Reservoir

As is evident from the field notes, I was quite worried that Montañuelas (and other towns around the lake) would be totally cut off by the floods, landslides, and road outages unleashed by Mitch. I also expected that, in the "big picture" of the national-scale disaster affecting Honduras, restoring roads to Montañuelas would not rank high on the list of government priorities. I was focused on a worst-case scenario of diminishing food supplies in the town. Most poor, rural households in Honduras—like those around the reservoir—lack any kind of financial cushion and generally rely on family connections, patronage (personal relationships with the relatively well-off), and merchants who will sell on credit to get by during tough times. But if times turned uniformly tough, as they promised to do with Mitch, it was not clear if these coping mechanisms would remain viable.

This is the social essence of a disaster: an event or events that push people's coping capacities beyond "normal" limits (Oliver-Smith and Hoffman 2002:4). Although Mitch had not hit at the worst time—most households had stocks of maize harvested, though they were very low on beans—there is clearly no "good" time for such a massive disaster. However, if the storm had hit (say) in August, before the maize harvest and when foodstocks are chronically low, then the impact could have been far worse. It is a fact of life in contemporary rural Honduras, and in most rural areas worldwide, that former patterns of self-sufficiency have been altered as households and communities are increasingly linked to broader circuits of exchange of goods and services. Rural areas retain more self-sufficiency compared to urban dwellers, most of whom are virtually totally dependent on the market for their livelihoods and well-being. Hence rural dwellers have traditionally had the ability to draw on local resources to "weather the storm." At the same time, the remoteness of rural areas makes their recovery more precarious and of lower priority than the needs of easily mobilized urban dwellers who live close to infrastructure and centers of power. In other words, rural and urban people demonstrate different patterns of "vulnerability" (Blaikie et al. 1994:9) and so exhibit contrasting mechanisms of coping. Rurality is a mixed blessing: people may have subsistence resources to draw on, but their isolation from centers of power makes organized efforts at recovery more expensive, more time-consuming, and of lower national priority.

The prospect of an extended period of isolation led to the decision, taken in consultation with local leaders and a few merchants, to make a trip to the site of the El Cajón dam and attempt to purchase supplies that would tide the community over and, equally importantly, to make contact with government authorities, remind them of the plight of the lakeside towns, and try to get some sort of routine provisioning of goods via boat. The reservoir is not a major or routine means of commerce (boat traffic is relatively rare), so this would require some planning and effort involving local and national authorities. So, early in the morning on November 2, 1998, Gumercindo Avila and I left Montañuelas and headed for the ENEE facilities at the El Cajón dam site. We carried about USD 100 collected from three merchants in town (Lila, Joaquín, and Efraín, mentioned in notes below) to buy supplies—sugar, rice, flour, beans, and cooking oil—to be distributed upon our return.

11/2/98

9:28 P.M. ENEE housing, El Cajón

Yesterday's meeting in Montañuelas produced a letter [to the ENEE asking for help] signed by the community's political leaders. Gumercindo and I geared up for our trip to El Cajón. Woke up at 4 A.M. this morning. Had coffee and bread. By 5 A.M., still dark, we were leaving the house, heading down the road to . . . Terreritos. . . . Along the road there were 5 or 6 mini-landslides (nothing like the massive landslides at the ENEE) with knocked down pines. Enough to impede horse and vehicle traffic, though. . . . Anyway, the walk [was] about . . . four hours total from Gumercindo's house to Terreritos. . . . Gumercindo took me to some *primo*'s [cousin's] house where I sat and watched a *ternero enredarse* [a calf tangled up] tied to a tree, a highly mobile and feisty herd of horses ran back and forth through the town, pigs rooting around everywhere . . . and an old man (out of sight) coughed his lungs out. Meanwhile, *guirros* [kids] were sent out to find someone to row us across the suddenly large lake.

By 9 A.M. we were heading down to the lake with Francisco, 70 years old, . . . who proceeded to row us 1 hour and 40 minutes across the lake. We set out at 10 A.M. and arrived at 11:40. The old man rowed the entire way, except for 20 minutes when I spelled him. The lake is big, drowning young pines and lots of other vegetation.

It is nearly 10 P.M. and I am out of gas. Gotta sleep. Tomorrow I hope to buy supplies in Santa Cruz and push for their shipment to Montañuelas.

Note: While slightly out of chronological sequence, the following entries elaborate on my arrival with Gumercindo at the El Cajón dam on November 2.

When Gumercindo and I first arrived at the ENEE property, we were dropped off where the Agua Finca Saint Peter [an experimental aquaculture project] has their fish raising nets, etc. This area was virtually unrecognizable compared to earlier visits because of the high level of the lake. For example, the dilapidated school bus that the fish farm used to store stuff in was under several meters of water—out of sight. Gumercindo and I got off the row boat and walked up a little hill where we encountered personnel from the fish farm measuring out rations for the fish and generally continuing their routine. They informed us that the road linking this area with the rest of the dam installations was closed by a landslide and impassable even by foot. Fortunately, a boat from the fish farm was leaving to go around the point to the dam site to pick up materials and communicate with Tom Ryan, the gringo manager of the fish farm. We hopped on the boat and found that the new place to embark/disembark was a steep cliff about 30 mts tall right near the dam. The boat moored there and Gumercindo and I scrambled up the hill where we ran into Tom Ryan.

Tom Ryan was at the top of the cliff face waiting to provide direction to his workers. I went up to him and told him about the situation in Montañuelas, my mission, etc. He explained about conditions in the outside world—a mess—and the condition of ENEE roads to the dam—closed. He said that if we could get supplies down to the dam, Agua Finca Saint Peter would help in getting supplies to communities around the lake. This was my first indication that getting supplies to Montañuelas would be more complicated than I initially thought. The offer of a boat proved to be necessary as we later found out that the ENEE had sent their boats to the coast to help with rescue operations there.

After talking with Tom Ryan, Gumercindo and I began walking from the dam site to ENEE offices. This involved crossing several major landslides, including one very close to the dam itself. We were also impressed by the amount of water pouring out of the flood gates of the dam. . . . You could literally feel the ground shake from the impact of the water. We then continued on down the road, marveling at the numerous landslides that completely covered the road and spots where the road appeared on the verge of giving way. We walked in the bright sunshine (no rain) for at least an hour, probably more like 90 minutes when we encountered the first military checkpoint, where we stopped to chat with the soldiers. While we were talking, up came an ENEE truck with . . . Roger Mendoza, an agronomic engineer who works on the ENEE natural resources management project who both Gumercindo and I know. He was on his way to visit the dam headquarters so we hopped in the truck and went with him. I must have spoken with him about conditions in Montañuelas, but I do not remember the particulars of the conversation. He also probably told me about the ENEE boats being gone. But I also recall him being extremely concerned about Choluteca, the area where he hails from, which he said suffered massive destruction at the hands of the hurricane [see Barrios, chapter 7 in this volume, for a discussion of Choluteca].

Leonardo Deras is the boss at El Cajón and where Mendoza was heading. I went into dam headquarters with Mendoza to deliver my letter from . . . Montañuelas requesting ENEE help. Deras received us and the letter, looked it over and promised his help in getting supplies, but no boats. It was evident that Deras was extremely busy with numerous management tasks at the dam and crisis managing ENEE endeavors. I almost felt bad adding another variable to his overburdened situation, but I was under the impression from both Mendoza and Deras that no one had given the situation of the lakeside communities serious thought. Again, Deras promised the ENEE's help and added that opening a road to the dam site was a top priority, one which dovetailed nicely with our needs.

Once I had touched base with Deras and gotten him on board, . . . I headed off with Mendoza, et al., and Gumercindo to the office of "*Cuencas*," the river basin management office where Mendoza works. There Gumercindo and I hung out waiting for a ride to Santa Cruz. We eventually caught one waiting by the side of the road from an ENEE vehicle heading to Santa Cruz. There Gumercindo and I checked a couple of wholesalers for the availability of sugar, flour, and rice, our main items for purchase. We also looked up Selvin, Gumercindo's son, who is in the military and currently posted to the local police station in Santa Cruz to help with rescue operations. He filled us in on some of the hardest-hit areas around Santa Cruz and his participation in rescue efforts, including rounding up orphans and "using a teaspoon to scoop someone's brains back into their smashed skull." . . . We also went to the local radio station in Santa Cruz to have an announcement read that we were in Santa Cruz and heading back with supplies. The shops seemed to have everything we wanted, though there were some quantity limits on some items. Shopkeepers also indicated that they were being regularly provisioned by San Pedro and that the next day there would be even greater quantities available. Gumercindo and I decided that we would postpone our buying until tomorrow and found a ride back with an ENEE vehicle. . . . Gumercindo and I decided that he would head back to Montañuelas and report on our progress and have someone waiting at lakeside to help with provisions. Of course, it was still far from clear that we would be able to get provisions to the lake's edge, as the roads to the dam were closed by landslides and vehicle access was a definite necessity. . . . Lucas [ENEE liaison with local communities] also met with Gumercindo and me and told us not to worry, that he would find a way to get provisions to lakeside. Just get the stuff and he would be sure it got there. . . . Then I retired to my room to write the above recorded notes and crash.

11/3/98

4:21 P.M. Embarcadero Montañuelas [lakeside area below Montañuelas]

I just arrived, about 20 minutes ago, at the embarcadero of Montañuelas. I just helped load two sacks of sugar, one sack of rice and one of flour onto the mules of Pedro. I am now sitting on the rest of the provisions: batteries, candles, beans, salt, *manteca* [lard], coffee—waiting for another mule to carry it uphill. The embarcadero is absolutely unrecognizable, the lake has risen so far, so fast (289 masl today; 262 masl before Mitch). I have just passed a rather harrowing day. Moments of boredom and moments of danger, moments of pleading, moments of demanding, to get these provisions here. The bitch is that all this effort will not begin to supply the needs of this town. The town could suck up this stuff like a sponge and hardly notice. But at least I planted the seed in the mind(s) of the ENEE to open up a route to supply towns along the lake. And judging by some reports, there are towns on the Yoro side [north side of reservoir], around Chilistagua . . . that were really wiped out. So to attend to their needs will be a top priority.

I started out today with Gumercindo knocking at my door at 5:45 A.M. anxious to get started or at least get a cup of coffee. . . . By this time we had decided that Gumercindo would head back to Montañuelas ASAP while I stayed on to purchase provisions and tried to (a) get supplies to the lake and (b) tried to get them up-lake to Montañuelas. The purchasing of supplies was not too tough. After dropping off Gumercindo at the first *derrumbe* [landslide], Ismael [ENEE driver] and I headed to Santa Cruz.

I bought what I could in Santa Cruz, then my driver disappeared on me. After waiting around on the corner (dog got hit by car, blood on the road) I went to look for him. Found him running emergency errands for the mayor. Eventually got a lift from Major Bandares of the 14th Battalion, who took provisions and me back to the ENEE. I strained my back loading 100-pound sacks onto the Army truck. We unloaded at the Watershed Management office. . . . Deras got the road to the dam open—a little trail through the massive landslides. . . . Once the road to the dam site was opened, we got a truck to take me, Ricardo Palma (agronomist technician of Mal Paso), his mother and provisions to the dam site. There was a *lancha* [skiff] of Agua Finca Saint Peter tied up at the provisional embarcadero of the dam. . . . There was rope, a boat and gasoline—all provided by Agua Finca St. Peter. It took us an hour to load the boat down the steep, 30 meter cliff between where the supplies were dropped off and the boat. Ricardo Palma lowered the sacks down to me, waiting precariously on the cliff face. I would receive them, then half haul them, half roll them to a point only about 10 feet above the boat and lower them down [to the boat]. Skittering up and down the cliff and hauling 100-pound sacks with a bad back was no fun. . . . The last load down was Ricardo and his mother. Finally we got everything and everyone in the boat and took off. . . . The boat was VERY tippy . . . and seemed about to roll over any second. We went to the fish farm and moved the people and provisions into their big Gulf of Fonseca cruiser. . . . We headed . . . up the lake to here. Saw . . . many landslides on the hills around the lake, including a particularly nasty one over in the Quebrachal area near Majadas. Pedro and his mule were here to meet us, sent by Lila (a merchant), wise woman that she is! Pedro helped us unload the boat. Then loaded up two mules and went away. That leaves me here, swatting mosquitoes in the waning light, guarding the last of the provisions. Me and my aching back! It is after 5 P.M. and will be dark soon. I will have to head up the hill soon whether the mule is back or not!

11/4/98

Montañuelas

Well it got to be 5:30 P.M. yesterday and Pedro had not shown up, so I headed up the hill. Ran into Pedro halfway up, on his way down to retrieve the last load. . . . I arrived in town about 6 P.M., beat and wrung out by the long day and experience. Got to the *Centro Comunal* [community center] and there were the four sacks sitting outside the door. No sign of nobody. As I was walking away, Professor David [local teacher] and Roberto appeared. They seemed puzzled and concerned that I wanted to store the provisions in the Centro Comunal rather than turn it over immediately to the shopkeepers. I explained that I wanted to meet with the shopkeepers first, to settle accounts money-wise and discuss guidelines for the sale of the goods to avoid hoarding. I mentioned that some items, sugar for instance, would probably have to be rationed. They mentioned that there was a community-wide meeting tomorrow (today) to deal with the situation.

From there I went to greet Joaquín [another merchant] and tell him of the situation and my plan to meet with shopkeepers. He seemed agreeable, but would not be around during the day to settle accounts. Then to Lila's to repeat my message. . . . She seemed to be OK with everything. Efrain showed up and the story was the same.

I then went to Gumercindo's to rest and compare notes. . . . Eventually Prof. David came by to look at my copy of the newspaper. We talked about the situation in the country, Montañuelas' relatively privileged position—virtually undamaged. I talked about some of the issues to discuss at the meeting—opening the road to Terreritos, sending another delegation to the ENEE to secure their help, bring more provisions, etc.

This morning, Gumercindo got up at 4 A.M. to buy some meat from a cow being butchered by Efrain. I stayed in the hammock for a luxurious morning until 6 A.M. . . . Then I met with (Montañuelas mayor) Isaías. Briefed him on my trip to the ENEE and Santa Cruz. Tried to get him to form an agenda in his mind for the meeting this afternoon. He wants to organize a shipment of maize from Montañuelas to La Libertad as a show of solidarity with those in need there. That is a good idea, but there are many other issues to discuss, too.

Then in the morning about 11 A.M. I met with Lila, Graciela (Joaquín's wife and the person who really minds the store) and Efraín, the three shopkeepers who gave me money to buy provisions in Santa Cruz. There, we settled accounts, decided on the division of the provisions, paid my minimal costs for the trip (lake crossing, food, cigarettes for Gumercindo). I also suggested prices and conditions for the sale of the goods. For example, I suggested that sugar be rationed to one pound per household, with Lila selling to Barrio Arriba and Efraín to Barrio Abajo. The shopkeepers agreed to all the conditions I proposed. So we settled accounts. I suggested we leave the provisions in the Centro Comunal until the 3 P.M. meeting, to explain to people the situation of how the stuff got here and the conditions of sale. And to inform them to expect price increases in the future. We'll see who shows up at the meeting.

Well, about 25–30 people showed up at the meeting. A *Comité de Emergencias* [Emergency Committee] was formed. Its focus, for now, is to aid members of nearby communities affected by the storm.

The meeting was typically Honduran. Started late. Coalesced slowly, as people hung around outside, chatting in small groups and generally milled around. Finally, around 3:40 or so, Isaías called the meeting to order. He noted the sparse attendance and the generally negative attitude of most people in Montañuelas toward organizing for the good of the community. Spoke of the need to help people in La Libertad. Talked about my trip to the ENEE and then turned the meeting over to me. I spoke about the difficulties facing Honduras at the national level. The willingness of the ENEE to help lake communities, but their limited capacity to do so.

The feasibility of opening up a route of communication via Terreritos. The logistical support provided by the ENEE, the battalion and Agua Finca St. Peter. And, finally, about the need to prepare, the need to organize, to act in the face of difficult circumstances.

In short, the need to form an Emergency Committee. I then discussed the delivery of provisions to Montañuelas that I had carried out. Spoke of the need to ration sugar and of how the prices of goods were set. I noted that these prices were artificially low, did not reflect full transportation costs (e.g., the boat ride from the dam to Montañuelas) and that in all probability future commodities would probably cost more. This was the last shipment at pre-Mitch prices. I told them that productive capacity in the country had been reduced 70 percent and that scarcity was coming. Get prepared, or suffer the consequences. I think my plea fell on deaf ears. After I was finished speaking, Lila asked if she could please take her goods now.

As she and her fellow shopkeepers moved their stuff out, some people also began to leave. It was in that anticlimactic moment that we attempted to form the Emergency Committee. About 15 people volunteered to serve, but the focus was on voluntary humanitarian assistance for those most affected by the storm, not on preparing a plan to deal with problems in Montañuelas. I did not volunteer for the Emergency Committee or to help in the collection of maize, as I wanted local people to step up, especially given my not-too-distant departure. But I was pressured into joining and helping and agreed to do so. There is no evidence of a concerted effort to assure the food supply here. Perhaps that is as it should be, but I think things will get ugly here in the next week or ten days. Perhaps I am wrong. Maybe supplies will start trickling in from Lajas/La Libertad/Comayagua. People here seem to think so. But I think supply will be weak and subject to being bought up by a few people, leaving most people in the rough. This will further weaken and divide the community between the few haves and the many have-nots. That is my pessimistic prediction. [*Note:* People turned out to be right; no serious shortages occurred during my stay.]

Summary of Events "After the Flood" around the Reservoir

The preceding field notes recount efforts to establish a route for supplies into Montañuelas and other lakeside communities in the chaotic days immediately following Mitch. With roads into the region cut off, the lake suddenly took on unprecedented importance as a transportation route. But since so few people have boats, this left communities dependent on the goodwill of the ENEE and a few others: a precarious position, given the history of conflict between the ENEE and local lakeside communities.

The field notes also convey the contrasting reactions to this disaster: my focus on self-preservation and provisioning of the community versus the much more laid-back reaction of local campesinos, whose primary thought was to help others in need (specifically, to send food and other goods to the hard-hit communities in and around La Libertad). Again, this is a central tenet of the anthropology of disasters: "Disasters are both socially constructed and experienced differently by different groups and individuals, generating multiple interpretations of an event/process" (Oliver-Smith 2002:25). How can we explain the contrasting reactions to the disaster exhibited by the people of Montañuelas and by me as participant-observer?

It may be that the rural poor of Montañuelas (and elsewhere) react to adversity more stoically and calmly. Perhaps they are inured to the threat of deprivation because they live with it routinely. Most of these households are frequently on the edge of survival and have well-developed coping mechanisms to deal with that condition. These mechanisms are both psychological and economic. Psychologically there is a sense of detachment and resilience that leads people to feel they can endure the hardships that life deals them. While I was in a dither about the possibility that access to material goods might be interrupted, this was less of a concern for the vast majority of people with whom I spoke. If supplies failed to show, they would simply do without. That the Honduran state was crippled and incapable of responding to their needs was, I suppose, no news to them. When has the state ever been responsive to their needs? (Never!) Many households face scarcity on an almost daily basis and so—unlike my own case—the threat of scarcity does not make them anxious nor move them to action.

It was truly inspiring for me to see that the first organized response of the town was not provisioning their own needs but rather assisting those more severely affected by the disaster than they. Rather than worrying about opening up the roads or setting up a lake-based distribution network, the nascent Comité de Emergencias in Montañuelas chose as its first priority collecting disaster assistance, in the form of maize donations, to send to heavily damaged La Libertad and surrounding villages, which the radio reported as being severely affected by mudslides with attendant loss of housing and life. As this was transpiring I was truly baffled and, at the same time, moved. One might conceptualize this as a "moral economy of disaster" (Scott 1976; Oliver-Smith, chapter

1 in this volume) in which people—especially poorer people—engage in a kind of extended reciprocity based on compassion, the expectation of future help, and attachments to community and place.

This account also highlights the importance of media, especially radio, as a means of shaping people's response to the disaster. The fact that La Libertad's plight was highlighted on national radio and that the mayor, Andino (whom most people knew personally), was interviewed heightened local perceptions regarding the need to act. La Libertad's disaster was their disaster. The moral economy of disaster based on ties to a local region and sense of place has not been systematically explored as an asset and strategy for coping with disaster; evidently, it is underappreciated by international purveyors of disaster assistance. La Libertad's high-profile damage also heightened national response to the troubles afflicting the local region—and, by extension, Montañuelas—and probably hastened efforts to restore roads and otherwise respond to the regional effects of Mitch.

The next group of field notes describes efforts to collect relief supplies in Montañuelas and my eventual trip to Tegucigalpa as I ran out of money. Though the experience is instructive of life in rural Honduras, I have edited out my search for centavos to stick more closely to the Mitch-related narrative. In reading about the bus ride from Comayagua to Tegucigalpa, keep in mind that the bus was traveling the main road of all Honduras, one that connects the capital city of Tegucigalpa to its industrial center, San Pedro Sula. Those familiar with Honduras know that this "major artery" is just a two-lane blacktop road that would be considered a secondary road in the United States. We are not talking about an interstate highway here! My destination in Tegucigalpa was the home of Nelson and Mercedes Bendeck, my "other family" in Honduras, to whom I am related by marriage.

After the Flood: Tegucigalpa and Back

11/5/98

Montañuelas

So I am running out of dough. I will have to try to get to Tegucigalpa, then come back here for one last look. Since Rodrigo had said he was going to La Libertad tomorrow, I went back to the shack and packed up. Basically the evacuation pack, plus. I am taking all my notes, tapes, maps, photos, etc—everything essential to my work.

In the afternoon, I went house-to-house with other members of the Emergency Committee asking for relief supplies for people made homeless by Mitch. I was not looking forward to this experience, but it was actually interesting. I was assigned the part of town I know least, but now I know it better. The response of the people to our plea (I was on a team with Jeremías, Edelio, Virgilio, and Carlos, the gay teacher) was very moving. Here we were, asking people—many dirt poor—to give something to help the *damnificados* [people affected by the disaster]. Almost all people responded positively—anywhere from 20 to 200 pounds of corn. Only three houses said no: two of the three lost their milpas to the lake and the third was a poor female-headed household. Met many people I had previously not known. We went house-to-house from 3–5:30 P.M.—dark, and collected pledges for 9.6 cargas [nearly a ton] of maize, plus three houses that promised an undetermined amount of maize.

After collecting, we turned in our list to Nayo who is coordinator of the Emergency Committee, and I headed back to the shack. . . . On my way back to the shack I ran into Rodrigo. He's not going to La Libertad tomorrow after all but on Saturday (day after tomorrow). So I am prematurely packed but still determined to go.

11/6/98

Montañuelas

At 4 P.M., the Comité de Emergencias met with the goal of finding two or three cars to carry the 18 cargas of maize [collected in Montañuelas] to La Libertad and Quebrada Amarilla [nearby town hit by a large landslide]. I went with Edelio, Dagoberto, and Julio to El Encinal. Jaime is out of gas and Baudilio is broken down. So, no help there. El Encinal has not been canvassed for donations. Adrian said he would do this in the next day or so. . . . Tomorrow, to La Libertad and beyond to Comayagua and Tegucigalpa. Should be interesting to see hurricane damage. Water service was restored yesterday in Montañuelas. Weather has been mostly sunny with occasional showers, light rain since Mitch left 4 or 5 days ago. It is supposed to turn "cold" and rainy in the next few days.

11/8/98

Tegucigalpa

Yesterday I did the fabled trip from Montañuelas to Tegucigalpa. A stretch under the best of circumstances, but in the post-Mitch emergency, definitely an adventure. Rodrigo, one of the richest men in town, with the best truck (a '94 Toyota Land Cruiser pick-up) finally left town at about 9:30 A.M. He bought maize for 150 lempiras per carga in Montañuelas and sold it for 220–230 lempiras/carga in Las Lajas—a trip usually of 45 minutes, but which took twice that long because the dude drives slow as molasses and due to the bad conditions of the roads—small slides, trees down, rutted, etc. Then down/up the road to Montaña del Indio, the alternate route from Lajas to La Libertad. Road narrow and only recently made passable after closure by numerous landslides. Across the valley one could see where the old road via Valle Bonito used to be, now closed by truly massive *derrumbes* [landslides] happening over there. That road is impassable and unrecoverable—will have to build a new road from scratch. Rodrigo drove painfully slowly and the clock was ticking. . . . Took some photos of landslides and wrecked roads, bridges. . . . It was nearly 2 P.M. when we got to La Libertad. My first view of the destruction of La Libertad. The entire riverfront area was totally devastated—roads, shops, houses destroyed. But virtually all damage was confined to a 500 meter strip on either side of the river—the little, insignificant Río Frío. What was once the tree- and building-lined edge of the river is now a boulder strewn *playa* [beach] of river rocks and wrecked buildings. Unbelievable. We forded the now normal river as a bulldozer worked to keep the passage open. I . . . rushed off . . . to catch the bus for Comayagua which was leaving at that moment. . . . The bus ride was also painfully slow. The road did not seem to be in such bad shape, but we stopped for gas, for *leña* [firewood], for everything and everybody. Consequently, we did not get to Comayagua until after 4 P.M. The bed of the Humuya River outside Comayagua was scoured out to about 2 km across, filled with sand, rocks, downed trees and debris. This pretty much describes all the river and quebrada beds in the Comayagua valley.

I . . . missed the last direct bus to Tegucigalpa. I got to the terminal at 4:10 P.M. and the bus left at 4. So I quickly flagged a cab outside the bus station and rode out to the highway and got on a bus from Siguatepeque headed for Tegucigalpa. Struggled aboard with my two backpacks and map tube. Settled in for the ride and asked my seat companion how much the fare to Tegucigalpa was. He informed me that the bus was not going to Tegucigalpa. It would only go to where the road was cut, then we would have to walk across the impassable portion of the road, to catch a bus on the other side. . . . I was surprised to hear this as I had read in today's paper that due to a "titanic effort" the government had restored the road connection from Tegucigalpa to San Pedro Sula, with only a few detours around Santa Cruz. All the derrumbes between Comayagua and Tegucigalpa were supposedly fixed and "*no había interrupciones del tránsito*" ["traffic flowed uninterrupted"]. I hoped my seat companion was wrong, but trusted his information more than the newspaper. We cruised at a good clip across the valley. Bridges were eroded from the pounding they had taken during the storm, river courses washed out and debris filled, but passable. Started up the big hill heading to Tegucigalpa. Made it about 2/3 of the way up, and then, sure enough, the bus stops, and . . . people fight to get out and start hiking madly for the bus somewhere on the other side.

The landslide was truly extensive. A flow of that white sandy volcanic ash that lines this section of the highway. I . . . started hoofing it at a brisk pace uphill past a lllllooonnnnggg line of backed-up traffic—mostly semi-trucks, but a fair amount of car traffic, too. I walked fast and it must have been at least half an hour walk in the waning light. Then I got to the actual derrumbe, road washed out, covered with spongy, white ash, with a large tanker truck stuck in the middle of the derrumbe, with heavy equipment crawling around it trying to extricate the truck. Semi-trucks and cars lurking, hovering, waiting for a chance to get through. This was around Km 44. I didn't even stop to take a picture (I knew I would regret that) as I was in a hurry to try to catch whatever bus might be waiting on the other side. The prospect of spending the night along the side of the road in the mountains did not thrill me. I had not eaten, drunk, or peed since Montañuelas (ate an orange in Lajas). But I pressed on up the hill, passed the hundreds of waiting vehicles, in an Exodus-like scene. There was a small bus parked on the road up ahead with people streaming in the doors. I was afraid to even stop to pee, fearing I would miss the bus. I got a seat in the very back of the bus and settled in as the bus finished filling up with standees. The ride was amazingly fast, as night fell. We rode . . . into Tegucigalpa/Comayaguela. Heeding the advice of the woman sitting next to me, I got off the bus somewhere in upper Comayaguela and caught a taxi to Nelson and Meches' house. The ride took me to the Parque del Obelisco,

> which had flooded, across a damaged bridge, and past shops along the Blvd. de la Comunidad Económica Europea, where people were shoveling mud and debris out of their stores. I arrived . . . at the foot of the hill to Nelson's house at about 6:30 P.M. . . . Nelson and Meches (N&M) and I swapped hurricane tales. According to N&M, the rivers here rose in a matter of hours in the middle of the night and wiped out bridges, flooded houses and swept away entire neighborhoods. According to Nelson, business is pretty much at a standstill.

The trip from Montañuelas to Tegucigalpa was a clear indication of the level of Mitch's destruction and the havoc it was raising with the country. The severing of the main road and the inability to open it five days after the storm's passage clearly demonstrated that the country was massively affected. Hiking from one bus to another across the landslide was an inconvenience for me, but for the country it represented a major disruption of essential transportation, commercial, and communications services. At the same time, there were stirrings to restore services. The U.S. government promised a "*puente aereo*" ("air bridge") to fly supplies into Palmerola, the U.S. airbase built in the early 1980s to supply the Contras and serve as a logistical center and listening post in our counterinsurgency war of those times. I was glad it was finally coming in handy for some constructive purpose.

My impressions from the trip were confirmed over the next several days in Tegucigalpa. Tegucigalpa was hit hard by the storm, with landslides wiping out entire hillside neighborhoods and with massive flooding of the low-lying areas adjacent to the two usually innocuous "rivers" that transit the city. As described by Ensor and Ensor (chapter 1 in this volume), rainfall from Mitch contributed to the breaking of a small dam upstream of the city at the height of the storm, creating a raging flash flood that tore through the city in the middle of the night of October 31–November 1. This torrent was blocked by landslides that dammed the river, causing further flooding and devastating the housing located on these precarious slopes. One week later, the city was still struggling to recover from the incredible devastation. Yet later fieldnote entries (chronicling my return trip to Montañuelas) indicate that Honduras was dealing, however haltingly, with the immediate crises caused by this massive disaster: the restoration of roads and transportation services.

11/9/98

Tegucigalpa

Went to the Instituto [Honduran Institute of Anthropology, IHAH] today. I had tried calling without success—no answer—so I took a cab over. The flood hit the DIPPSA gas station and La Colonia supermarket hard. Two other buildings collapsed on the corner and from there to the river, down by the Parque La Concordia, was even further devastation. I found IHAH to be at work, but barely. . . . The visit to the park also presented another panorama of destruction, like that which I witnessed yesterday in Comayaguela. (See below.)

After IHAH, I . . . briefly met with Hector Barreto, ex-head of CIAT-Laderas [an agricultural development project]. . . . Barreto mentioned that all projects seemed to be on hold as people adjust to the new reality of post-Mitch Honduras. Amen to that. . . . Called the U.S. Embassy and my Fulbright contact, Stedman Howard. He will be tied up with visits by George Bush (just left), Tipper Gore (coming tomorrow), and Hillary Clinton (comes Friday). I told him that IHAH was down. That I planned to go back to the field—he was surprised I had even gotten out! And I mentioned I would like to do some volunteer work in disaster relief when I return to Tegucigalpa in late November. He said that was feasible and to come see him then. . . .

Yesterday I went down to the flooded area of Comayaguela with Meches. . . . The city—Comayaguela—was flooded about three blocks in from the river: Calle Real, Avenida 1 y 2. Virtually all of the adobe buildings were wrecked. Cars piled up in heaps, buses in the river bed, water up to the power lines and second story of buildings. Stench of rotten mud . . . [at] the Puente Carías . . . we had to pass a mound of rotten meat near the Mercado San Isidro—any humans in there? Smell made me gag. People picking through muddy garbage for shoes, clothing, anything of value. Also passed by the (former) residential barrio of María Cristina, which lost about ten square blocks of houses to the flood. The same scene repeated today in Barrio Abajo/Parque Concordia area.

11/11/98

ENEE housing at El Cajón

Yesterday . . . around mid-day I got in a discussion with Meches about rumors of aid corruption here that are floating around the Internet. We both agreed that such rumors are destructive, but we admit that neither of us knew enough about aid administration to say if such rumors are true or not. Unfortunately, the tendency here is to believe the worst (with some justification!). This sent Meches into a whirlwind of activity and phone calls to alert relevant and competent people here about these rumors, to investigate them and, where unsubstantiated, to deny them vigorously and articulately. Mitch is a top story on international news. Ted Koppel is here. Tipper Gore, George Bush, Hillary Clinton. It's a Big Story. . . .

Today I woke early, showered and packed, getting ready to go back to Montañuelas. Got a ride from Nelson to Hedman Alas bus line. Bus ride was fairly uneventful. The road from Tegucigalpa to San Pedro Sula is now open. The big landslide that had closed the road has been patched over. There is one detour around Lake Yojoa. . . . I counted 18 landslides on the road between Tegucigalpa and the detour. Got out in Santa Cruz de Yojoa and used Nelson's 500-lempira donation to buy 50 lb of sugar, 50 lb of beans, 1 lb of coffee, and 10 lb of potatoes. Spent 80 lempiras transporting it to ENEE. . . . Eventually I made it to the Manejo de Cuenca offices. I ran into Eric Estrada there, an ENEE engineer, and he provided immediate logistical help—a car—to take me and the goods to the lake to hopefully catch a boat to Montañuelas.

11/12/98

Montañuelas

Today I left ENEE for Montañuelas. The road to the lake's edge is now open. No longer necessary to scramble down a cliff. . . . I arrived at the Embarcadero of Montañuelas with 110 pounds of provisions and fortunately there was someone there passing maize across the lake by lancha and sending it up the hill by horse. He made room on a horse for the beans and sugar and also my green backpack and up the hill we went with a *cipote* [kid]. . . . Got up the hill, helped the cipote unload, took goods to Leonardo's house, who is coordinating distribution of aid to surrounding communities.

Life in Montañuelas had returned to some sense of normalcy in the immediate aftermath of Mitch. Road connections were reestablished much more quickly than I had anticipated. The disaster in La Libertad had (ironically) raised the profile of the region and its priority for assistance. Also, because La Libertad and the mountainous areas between it and Montañuelas are important coffee-producing areas, there was a concerted effort to reopen the roads so that the soon-to-be-harvested coffee could get to market—an economic priority of national importance. The national coffee producers' association, AHCAFE, helped to pay for the road repair. The prolonged period of isolation and scarcity in Montañuelas that I had anticipated never did materialize.

I spent another couple of weeks in Montañuelas finishing up my work, which no longer seemed trivial given that the most acute phase of the Mitch emergency had passed. Hurricane Mitch clearly caused hardship in this part of the countryside, but among people accustomed to hardship there was no choice but to soldier on: to harvest what remained of the rain-soaked milpa, to gather firewood, to prepare the day's tortillas and beans "*sí hay*" (if there are any). If not, there is always tortillas and salt, the dietary last resort of the poor in rural Honduras.

In reality, however, things never really returned to "normal" in Montañuelas. There were several longer-term effects of Mitch, some positive and some negative. Hundreds of millions of post-disaster assistance dollars poured into the country, managed by a plethora of nongovernmental organizations (NGOs). (See Ensor and Ensor, chapter 2 in this volume; Fuentes, chapter 7 in this volume.) Some of that aid trickled down to Montañuelas, bringing NGO personnel with it. There was a project to build a new school and improve household sanitation—basic development work, but definitely accelerated by the provision of disaster relief. It is a mantra of disaster specialists, such as those contributing to this volume, that relief efforts should be managed so as to create development, not dependency. The construction of the school and sanitation facilities, funded externally but performed by local people, seem to be examples of this. Of course, a school is more than a building; its social benefits depend on quality teachers, supplies, and so forth. It is not clear if this school will be sustained, though it was operational on my last visit to Montañuelas in 2004.

On the downside, immediate post-disaster relief had a strong negative effect on the national and local agricultural economy. Food donations flooded the market, depressing prices for maize and causing a great disincentive for local farmers to produce. Several of the poorer families I knew, landless campesinos for whom agriculture was a marginal economic activity (though it normally supplied their subsistence needs), stopped planting maize for several seasons after Mitch, preferring to live on handouts. This was an entirely rational decision, but one that embodied the very dependency that disaster aid strives to avoid. For just this reason, the jury is still out on the benefits of food aid. It may stave off a food emergency but, unless carefully managed, it can damage the productive capacity of a country.

Conclusions: Pateando al Perro

A former colleague of mine, Uruguayan economist Carlos Seré, had a refrain that went something like this: "Si quieres ver si el perro está vivo, patealo." If you want to see if the dog is alive, give it a kick. By this he meant that one excellent way to see how a society works is to introduce some change. Hurricane Mitch certainly qualifies as "kicking the dog" in the Honduran context. Oliver-Smith (chapter 1 in this volume) expresses this same thought in more elegant terms: "disasters like Mitch focus with uncommon intensity the widest possible variety of . . . processes and events of social, environmental, cultural, political, physical, and technological natures. . . . All dimensions of a society's structure and the totality of its relations with the environment become involved." As this volume amply demonstrates, analyzing the reaction of Honduras and its population to Mitch provides a superb lens for understanding Honduran society.

The key analytical conclusion drawn from my experience of Hurricane Mitch is this: Do not underestimate the resilience of households and communities in coping with apparent crises. This is not a prescription for neglect; rather, it is a call to build on household and community resilience when devising strategies to cope with disasters. It also calls our attention to the necessity of clearly distinguishing those communities most severely affected by disasters, where usual coping mechanisms are no longer viable, from those that can still manage to adapt to difficult circumstances. Aid efforts need to focus on those who have lost homes, suffered physically, or lost access to essential services. If this principle is neglected, then national-level responses (or international aid efforts focused on the national level) have the potential to do real harm. A case in point is the provision of massive amounts of food aid in the wake of Mitch, which drove prices down and left farmers—both marginal and commercial—with little incentive to produce.

As is true of development efforts generally, relief efforts should avoid doing things *for* people and instead provide the resources necessary to enhance people's ability to cope with their circumstances. Such efforts must be sensitive to the existing cultural context, recognizing where this context constrains the majority's well-being and when it serves as a resource and means for coping with life's vicissitudes. The campesinos of the El Cajón region do not routinely look to the state for help in coping with the difficulties they face. They are skeptical, and rightly so, of the state's ability to deliver: on promises, on benefits, on the type of assistance folks need to improve their lot. As in many other countries, in Honduras the state—far from being a neutral arbiter of social conflict and an institutional mechanism for delivering social benefits and goods—is itself a resource and is in play and "up for grabs" for those with the means to enter this contest. It is my impression that the rural poor in Honduras, while not despairing of the state's capability, know better than to *rely* on the state: not on a daily basis and certainly not in an emergency. The state does best at managing the basic services and infrastructure of the nation (roads, dams), whereas communities and households are better able to ensure provision of the private goods and services necessary for survival. In the El Cajón region, state assistance in the form of providing a temporary means for the distribution of food (i.e., ENEE water transport on the lake) was important in the immediate aftermath of Mitch. No single community or household could perform this function. Likewise, restoring road service was and is an important state service. Beyond that, communities need to participate actively in determining relief/development priorities and in performing the work needed to achieve these.

Finally, it is worthwhile to highlight once again the moral economy of disaster evidenced by the people of Montañuelas. Their first impulse was to reach out to help their neighbors. This response may well represent an underappreciated resource for coping with disasters even in the poorest of countries. We often conceive of aid as a one-way flow from the rich to the poor, whether we are discussing countries, communities, or households. The response of the people of Montañuelas—to collect maize and deliver it to those more severely affected by Mitch—exemplifies an important resource that should be built upon in disaster assistance. Their response to the crisis represents a possibly universal urge to balance receiving with giving (see Williams 1995 for a discussion of this impulse in circumstances radically different from these). At the very least, aid organizations should recognize the importance of local participation in disaster relief/development efforts, if for no other reason than to combat a sense of dependency that would ultimately undermine the physical and mental well-being of inhabitants. Putting participatory disaster responses in place is a huge institutional challenge in social and political contexts that do not routinely depend on these mechanisms. It is ironic that the extraordinary circumstances of disaster situations introduce the possibility of this work being accomplished. Yet as this chapter points out, even if national institutions are lacking, local communities often have both formal and informal institutions that can be mobilized for immediate response to disasters and, perhaps, longer-term building of participatory organizational structures. This latter prospect should be an explicit goal of disaster relief efforts everywhere.

Note

1. Research reported on in this chapter was supported by the Council for the International Exchange of Scholars, the National Geographic Society Committee for Research and Exploration, Mississippi State University, and California State University, Chico; it was carried out with the permission and sponsorship of the Instituto Hondureño de Antropología e Historia (IHAH, the Honduran Institute of Anthropology and History), Dr. Olga Joya, director. Special thanks to Gumercindo Avila and family for their support, friendship, and insights during my research in the El Cajón region as well as to the people of Montañuelas for the example of their generosity.

References

Blaikie, Piers, Terry Cannon, Ian Davis, and Ben Wisner. 1994. *At Risk: Natural Hazards, People's Vulnerability and Disasters.* New York: Routledge.

Hawker, Patrick. 2000. *A Review of the Role of Dams and Flood Management. World Commission on Dams.* Wiltshire, UK: Halcrow Water.

Loker, William M. 2004. *Changing Places: Environment, Development and Social Change in Rural Honduras.* Durham, NC: Carolina Academic Press.

Oliver-Smith, Anthony. 2002. "Theorizing Disasters: Nature, Power and Culture." In *Catastrophe and Culture: The Anthropology of Disaster,* edited by Susannah Hoffman and Anthony Oliver-Smith, 23–48. Santa Fe, NM: School of American Research.

Oliver-Smith, Anthony, and Susannah Hoffman. 2002. "Introduction: Why Anthropologists Should Study Disasters." In *Catastrophe and Culture:*

The Anthropology of Disaster, edited by Susannah Hoffman and Anthony Oliver-Smith, 3–22. Santa Fe, NM: School of American Research.

Scott, James C. 1976. *The Moral Economy of the Peasant: Rebellion and Subsistence in Southeast Asia.* New Haven, CT: Yale University Press.

Williams, Holly Ann. 1995. "There Are No Free Gifts! Social Support and the Need for Reciprocity." *Human Organization* 54, no. 4: 401–9.

5
Post-Disaster Reconstruction
An Opportunity for Political Change

Vilma Elisa Fuentes

Post-disaster reconstruction is fundamentally a political event that can have very discernible political outcomes. Ideally, the most devastated areas or individuals in a country should receive a high level of government assistance soon after the initial shock of the event has subsided. But this is often not the case. Corruption or clientelism may taint the distribution of aid, channelling most of it to powerful or well-connected individuals in a country. Governments also may choose to prioritize reconstruction projects for regions and social sectors that are critical for reactivating the economy, rather than for those most severely affected by the event. As a result, traditionally neglected regions or social groups may continue to be marginalized during this period (DeVries 2000; Olivo Díaz López 2002; Ensor, chapter 6 in this volume). The manner in which reconstruction decisions are made and aid is distributed significantly affects their impact. If only a small number of individuals within the central government are making reconstruction decisions, then the process will tend to reinforce centralized or authoritarian state structures and be more susceptible to corruption. If, however, these choices are made in a transparent and participatory manner, then this special period may contribute to a process of democratization. What can be done to ensure that reconstruction unfolds in this latter form, especially in countries that have frail or nonexistent democracies? The case of Honduras suggests that both civil society and international donors can play a critical role in determining how reconstruction unfolds and its political impact. Both groups can help advance democracy during the post-disaster period if they organize, work closely with each other, and jointly demand political changes.

Research reveals that natural disasters often challenge existing political structures and pose an opportunity for change. They do so by increasing the number of citizen demands while simultaneously reducing a government's response capabilities (Olson 2000). Cuny (1983:54) explains that "disasters often highlight the social struggles in society and underscore the inherent inequities within a political system. Earthquakes and hurricanes, for example, affect a disproportionately high percentage of the poor in developing countries. . . . A disaster makes it very evident that the poor are vulnerable because they are poor." Longitudinal studies by Drury, Olson, and Shefner show that countries with an inequitable distribution of wealth and/or a history of social or political strife tend to experience a rise in political conflict after disasters (Drury and Olson 1998:153–61; Shefner 1999:137–90). The incidence of such politically unsettling events "may throw into question the very legitimacy of the authoritative allocation process itself—the regime" (Olson 2000).

Case studies reveal that the political systems of several Latin American countries have been destabilized by natural disasters during the last half-century. The disasters highlighted the corrupt and authoritarian tendencies of existing governments and encouraged the creation of organized groups (or invigorated existing ones). The civil society so revitalized has challenged those in control of the state and often demanded a political regime change.

The 1972 Managua earthquake set in motion forces that eventually led to the demise of the Somoza regime and gave rise to socialism there (Black 1981:58–62; Drury and Olson 1998; Gawronski 2000). Black (1981:58) argues that "the importance of the earthquake as a pivotal moment in the disintegration of Somocismo can hardly be overstated." In the aftermath of the disaster Somoza, the National Guard, and members of the ruling triumvirate were involved in several incidents of corruption (Somoza 1980:3–22; Booth 1981:89, 93; Anderson 1982:155–56).[1] Although such behavior may have been accepted or may have typified the Nicaraguan political system during normal times, citizens were unwilling to tolerate corruption during the emergency and reconstruction periods (Olson and Gawronski 2001).[2] The press exposed and denounced such behavior (Daly and Lynn 1990:49), and business elites—which until then had offered tenuous support to Somoza—turned against him (Booth 1981:81; Dunkerley 1988:235–36). Meanwhile, dissatisfaction with the regime grew among the lower and middle classes, who increasingly demanded fundamental political changes in their country (Booth 1981:84, 113, 124–25, 277). All of these factors revived and strengthened support for the Frente Sandinista de Liberación Nacional (FSLN), a guerrilla group that had been "presumed dead since 1970" (Anderson 1982:156–59). The mounting opposition and the rise in political violence after the earthquake eventually led to a regime transition in Nicaragua in 1979.

The Guatemalan political system also was strained after a 1976 earthquake. Dunkerley (1988:469) notes that "the political impact of the earthquake was sharp if not—in the short term—quite the same in form as that in Nicaragua four years earlier." Part of the problem arose from the government's mishandling of emergency and reconstruction assistance. Although approximately 25,000 Guatemalans were killed and 1.25 million were left homeless, the government offered only scant relief to the highland Mayan communities that had been most affected by the disaster. In addition, the government persecuted missionary and other humanitarian groups who tried to supply needed help to these areas independently of official state channels (Schlesinger and Kinzer 1983:249). Peasants in affected areas of the country responded by organizing, criticizing the government, and articulating their demands better than ever before. Meanwhile, several companies took advantage of the post-disaster crisis to lay off hundreds of workers and thus weaken labor unions. Workers responded by consolidating themselves into a united front, demanding that their labor rights be secured and that the government respond to the needs of disaster victims (Fernández 1988:207–15). Jonas (1991:124–25) notes that "some of the most important, urban-based movements" in Guatemala emerged "from the rubble of the massive earthquake of 1976. . . . Not long after the earthquake, when the potential of these organizations became clear, the repression began." Eventually, this post-disaster organization and the state's response to it helped strengthen the Guerrilla Army of the Poor, which gained much of its support from those highland communities most affected by the disaster. Unlike the FSLN, this guerrilla group was unsuccessful in overthrowing the government or prompting a regime transition in Guatemala. Instead, the increasing discontent and organization among civil society groups here led to a prolonged civil war.

The 1985 Mexico City earthquake also contributed to the emergence of a strong though nonviolent civil society that challenged the undemocratic nature of the state. A dramatic and spontaneous upsurge in organized groups arose after the earthquake. Their prompt and coordinated response to this crisis contrasted sharply with the government's slow and corrupt mismanagement of emergency assistance (Tavera-Fenellosa 1999; Gawronski 2000). The number of nongovernmental organizations (NGOs) in Mexico also increased after the 1985 earthquake

(Fox and Hernandez 1992:165–208). Many of these civil society groups eventually united into the Earthquake Victims Movement, which effectively "undermined the repressive discourse with which the government justified its exclusion of citizens from local government, challenged the legitimacy of the political status quo in the Federal District and opened the door for the democratization of . . . Mexico City" (Tavera-Fenellosa 1999:108). Although neither the earthquake nor these emergent groups radically altered the national political system, they accelerated sociopolitical changes that had already been underway in the capital and thus contributed to the democratization process in Mexico.

Although disasters can serve as catalysts for political change, they do not always serve this function. If well managed, these events may legitimize rather than destabilize a government or system of rule. The Argentine military's adept response to the 1944 San Juan earthquake helped the recently installed military junta legitimize its undemocratic hold of government. Perón's seemingly compassionate role and involvement in relief efforts helped him rise in popularity and gain political control of Argentina soon after this event (Healy 2000). Similarly, in 1974 Hurricane Fifi helped the military solidify and extend its political control in Honduras. Although massive corruption diminished the effectiveness of the foreign aid that was received, the military government responded to this disaster by implementing an agrarian reform law and distributing land to thousands of Hondurans, many of whom had been adversely affected by the hurricane. This enabled the military to gain the support of the peasants and remain in power until the early 1980s. The political effects of disaster, in other words, need not lead to a deepening of democracy. Disasters may also help to strengthen authoritarian or highly corrupt practices.

What accounts for such differences in the political impact of a disaster? The case of Honduras suggests that the level of civil society organization and international donor oversight are both critical to understanding the political effects of disaster. There will be few domestic challenges to the government or regime in power if civic groups do not use this window of opportunity to strengthen their organization, coordinate their activities at a national level, and begin demanding fundamental political changes. International donors play a crucial role during this period. They can oversee the reconstruction process, help curtail the incidence of corruption, and demand that governments receiving aid initiate democratic reforms. They also can support the work of civic groups and legitimize their actions and demands by working closely with them.

The use of *conditionalities* has been one of the principal ways through which bilateral and multilateral agencies have encouraged aid-recipient countries to undertake structural reforms. A conditionality "entails offering a benefit if . . . the receiver takes specific actions (or refrains from taking actions [of] which the donor disapproves)" (Nelson 1992:10). These benefits may be economic, as when an international agency offers a loan to a developing country on the condition that certain public policies be adopted. Or the incentive may be political, as when the European Union makes membership in its organization contingent upon having a stable democracy (Pridham 1991, 1999; Huntington 1993:87–91).

Donors have promoted democratization not only through the use of such conditionalities but also by disseminating a specific political discourse. Politicians and civic groups in developing nations increasingly speak of the need to make governments more democratic, accountable, and participatory. The ideas disseminated through such a discourse can help change a state's conception of development (Finnemore 1996). Although the degree of actual commitment to these goals among those who profess them may be questionable, the mere fact that this language is being employed is politically significant. As Barrios (chapter 7 in this volume) points out, discursive practices can have an impact on the constitution of reality (see also Yee 1996:86). In order for democracy to advance, it must be preceded by a discussion of this process. Of course, the mere use of a particular discourse does not ensure that those employing it will act in concert with what they profess. Governments may alter their discursive practices for instrumental reasons, but eventually they may come to accept the validity of what they profess (Risse, Ropp, and Sikkink 1999). More importantly, the use of a particular discourse becomes the basis for assessing the politicians who employ it as well as the regime they represent. Politicians who speak of democracy, government accountability, and reducing corruption will likely be judged by international actors and their constituents on the basis of these concepts. Political language also helps frame the nature of political interactions. It "lends representative legitimacy to some social interests more than others, delineates the accepted boundaries of state action . . . and . . . privilege[s] some lines of policy over others" (Hall 1993:289).

The degree of donor influence over national governments, whether by conditionalities or use of a particular discourse, depends on the needs of the recipient country and the extent of its cooperation with donors. Highly indebted or aid-dependent countries will be more vulnerable to donor conditionalities and pressures than those experiencing a steady level of economic growth based on a diversity of competitive exports. Crisis events seem to heighten donor influence on developing countries by augmenting citizen demands on the state while dramatically increasing foreign aid to a country. Multiple donors who together offer billions of dollars in assistance will have a greater impact than a few donors who offer aid packages of only a few million. Moreover, if donor organizations collaborate with each other to demand the same set of political reforms from a recipient country, they will increase the likelihood of achieving that goal.

Although bilateral and multilateral donors can exert significant influence over a country receiving aid during a post-disaster period, they do not determine the nature of politics there. The interests of local elites and the actions of civic groups both mediate the extent to which international donors can affect national-level politics. Democratic reforms favored by foreign donors are more likely to be realized if there is strong grassroots support for such changes. In an effort to appease international donors and organized groups in society, national politicians may accede to the demands placed before them, adopt a new political discourse, and eventually institute reforms that contribute to the democratization of a country. The case of Honduras clarifies this argument.

Initial State Reaction to the Disaster

When Hurricane Mitch struck Honduras, the country's government was wholly unprepared to meet the immediate needs of disaster victims. As discussed by Ensor and Ensor (chapter 2 in this volume), the national emergency management agency, the Comisión Permanente de Contingencias (COPECO), lacked the funds, personnel, and equipment to confront the emergency.[3] Although it counted on several helicopters and planes, the agency's operations chief was forced to acknowledge just a few days after the storm that it needed twice as many air vehicles in order to manage rescue operations adequately just along the Northern Coast (La Prensa 1998a). Consequently, the overburdened Honduran state was unable to offer some regions of the country emergency assistance even after they requested it (DeVries 2000). This prompted communities in different parts of the country to self-organize and develop their own survival strategies.

Meanwhile, state agencies distributed humanitarian aid at a painstakingly slow pace to those most in need (Olson 2001). Some citizens were still trapped on rooftops two weeks after the storm, and many of those housed in temporary shelters did not receive food shipments or other humanitarian assistance for more than three weeks. The paucity of aid distribution caused many to question the government's ability to distribute foreign aid efficiently, fairly, and with transparency. The human rights commissioner, Leo Valladares, expressed the fear that corruption would hinder the state's relief efforts and reminded the public that Honduras had been rated as the second most corrupt country in Latin America earlier in 1998.

The increasing domestic and international concern over the government's capacity to administer aid led President Carlos Flores (1998–2001) to give the task of receiving, managing, and distributing foreign assistance to both Catholic and Evangelical Churches on November 17, 1998. Since the Catholic Church was the largest of these religious institutions, it assumed the bulk of this responsibility. In some areas the Church worked through a strong network of Delegates of the Word[4] and Christian Base Communities; in others, it created new community organizations to carry out relief work (see Humphrey 1997:28). Although the Catholic Church had become a key protagonist in the emergency phase, both the Honduran Catholic Bishops Council and the CARITAS Council continually stated that the Catholic Church should only cooperate in the emergency and reconstruction process, not manage it. These religious leaders were hopeful that the Church's work would help strengthen the Honduran state. They believed that the best way to achieve this was by strengthening civil society and encouraging it to become more active in the emergency and reconstruction process.

Although President Flores gave Honduran churches the task of distributing emergency assistance, he attempted to centralize state power in order to confront the crisis. On October 29, 1998, just two days after Mitch made landfall, President Flores declared a state of emergency and ordered the armed forces and National Police to take possession of affected Atlantic Coast areas in order to prevent looting and maintain order. He also began ruling by decree in early November 1998 so that members of Congress could remain in and better assist the communities that they represented. Flores suspended civil liberties on November 3 and imposed a fifteen-day curfew from 9 P.M. to 5 A.M. Two days later, he announced that a group of technocrats had begun drafting a national plan for reconstruction. The government's work on this document was highly secretive. Few people knew who was working on it or what the plan would entail. Once the Congress was recalled, it facilitated the president's centralization of power. The Congress approved the executive decree suspending civil liberties and extended the nighttime curfew until the end of November. It also quickly approved a bill—the Law for Administrative Facility—submitted by the executive that allowed the president to modify the national budget, prioritize state expenditures, bypass regular bureaucratic channels, and form a Special Cabinet for National Reconstruction. This effectively institutionalized a highly centralized reconstruction process. On November 25, 1998, Flores began to organize his new cabinet.[5] This group of five ministers was expected to supervise the development and monitor the implementation of the government's reconstruction plan. Municipal governments as well as those ministries not represented in the new cabinet were required by law to implement the master plan even though they were not guaranteed participation in its design (La Prensa 1998b). Mayors and congressional representatives found it increasingly difficult to access members of the Reconstruction Cabinet or have any influence on them in the first few months after Mitch.

International donors began working closely with the Honduran government shortly after the disaster in order to facilitate the process of recovery. The World Bank established a Central American Emergency Trust Fund with the contribution of several donors in November of 1998 to help countries affected by Mitch continue to make debt repayments (World Bank 1999). This enabled Honduras to channel the millions of dollars normally spent on repaying foreign loans to relief and emergency work. In December 1998 the Inter-American Development Bank (IADB) began coordinating longer-term recovery work by hosting a Consultative Group meeting on the Reconstruction of Central America in Washington, DC. This marked the beginning of international donor coordination to assist Honduras. Representatives from major bilateral and multilateral donors met the Central American presidents to discuss the region's needs and coordinate the international community's commitment to reconstruction. Attendees agreed that reconstruction should be seen as an opportunity to pursue a more sustainable development than what had been achieved in the past. They decided that reconstruction should contribute to a broader process of (1) lessening ecological and social vulnerability, (2) reducing foreign debt, (3) achieving greater social equity, (4) promoting decentralization, (5) increasing civil society participation, and (6) encouraging good governance.[6] Another Consultative Group meeting was scheduled for May of 1999 in Stockholm, Sweden. Unlike the December meeting, this second gathering was to include civil society groups. Central American governments were asked to draft reconstruction plans in consultation with these civil society groups and to present the plans in Stockholm, where donors promised to announce their financial commitment to the region.

Although participants at the Washington meeting committed themselves to improving the nature of governance in Central America, the Honduran government initially did little to change its authoritarian and centralist tendencies. President Flores replaced Foreign Relations Minister Fernando Martínez in early January of 1999 after he criticized the unproductive nature of the Reconstruction Cabinet and the lack of competitive bidding for new projects.[7] Martínez claimed that the Reconstruction Cabinet tended to act like a coffee-break club during this early period: he claimed that members merely discussed reconstruction in abstract terms instead of tackling significant policy matters. Meanwhile, contracts for reconstruction projects were being granted to friends and family members of senior-level political officials. Martínez suggested that these be audited and subject to a competitive bidding process, but his views were dismissed (see La Prensa 1998c; Jeffrey 1999:32). Martínez resigned from the Reconstruction Cabinet in late December 1998, only to be discharged from his ministerial post a few days later. President Flores also resisted attempts at promoting decentralization. He refused to transfer 5 percent of the national budget to the country's municipal governments, as mandated by law. He (and other national-level government officials) claimed that municipal governments lacked the capacity to administer these funds. Consequently, only 1.7 percent of the 1999 budget was distributed among these local public entities. The Flores government did agree to allow civil society participation in the drafting of the Reconstruction Plan, but only from groups represented in the Foro Nacional de Convergencias (FONAC)—a corporatist body formed just a few months before Hurricane Mitch.

The Reinvigoration of Honduran Civil Society

Honduran civil society responded to the increasingly closed and centralized nature of Honduran politics by organizing and considering how it could best address the challenges of reconstruction. CARITAS, the Catholic Church's development agency, decided to invite leaders of several civil society groups to meet in December 1998 to begin a public discussion on what reconstruction should entail. Several professionals, intellectuals, and civic leaders had been arguing since the onslaught of Mitch that socioeconomic and environmental factors had contributed to the country's recent natural disaster. Informally and through newspaper editorials, these individuals argued that the process of reconstruction should try to transform these pre-existing conditions, not simply rebuild houses and infrastructure. However, there was no structure or unity to these disparate views. Father Germán Calix, the executive director of CARITAS, believed that civil society groups would have united on their own without his group's intervention. But because CARITAS, and the Catholic Church more generally, were playing such a large role in relief work, he and other Church leaders thought they could facilitate a dialogue among civil society groups and encourage them to begin thinking more formally about reconstruction. The December reunion did not seek to unite all civil society groups in Honduras. In fact, most of the traditional, mass-based organizations in the country were excluded from this meeting. CARITAS merely invited those organizations (most of them NGOs) with whom it had coordinated development projects in the past. The attempt to unite development-oriented NGOs seemed logical at the time, since these groups (together with municipal governments) were the ones leading much of the grassroots emergency work. Those who attended the meeting formed working groups dedicated to discussing education, health, housing, agrarian reform, and other such topics. These brainstorming groups continued to meet on various occasions during the following weeks.

At the end of 1998, labor unions, peasant cooperatives, and other mass-based organizations also began meeting through the government-led FONAC in order to discuss the issue of reconstruction. The Honduran government had experimented with several such corporatist arrangements throughout the 1990s. But these instances of citizen participation had been evanescent, and those present were simply "co-opted"; this contributed to the fragmentation and weakening of traditional mass-based groups and not to their political empowerment (Pino 1992:20–26). FONAC was almost identical in form to its predecessor, except that it had a permanent meeting site and office personnel. This group's ability to affect government policy was severely limited: FONAC's agenda was influenced by the executive branch of government, which ultimately decided whether to accept or ignore any recommendations. Several individuals at these meetings explained that the government's influence on FONAC's agenda led the organization to prioritize issues that were not those considered to be most important by Honduran citizens. For example, although FONAC designed and presented a reconstruction proposal in early 1999, the organization's resources were channelled to other matters soon thereafter. This limited FONAC's ability to follow through on its proposals.

The Asociación de Municipios de Honduras (AMHON; Association of Municipalities of Honduras), one of the organizations represented in FONAC, was reinvigorated during this post-disaster period. AMHON had been established in 1962 to represent mayors and municipal governments before the state. But rather than achieve this task, the executive traditionally had used AMHON to manipulate local governments. AMHON had been reorganized in the early 1990s with the strong financial and technical support of foreign donors. It soon became a strong advocate of decentralization. The group had lobbied for and achieved electoral reform in Honduras in the 1990s but had failed to increase the financial and administrative autonomy of local governments. AMHON set out to achieve both of these goals after Hurricane Mitch, arguing that municipal governments had proven during the post-disaster emergency period that they were better able to respond to citizen demands than was the central government. AMHON drafted its own proposal for reconstruction based on municipal government needs. It also demanded that the government transfer 5 percent of the national budget to municipalities as required by law. Initially, President Flores' administration ignored the organization and refused to transfer more funds to municipal governments. Instead, it passed laws to weaken their fiscal independence. AMHON responded by increasing its lobbying activities and, in 2000, filing a lawsuit against the central government for its refusal to transfer the legally mandated funds. By the end of the century AMHON had become the most active municipal association in Central America, possessing both the technical and political capacity to lobby for decentralization and to promote mayoral interests (García González 2001).

While FONAC worked on its reconstruction proposal, CARITAS held a second general meeting of civil society groups in January of 1999. Those present agreed to create a more formal, broad-based coalition that came to be known as INTERFOROS. Although CARITAS had encouraged the unification of civil society groups not represented in FONAC, it adopted a less proactive role toward these organizations once INTERFOROS was formed. INTERFOROS initially comprised CARITAS, the Foro Ciudadano (Citizen's Forum), the Foro Social para la Deuda Externa (FOSDEH), the Federación Privada de Organizaciones en Desarrollo (FOPRIDEH), ASONOG (the Asociación de Organizaciones No Gubernamentales), and various women's groups. Several labor, peasant, and indigenous organizations—some of which were part of the government-led FONAC—also asked to be incorporated into INTERFOROS in February 1999. By the middle of 1999, INTERFOROS encompassed twelve networks that together represented approximately 575 base groups. INTERFOROS began to work more closely with grassroots groups in 2000. Two years later, INTERFOROS was reorganized to represent eight regional (instead of twelve issue-oriented) civil society forums. This essentially decentralized the group's decision-making power (Comisión Ad Hoc de la Sociedad Civil 2002:107). Some of the members of INTERFOROS had united in December of 1999 to denounce President Flores for continuing to rule by decree. As a result of their protests, the president stopped this authoritarian practice at the end of that year. Now, these groups joined forces once again to draft a reconstruction proposal.[8] The document, which was submitted to the government in mid-March of 1999, emphasized the need to strengthen the country's democracy, institute citizen controls on government, decentralize power, alleviate Honduras' foreign debt, and develop new agrarian and economic policies that were less detrimental to the poor.

Surveys conducted at the end of 1999 and in 2000 with thirty-eight leaders of second- and third-level civil society groups[9] confirm that there was greater organization and cooperation among Honduran civil society groups after Mitch than previously (see table 5.1). Whereas half of those consulted had worked with other civil society organizations only sporadically before the disaster, approximately 47 percent were doing so on a weekly or biweekly basis a year after the storm.

Table 5.1 Reported Cooperation among Civil Society Groups

How frequently did your organization work with other civil society groups before Hurricane Mitch?	
Weekly	10.5%
Biweekly	7.9
Monthly	23.7
Sporadically	50.0
Never	5.3
Don't know	2.6
How frequently has your organization worked with other civil society groups since Hurricane Mitch?	
Weekly	21.1%
Biweekly	26.3
Monthly	36.8
Sporadically	13.2
Never	2.6
Don't know	0

Table 5.2 One-Sample *t*-Test Comparing Reported Levels of Civil Society Participation in 2000 with the pre-Mitch Period

	t	*Df*	Significance (2-tailed)	Mean difference	95% confidence interval of the difference
Test value = 1.68	4.773	37	0.869	0.000	0.47 lower; 1.17 upper

Note: Test value represents the mean of survey participants' perceptions of how frequently their organization cooperated with other civil society groups before Hurricane Mitch.

A one-sample *t*-test determined that there was a significant difference between the level of intragroup cooperation reported for both time periods (see table 5.2). Not surprisingly, 71 percent of those questioned said that it was easier to cooperate with other civil society groups than it had been before Mitch. Moreover, nearly 37 percent of them reported that their organization's membership had increased after the disaster. Several new civic groups also arose during this post-Mitch period. A 2002 study of Honduran civil society reported that 298 second- and third-level civil society organizations were registered with the government (i.e., obtained their *personería jurídica*) from January 1999 to July 2001. Their yearly rate of inscription was almost twice what it had been from 1991 to 1998 (Comisión Ad Hoc de la Sociedad Civil 2002:34). The new numerical strength and unity of Honduran civil society enabled it to challenge the state more forcefully and to reinforce international calls for political change.

The heightened level of organization and political activity among Honduran civil society groups—together with donor pressure to incorporate their views into government decision making—led the Unidad Nacional de Asistencia Técnica (UNAT), the technical office in charge of drafting the government's reconstruction plan, to meet with representatives of INTERFOROS, FONAC, AMHON, and other groups in March 1999. Hundreds of people attended this meeting. Unfortunately, UNAT's meeting was not designed to obtain much citizen input regarding the reconstruction plan. The government presented an outline of its master plan through slides and overheads, and those present were then allowed to comment on what they had seen. The structure of and large number of people at this gathering allowed little room for civil society participation in the decision-making process. However, those present were able to persuade the government to think more about transformation, not merely reconstruction. Based on these general suggestions, the government slightly altered its reconstruction plan (beginning with its title). It then held another meeting with civil society groups, in early April 1999, at which it presented the Master Plan for National Reconstruction and Transformation. This plan estimated that approximately USD 4 billion were needed to rebuild the country—a sum the government hoped to obtain at the upcoming meeting with donors in Stockholm.

Shortly after the government published its reconstruction plan, Human Rights Commissioner Leo Valladares issued a report alleging seventeen cases of foreign aid mismanagement by high-ranking public officials during the immediate aftermath of Mitch. The government responded by harshly criticizing Valladares for tarnishing Honduras' foreign image and hindering its ability to contract funding. Within days, President Flores sent a bill to Congress (it was formally introduced by a Liberal Party congressman) that proposed reducing the human rights commissioner's term from six to four years and limiting his mandate to investigating only cases of human rights abuses. Essentially, this would have prevented the commissioner from investigating cases of corruption. The Congress, then dominated by President Flores' Liberal Party, approved the constitutional reform on April 20, 1999, with 28 votes in favor, 26 against, and 74 abstentions. Honduran civil society responded with outrage. FONAC, INTERFOROS, and other civic groups publicly denounced the government's actions and demanded that the commissioner's term and mandate be left unaltered. Meanwhile, several mass-based groups prepared to launch public protest activities. The political influence of Honduran civil society was reinforced by international pressure. Foreign ambassadors and representatives of multilateral institutions met with the president of the Congress and other senior-level officials to urge the legislature to reconsider its recent vote. President Flores responded by publicly condemning the recent legal decision. Meanwhile, the president of the Congress promised to reconsider the bill and tried to convince the media that Flores had not proposed it. With hundreds of protesters in the streets, Congress unanimously voted on April 27, 1999, to leave the human rights commissioner's term and mandate unchanged (see also Jeffrey 1999:28–35).[10]

In the midst of this political crisis, President Flores tried to polish the government's image by inviting representatives of the Foro Ciudadano to meet with him on April 26, 1999. The Foro Ciudadano is a civic organization composed of distinguished intellectuals who for several years had been lobbying for the need to deepen democracy and reform existing political institutions in Honduras. The group had not only denounced the congressional attack on the human rights commissioner, it had also launched a barrage of criticism against the government during the preceding months. Moreover, the Foro Ciudadano had drafted a series of recommendations on how to improve the country's political system and integrated these into INTERFOROS' reconstruction proposal. President Flores sought a dialogue with the Foro Ciudadano (rather than the broader INTERFOROS, of which it was a part), most likely because one of its key members, Victor Meza, was his former legislative advisor. The president may have intended to use this personal association to co-opt and pacify the group. Instead, the Foro Ciudadano adeptly used its meeting with the president to pressure the government into committing to a series of reforms. These reforms sought to (1) ensure transparency in the management of public affairs and resources, (2) increase both civil society and municipal government participation in public decision making, and (3) reduce Honduras' social and ecological vulnerability. President Flores and all members of the Reconstruction Cabinet committed themselves to pursuing these goals by signing a seven-page declaration on May 20, 1999, and Flores agreed to add this agreement as a supplement to the Master Reconstruction Plan.[11]

Despite this apparent willingness to discuss and accept several civil society demands, the government continued to ignore INTERFOROS. Representatives of this group had been unable to meet the president and had held only a few meetings with members of the Reconstruction Cabinet. When INTERFOROS submitted its reconstruction proposal to the government in mid-March, they were told that the Master Reconstruction Plan was already completed and could not be altered to accommodate their suggestions. The president's subsequent meeting with the Foro Ciudadano caused a rift between this group and INTERFOROS. Members of the latter felt that the Foro Ciudadano should have asked them to participate in this session; the Foro Ciudadano countered that the president had not asked for a dialogue with this larger group. As a result of this disagreement, the Foro Ciudadano withdrew from INTERFOROS in May of 1999.

Nevertheless, Honduran civil society continued to pressure its government and donor agencies to approach reconstruction with a new vision. Two days before the second Consultative Group meeting was set to begin, Central American NGOs and civil society organizations met with their North American and European counterparts in Stockholm to discuss how they could participate in reconstruction. Those present emphasized the need to transform existing socioeconomic and political structures. They suggested that international donors develop multiple follow-up mechanisms to ensure the active participation of civil society in the implementation and supervision of reconstruction. They also asked that conditionalities be attached to the aid offered by these donors in order to reward governments that developed formal participatory mechanisms.

The second Consultative Group meeting took place May 25–28, 1999. Approximately fifteen leaders of Honduran civil society groups attended this event. Most represented traditional organizations such as labor unions, women's groups, and peasant organizations. However, newer groups such as INTERFOROS and the Foro Ciudadano also sent delegates. The Honduran government had met all of these organizations either directly or via FONAC before Stockholm, but its relationship with INTERFOROS remained tense. Moreover, despite its attempts to inform and involve civil society in the reconstruction plan during the early part of 1999, many donors and civic groups continued to believe that the government was too closed and centralized. Donors hoped to use this meeting to encourage the Honduran government to continue cooperating with civil society and incorporating its participation in the reconstruction process. As a first step in this endeavor, forums were held on topics such as transparency and good governance, decentralization, and local development. These forums offered donor agency, national government, and civil society representatives the opportunity to meet and exchange ideas about how to achieve the reconstruction and transformation of Central America.[12] Donors also encouraged the Honduran government to improve its level of dialogue with INTERFOROS. At one point in the consultative group meeting, a Swedish representative invited President Flores to his chamber to meet Mauricio Díaz, the head delegate of INTERFOROS. This was the first time the president had agreed to meet with a representative of this group (see also Jeffrey 1999:35).[13] All of these events sent a clear message to the Honduran government that it had to do more to accommodate civil society. The Consultative Group meeting ended with the drafting and signing of what is simply known as the Stockholm Declaration. Signatory states agreed to the following goals:

- Reduce the social and ecological vulnerability of the region as an overriding objective.
- Reconstruct and transform Central America on the basis of an integrated approach to transparency and good governance.
- Reinforce the process of decentralizing governmental functions and powers with the active participation of the civil society.
- Promote respect for human rights as a permanent objective, giving special attention to promoting equality between women and men and to the rights of children, ethnic groups, and other minorities.
- Coordinate donor efforts—guided by priorities set by the recipient countries—and intensify efforts to reduce the external debt burden of countries in the region.

At the end of this Consultative Group meeting, donors pledged to give Honduras approximately USD 2.8 billion during a four-year period to finance relief, reconstruction, and transformation programs. In addition, the World Bank and IMF agreed to consider forgiving part of

Honduras' debt through their Highly Indebted Poor Country (HIPC) initiative.[14] All of this assistance was conditioned on the Honduran government's complying with the Stockholm Declaration. In order to ensure this compliance, donors created multilevel oversight committees (*grupos de seguimiento*). Foreign donors agreed to meet regularly, coordinate their reconstruction activities, and oversee the Honduran government's compliance with their conditions through these committees.[15]

Initially, the oversight committees were composed of major bilateral and multilateral donors as well as Honduran state officials. At the political level, the ambassadors or representatives of each donor organization met about once every month with the Reconstruction Cabinet to discuss how reconstruction was proceeding. Underneath them, a technical follow-up group was formed consisting of the development agencies of the major bilateral donors. These met on a weekly basis with their Honduran counterparts to analyze the Stockholm Declaration and develop standards for interpreting and applying it. These technical oversight committees helped establish thirteen sectoral groups within different government ministries that were charged with monitoring the actual implementation of projects. Civil society representatives were asked to form a part of these sectoral groups in 2000. This further legitimized Honduran civic groups and enabled donor agencies to develop a closer relationship with them.[16] These groups, together with the CPSC (see next section), also ensured that Honduras would not experience the misappropriation of reconstruction funds that occurred after Hurricane Fifi and was occurring in Nicaragua after Hurricane Mitch. It is most interesting that these oversight committees were not merely temporary responses to reconstruction challenges: they have continued to meet and remain active during the decade after Hurricane Mitch destabilized the country.

The Government's Response to Civil Society and Donor Demands

The Flores government initially responded to the increasing domestic and international pressure for reform by improving its level of transparency and creating new spaces for citizen participation in the reconstruction process. The Reconstruction Cabinet sponsored periodic meetings with civil society groups to inform participants of the amount of aid that had been promised and disbursed as well the progress on reconstruction projects. The content of the Stockholm Declaration, and how the government proposed to abide by it, were also discussed. In addition, the government periodically used local television stations to inform citizens of the progress it was making on reconstruction.

The government tried to involve civil society in the reconstruction process by creating the Comisión para la Participación de la Sociedad Civil en el Proceso de Reconstrucción y Transformación Nacional (CPSC). The CPSC was composed of two representatives from each of five organizations: FONAC, INTERFOROS, the Foro Ciudadano, AMHON, and the Honduran Private Enterprise Council (COHEP). The commission was expected to monitor reconstruction projects and to advise the Reconstruction Cabinet. It began meeting in October of 1999 and by the end of 2000 had developed a plan to undertake its work, made several recommendations to the government, and begun working on a Poverty Reduction Strategy (PRS). Although the Civil Society Commission increased citizen participation in government, it was temporary in nature: the group was disbanded at the end of President Flores' term.

The Flores government began working more closely with different interest groups through less formal means as well. Surveys conducted with Honduran civil society representatives at the end of 1999 and in 2000 revealed that 84 percent of the groups they represented had participated in a government-organized forum, commission, or consultative group after Mitch whereas only 55 percent had done so previously. Three quarters of those questioned also reported that they had more opportunities to express their opinions, discuss matters of concern to them, and make proposals before the government than in the past (see table 5.3). This improved level of dialogue led nearly 58 percent of those surveyed to believe that their organization had more political influence on the government than it had had before Mitch.

Although the national government took steps— after the Stockholm Consultative Group meeting—to promote transparency and ensure civil society participation in the reconstruction process, it continued to be plagued by problems of corruption. The Human Rights Commissioner issued a study in April of 1999 wherein it reported receiving 400 citizen complaints of judiciary corruption during the preceding five months (Infopress Centroamérica 2000b). Transparency International (2000) issued a report the following year that ranked Honduras as one of the most corrupt countries in all of Latin America. The U.S. Agency for

Table 5.3 Civil Society Groups' Participation in National Government Forums, Commissions, and Consultative Groups

	Percent of attendees	
Activity	Before Mitch	After Mitch
Expressed an opinion	55	82
Discussed an issue	53	74
Made a proposal	50	76
Voted	24	26
Made a decision	21	24
Implemented a project	24	29

Note: Test value represents the mean of survey participants' perceptions of how frequently their organization cooperated with other civil society groups before Hurricane Mitch.

Source: Secretaría de Salud de Honduras (1999).

International Development funded a nationwide study in 2001 to investigate these allegations. The study revealed that one in every five Hondurans had been victimized by acts of corruption during the previous year and that 62 percent of them had come to accept bribery as a means of facilitating bureaucratic transactions (Seligson 2001). Even more troubling was the study's finding that victims of corruption were less supportive of the country's political system, were more indifferent to democracy, and had less trust in public officials than those who had not been directly affected by these acts. A separate nationwide study funded by the World Bank that same year arrived at similar conclusions (World Bank 2002). All of these revelations led civil society groups and foreign donors to demand that government corruption be curtailed in Honduras.

President Flores responded to these denunciations by creating a Special Commission of Notables on May 2, 1999, to study problems within the judiciary system and suggest ways of addressing them. Twenty-two representatives from the Congress, civil society, and public agencies were invited to form part of this group (Infopress Centroamérica 2000b). Shortly after its creation, the Commission of Notables revealed several problems within the Honduran legal system suggesting that the Honduran judiciary was corrupt. In particular, it disclosed that arrest warrants had been issued to eleven former judges and that criminal charges had been brought before another eight of them during 1999. In addition, it reported that Honduran judges had illegally released 800 confiscated vehicles (Comisionado Nacional de los Derechos Humanos 2000:58). The Commission of Notables, civil society groups, and foreign donors jointly encouraged the Honduran government to consider reforms to its judiciary and electoral system (see Infopress Centroamérica 2000c).

President Flores also responded to domestic and international charges of corruption by creating a National Anticorruption Council in February 2001. The group was asked to study and make proposals on how to combat government corruption in general, not just that found in the judiciary system. The Anticorruption Council consisted of five government and five civil society representatives and was chaired during its early years by one of the most respected and nonpartisan Honduran citizens, Monsignor Oscar Andrés Rodríguez. The Council submitted an anticorruption strategy to President Flores in January of 2002. The plan proposed limiting political immunity for high-ranking political officials, depoliticizing the comptroller's office, and reforming the constitution so that plebiscites and referendums could be used to enhance citizen participation in public decision making (Comisión Nacional Anticorrupción 2000). Although the Anticorruption Council was intended to be only a temporary group, domestic and international pressure forced the National Congress to pass a new law that transformed this institution into a permanent one in 2002. The Anticorruption Council's strategy for combating government fraud and illicit behavior has been integrated into the government plans of all Honduran presidents since its creation. Although incidences of corruption continue to occur, the Anticorruption Council has been active in denouncing such activities and in monitoring the implementation of its proposal. Its activities even helped Honduras become the first country in Central America to benefit from President Bush's performance-based development aid program in 2007 (*Washington Post* 2007).

Civil society's new participation in government has led to several significant institutional changes. The National Congress altered the rules through which it selects Supreme Court judges in response to recommendations it received from the Commission of Notables and other civic groups. Instead of nominating magistrates on the basis of party recommendations—a highly politicized process—it agreed to choose these individuals from a list of names submitted by a new, independent nominating committee. First established on October 15, 2001, this committee includes representatives of several civil society groups and the Supreme Court of Justice (Infopress Centroamérica 2000d). The new judiciary selection process went into effect in 2002, a few months after the country's last election. The Congress also responded to pressure from civic groups to advance political reform, passing legislation at the end of 2001 that replaced the Tribunal Nacional de Elecciones (TNE) with a new, less politicized electoral agency: the Tribunal Supremo Electoral (TSE). Unlike its predecessor, the TSE is separate from the National Citizen's Registry (Registro Nacional de las Personas). The Congress also replaced the positions of three presidential designates (*designados presidenciales*) with that of a single vice president. This has reduced one type of senior-level clientelism as well as unnecessary bureaucratic expenditures.

The Honduran government has also taken several steps to decentralize power. AMHON and donor pressures eventually forced the government to begin transferring the legally mandated 5 percent of its national budget to municipal governments in 2004. In addition, the Ley de Municipalidades was reformed in 2000, significantly augmenting the fiscal power of local governments. It gave municipalities control over rural *ejidal* lands and granted them the right to sell forested areas that were not specifically designated for public use. Now municipal governments can use the profits from these sales to promote local development. The 2000 reforms gave municipalities the right to charge the central government interest rates for any delay in the funds transfers that are due to them. Although Honduran municipalities continue to have little control over public finances, they have achieved a significant amount of fiscal decentralization since the early 1990s as a result of foreign donor and domestic demands.

Domestic and international pressure also has forced the government to make a greater effort to combat poverty. The Honduran government consulted approximately 3,500 civic associations between 2000 and 2001 in order to gain input on how it should design a Poverty Reduction Strategy (Secretaría de Despacho Presidencial 2001). After the document was approved, a poverty reduction fund was created in April 2002 with funds that had once been destined to repay recently forgiven foreign loans. Although different government agencies are charged with implementing the PRS, their work is supervised and counseled by a new Poverty Reduction Consultative Group formed in September 2002 and consisting of five civil society and several local and national government representatives. This consultative group has developed a methodology for monitoring and evaluating the PRS in a participatory and decentralized manner and has started to implement many of the approved poverty reduction projects (Comisión Técnica 2003).

The Limits to Donor and Civil Society Activism

Although civil society's renewed political activism has led to significant political changes in Honduras since Hurricane Mitch, there have been limits to this process. First, different actors in Honduras have adopted divergent interpretations of what "citizen participation" means. The government tends to view it merely as a process for granting a voice to civic groups. Of course, the civic groups themselves tend to hold a more expansive view of participation, believing that it should entail the opportunity to make decisions and implement particular projects or policies. This difference in interpretation has limited the satisfaction of civic groups with recent political openings.[17]

Honduran civil society also continues to be plagued by internal division and a lack of institutional capacity. The Frente Solidario para la Defensa de la Soberanía Nacional, for example, has ceased to exist. Some former members of this solidarity front continue to cooperate but less formally or regularly than in the year after Mitch. Similarly, some of the founding members of INTERFOROS have withdrawn from this organization in order to pursue their own agendas. As explained by Ensor (chapter 6 in this volume), some groups have done this because they felt that they were not being properly represented by this broad-based coalition. Others have withdrawn from the group owing to personal differences with its leadership. Fernando Mudarra, head of the Spanish Cooperation Agency, noted that those civic groups who participated in the sectoral oversight committees to monitor reconstruction were not well consolidated. Each group wanted to do its own thing, and there was little cooperation among them.[18] Carlos Arita Valdiviesco, executive director of the Civil Society Commission, said his group was hampered by similar problems. Moreover, third-level civil society groups—the civic organizations that most frequently interact with the state—also tend to act autonomously from their members. This has led some analysts to question the representative nature of these organizations.[19]

Foreign donors also should not be seen as always responsive to citizen demands. International financial institutions have continued to demand the privatization of state-owned industries and other neoliberal economic reforms despite strong opposition from Honduran citizens. Similarly, the United States, which is Honduras' largest bilateral donor, has pressured the government to agree to a Central America Free Trade Agreement despite strong opposition from organized groups in Honduran society.

Conclusion

Despite the limitations just described, significant political changes have taken place in Honduras as a result of donor and civil society demands after Hurricane Mitch. Three successive governments have created spaces for civil society participation in public policy making. This participatory style of governing has transcended the mere process of reconstruction to include legislative reforms, poverty reduction, and other key aspects of the government's work. There has been an attempt to depoliticize the judiciary system and elections-monitoring agencies through key legislative reforms. In general, a process of political, fiscal, and administrative decentralization has been unfolding. All of this has allowed the Honduran political system to improve its fragile democracy. Although much remains to be done, much has been accomplished.

Several factors help explain why such democratizing reforms were adopted in Honduras. First, the very presence of a major natural disaster created a window of opportunity for change. Honduran citizens and foreign donors saw the rubble and destruction as an opportunity for altering much of what they viewed as flawed in this country before the disaster. Second, foreign donors played a critical role in encouraging the state to undertake political reforms. They shaped the development discourse of the post-disaster period and conditioned both reconstruction assistance and debt relief on the government's willingness to alter its structure and style of governing. Foreign donors also helped legitimize the demands of organized groups in the country by encouraging civil society to participate in the drafting and implementation of Honduras' reconstruction plans. Donors augmented their influence on the state by cooperating regularly with each other through oversight committees and by jointly demanding the same set of reforms. Had this level of coordination not been achieved, state officials might have been better able to avoid complying with the specific demands of a few donors. It is unclear whether Honduras would have experienced the political changes it has without the support and encouragement of civil society. The discussion presented by Ensor (chapter 6 in this volume) suggests that if civic groups are weak, as were women's organizations in Honduras before and after the disaster, then donors' insistence on reform may not result in major changes. However, if civic groups are well organized and pressure the government for the same reforms demanded by foreign donors, then the chances for significant transformations are enhanced. The lessons to be learned from Honduras are clear. Post-disaster reconstruction offers the opportunity for achieving political change, but this will not occur automatically. Civic groups must organize, cooperate with each other, and increase their demands on the state. Donors must condition their aid, coordinate their efforts, and oversee the reconstruction process; their actions may also help to invigorate and legitimate organized groups in disaster-stricken countries. The more that grassroots groups demand reforms and cooperate with donors to achieve them, the more likely it is that these changes will be achieved. It is hoped that the lessons to be learned from Honduras can be applied to other post-disaster situations.

Notes

1. Even Somoza acknowledged that some of his army officers engaged in looting, but he presented excuses for his own personal gain after the earthquake.

2. Olson and Gawronski have shown in the case of Mexico that, although incidents of corruption may be tolerated by citizens during normal times, they are not accepted during post-disaster periods. Citizen reactions to corruption charges in Nicaragua after the 1972 earthquake suggest that the populace there experienced a similar decline in tolerance for such behavior.

3. Interview with Arturo Corrales, Commissioner of COPECO, October 19, 1999.

4. It is estimated that there were over 10,000 Delegates of the Word in Honduras by the late 1990s.

5. The Reconstruction Cabinet was to be composed of the Minister of the Presidency; Minister of Finance; Minister of Public Works, Transportation, and Housing; Minister of Agriculture and Livestock; and Minister of International Cooperation. The Minister of Foreign Affairs and the president of the Central Bank were designated as special advisors to the new cabinet.

6. Interview with Jan Robberts, Counselor at the Swedish Embassy in Honduras, October 13, 1999.

7. Interview with Fernando Martínez, former Honduran Minister of Foreign Relations, February 28, 2000.

8. Interview with Conrado Lando, member of the Executive Committee of the Consejo de Trabajadores de Honduras (CTH), November 3, 1999.

9. First-level civil society groups are understood here as community-based groups. Second-level organizations represent multiple first-level groups, and third-level organizations consist of several second-level groups.

10. The information reported here was obtained from various newspaper reports published in April 1999.

11. Interview with Victor Meza, member of Foro Ciudadano, October 1, 1999.

12. Papers summarizing the results of these and other workshops can be obtained online from the IADB at http://www.iadb.org/regions/re2/consultative_group/toc.htm.

13. Conversation with Mauricio Díaz, representative of INTERFOROS, October 21, 1999.

14. Honduras qualified for HIPC in 2000.

15. Interview with Fernando Mudarra, Executive Director of the Agencia Española de Cooperación Internacional (AECI) in Honduras, September 1, 2000.

16. Interview with Fernando Mudarra, Executive Director of the Agencia Española de Cooperación Internacional (AECI) in Honduras, September 1, 2000; and interview with Duty Greene, economist for the Project Strategy and Support Office, USAID-Honduras, August 28, 2000.

17. These conclusions are based on interviews with dozens of civil society leaders and Honduran government officials during 1999 and 2000. A similar assessment is presented in Comisión Ad Hoc de la Sociedad Civil (2002:100).

18. Interview with Fernando Mudarra, Executive Director of the Agencia Española de Cooperación Internacional (AECI) in Honduras, September 1, 2000.

19. Cruz and Espinoza (2004:105–6).

References

Anderson, Thomas P. 1982. *Politics in Central America: Guatemala, El Salvador, Honduras and Nicaragua*. New York: Praeger.

Black, George. 1981. *Triumph of the People: The Sandinista Revolution in Nicaragua*. London: Zed Press.

Booth, John A. 1981. *The End and the Beginning: The Nicaraguan Revolution*. Boulder, CO: Westview.

Comisión Ad Hoc de la Sociedad Civil. 2002. *La sociedad civil en Honduras: Caracterización y directorios*. Tegucigalpa, Honduras: Banco Interamericano del Desarrollo y Agencia Sueca de Cooperación Internacional.

Comisionado Nacional de los Derechos Humanos (CONADEH). 2000. *Derechos humanos: Dos años de realidades y retos, 1998–1999*. Tegucigalpa, Honduras: CONADEH.

Comisión Nacional Anticorrupción (CNA). 2000. *Estrategia nacional anticorrupción*. Tegucigalpa, Honduras.

Comisión Técnica, Consejo Consultivo de la Estrategia para la Reducción de la Pobreza. 2003. *Propuesta del plan de trabajo del consejo consultivo de la estrategia para la reducción de la pobreza*. Internal memorandum, Tegucigalpa, Honduras (March).

Cruz, Anabel, and Jose Luis Espinoza. 2004. "Organizaciones de la sociedad civil en Honduras. De la consulta a la participación." Paper presented at the ISTR Sixth International Conference (Ryerson University and York University, Toronto, July 11–14), http://www.istr.org/conferences/toronto/workingpapers/cruz.anabel.pdf.

Cuny, Fredrick C. 1983. *Disasters and Development*. Oxford, UK: Oxford University Press.

Daly, Heyck, and Denis Lynn. 1990. *Life Stories of the Nicaraguan Revolution*. New York: Routledge.

DeVries, Gregory. 2000. "Post Hurricane Reconstruction in La Mosquitia, Honduras." MA thesis, University of Florida, Gainesville.

Drury, A. Cooper, and Richard Stuart Olson. "Disasters and Political Unrest: An Empirical Investigation." *Journal of Contingencies and Crisis Management* 6, no. 3: 153–61.

Dunkerley, James. 1988. *Power in the Isthmus: A Political History of Modern Central America*. New York: Verso.

Fernández, José Manuel. 1988. "Comunidades indígenas y conflicto social en Guatemala." PhD dissertation, Universidad Complutense de Madrid.

Finnemore, Martha. 1996. *National Interests in International Society*. Ithaca, NY: Cornell University Press.

Fox, Jonathan, and Luis Hernandez. 1992. "Mexico's Difficult Democracy: Grassroots Movements, NGOs and Local Government Alternatives." *Alternatives* 17: 165–208.

García González, Daniel. 2001. *La cuestión municipal en Centroamérica: Un desafío para la consolidación democrática y la modernización del estado*. San José, Costa Rica: DEMUCA.

Gawronski, Vincent. 2000. "The 1985 Mexico City Disaster: A Critical Juncture?" Paper presented at the XXIII Latin American Studies Association Conference (Miami, March 16–18) .

Hall, Peter A. 1993. "Policy Paradigms, Social Learning and the State: The Case of Economic Policymaking in Britain." *Comparative Politics* 25, no. 3: 275–96.

Healy, Mark Allen. 2000. "The Ruins of the New Argentina: Peronism, Architecture and the Remaking of San Juan after the 1944 Earthquake." PhD dissertation, Duke University, Durham, NC.

Humphrey, Chris. 1997. *Honduras Handbook*. Chico, CA: Moon Publications.

Huntington, Samuel P. 1993. *The Third Wave: Democratization in the Late Twentieth Century*. Norman: University of Oklahoma Press.

Infopress Centroamérica. 2000a. "Avanza proceso de reformas judiciales." *Infopress Centroamérica* (April 28).

———. 2000b. "CONADES revela corrupción en sistema judicial." *Infopress Centroamérica* (April 28).

———. 2000c. "Buscan medidas para mejorar el sistema judicial." *Infopress Centroamérica* (May 12).

———. 2000d. "Sociedad civil pide reformar ley electoral." *Infopress Centroamérica* (August 11).

Jeffrey, Paul. 1999. "Rhetoric and Reconstruction in Post-Mitch Honduraso" NACLA *Report on the Americas* 33, no. 2 (September/October): 28–37.

Jonas, Suzanne. 1991. *The Battle for Guatemala: Rebels, Death Squads and U.S. Power*. Boulder, CO: Westview.

La Prensa. 1998a. "COPECO planifica masiva operación aérea." *La Prensa on the Web* (October 31), http://www.laprensahn.com/natarc/9810/n29002.htm.

———. 1998b. "Conforman Gabinete de Reconstrucción." *La Prensa on the Web* (November 26), http://www.laprensahn.com/natarc/9811/n260010.htm.

———. 1998c. "Renuncia canciller del Gabinete de Reconstrucción." *La Prensa on the Web* (December 23), http://www.laprensahn.com/ natarc/9812/n23006.htm.

Nelson, Joan M. 1992. *Encouraging Democracy: What Role for Conditioned Aid?* Washington, DC: Overseas Development Council.

Olivo Díaz López, María-Jesús. 2002. "Relocating Morolica: Vulnerability and Resilience in Post-Mitch Honduras." PhD dissertation, University of Florida, Gainesville.

Olson, Richard Stuart. 2000. "Towards a Politics of Disaster: Losses, Values, Agendas and Blame." *International Journal of Mass Emergencies and Disasters* 18, no. 2: 265–87.

———. 2001. *The Storms of '98: Hurricanes Georges and Mitch—Impacts, Institutional Response, and Disaster Politics in Three Countries*. Natural Hazards Research and Applications Information Center, University of Colorado, Boulder.

Olson, Richard Stuart, and Vincent T. Gawronski. 2001. "Normal versus Special Time Corruption: An Exploration of Mexican Attitudes." *Cambridge Journal of International Affairs* 15, no. 1: 344–61.

Pino, Hugo Noe. 1992. "La concertación económico social y el primer año de la administración de Callejas." *Puntos de Vista: Temas Politicos* 1: 20–26.

Presidencia de la República. 2002. *Plan de Gobierno 2002–2006: Un compromiso con Honduras.* Tegucigalpa, Honduras: Gobierno de Honduras.

Pridham, Geoffrey. 1991. "The Politics of the European Community." In *Encouraging Democracy: The International Context of Regime Transition in Southern Europe,* edited by Geoffrey Pridham. New York: St. Martin's.

———. 1999. "The European Union, Democratic Conditionality and Transnational Party Linkages." In *Democracy without Borders: Transnationalization and Conditionality in New Democracies,* edited by Jean Grugel. London: Routledge.

Risse, Thomas, Stephen C. Ropp, and Kathryn Sikkink. 1999. *The Power of Human Rights: International Norms and Domestic Change.* Cambridge, UK: Cambridge University Press.

Schlesinger, Stephen, and Stephen Kinzer. 1983. *Bitter Fruit.* New York: Anchor Books.

Secretaría de Despacho Presidencial. Gobierno de Honduras. 2001. *Estrategia de reducción de la pobreza.* Tegucigalpa, Honduras: Gobierno de Honduras.

Seligson, Mitchell A. 2001. *Gobernabilidad y transparencia en Honduras después del Huracán Mitch: Un estudio de opinión ciudadana.* Tegucigalpa, Honduras: Casals & Associates.

Shefner, Jon. 1999. "Pre and Post Disaster Instability and Contentious Supporters: A Case Study of Political Ferment." *International Journal of Mass Emergencies and Disasters* 17, no. 2: 137–60.

Somoza, Anastasio. 1980. *Nicaragua Betrayed.* Boston: Western Islands.

Tavera-Fenellosa, Ligia. 1999. "The *Movimiento de Damnificados:* Democratic Transformation of Citizenry and Government in Mexico City." In *Subnational Politics and Democratization in Mexico,* edited by Wayne A. Cornelius, A. Todd Eisenstadt, and Jane Hindley. San Diego: University of California at La Jolla Center for United States–Mexican Studies.

Transparency International. 2000. *Annual Report.* Berlin: Transparency International.

Washington Post. 2007. "Honduras Losing Steam on Corruption Fight" (July 27).

World Bank. 1999. *Responses to Hurricane Mitch.* Washington, DC: World Bank.

———. 2002. *Governance and Anti-Corruption in Honduras: An Input for Action.* Washington, DC: World Bank.

Yee, Albert S. 1996. "The Causal Effects of Ideation on Policy." *International Organization* 50, no. 1: 69–108.

6
Gender Matters in Post-Disaster Reconstruction

Marisa Olivo Ensor

It is generally accepted that when disasters strike, the poor and socially disadvantaged are most vulnerable and least equipped to cope with the impact. The factors discussed in chapter 2 of this volume created interrelated and mutually reinforcing crises that resulted in the high levels of vulnerability of many Hondurans. Women, particularly poor women, have been disproportionately affected by the disaster's impact. Along with age and class, gender conditions the resources, roles, rights, and responsibilities assigned to women and men and is a crucial factor determining people's position in society. In turn, people's socioeconomic position affects their vulnerability to disasters and other crises (Bryant and Bailey 1997:28–29).

In spite of the human tragedy provoked by Hurricane Mitch, new opportunities for positive change also emerged from the destruction. This chapter examines the role that gender has played in determining the capabilities and constraints facing the Honduran population in their efforts to rebuild their lives after the devastation caused by the disaster. More specifically, it examines whether reconstruction initiatives in post-Mitch Honduras have transformed inequitable pre-existing conditions or merely reconstructed them. Findings indicate that, in spite of their presence in post-disaster interventions, women did not fully participate in the reconstruction process and their practical and strategic needs have not been fully met. On the other hand, the revitalization of women's movements in post-Mitch Honduran society—and the gender focus of the poverty alleviation measures recently presented by the Honduran government—have emerged as potentially positive trends.

Gender and Disaster Research

As Elaine Enarson (2000:4) notes, "gender shapes the social worlds within which natural disaster events occur." Furthermore, "to the degree that disasters are rooted in unresolved dilemmas of global development, gender and development issues are disaster mitigation issues" (Enarson and Hearn Morrow 1998:226). The International Women's Year (1975) and the Mexico City Conference that began the subsequent United Nations Decade for Women (1976–1985) were important events that gave impetus to the incorporation of women into development and humanitarian initiatives (Spring 1995:5). The declaration of 1995 as the year—in the United Nations' International Decade for Natural Disaster Reduction (IDNDR)—to focus on women and children as the "key to prevention" provided further impetus for researchers and practitioners to emphasize gender and age as key variables in disaster research and practice. The Beijing Platform for Action, adopted at the Fourth Conference on Women (1995), recognized that the impact of environmental disasters on women, as well as women's responses to disaster, needed to be further investigated. Five years later, the review and appraisal of the implementation of the Beijing Platform for Action (2000) identified natural disasters and pandemics (such as HIV/AIDS) as issues deserving of increased attention (UN/DAW and UN/ISDR 2001).

In response to findings from its review and appraisal exercises, the General Assembly's twenty-third special session, entitled *Women 2000: Gender, Equality, Development and Peace for the Twenty-First Century,* acknowledged an increase in casualties and damage caused by disasters. It also raised awareness of the inefficiencies and inadequacies—from a gender perspective—of existing approaches and intervention methods in responding to such emergency situations. This special session suggested that a gender perspective be incorporated into disaster prevention, mitigation, and recovery strategies. It also recommended that the United Nations system and international and regional organizations should assist governments in developing gender-sensitive strategies for their emergency responses and delivery of assistance to humanitarian crises resulting from natural disasters (UN/DAW and UN/ISDR 2001).

In spite of these encouraging efforts, much disaster research and practice continues to be characterized by what Bhatt (1995:3) has termed "*gender silence:* the failure to acknowledge, explicitly or implicitly, that disaster management is occurring on a gendered terrain." A narrow view of the causes and consequences of disasters leads to a focus on the purely physical, which ignores social realities and marginalizes gender concerns. In effect, traditional disaster research has rarely given priority to the role that gender plays in shaping the interactions between human groups and their social and natural environment. Consequently, the differential constraints and opportunities that women and men face in post-disaster reconstruction have tended to be ignored. Even when a gender focus is incorporated into academic analyses of post-disaster situations, it is often limited to examining the situation of *women* rather than (as during the initial stages of feminist and women's studies) gender *relations*. More recently, a growing body of literature has illustrated both the theoretical and practical significance of adopting a gendered approach to the study of disasters (Peacock, Hearn Morrow, and Gladwin 1997; Enarson and Hearn Morrow 1998). Following this perspective, a number of studies suggest that the capabilities and constraints facing the Honduran population in their efforts to rebuild their disaster-stricken communities are clearly differentiated by gender (Delaney and Schrader 2000; Gomáriz 2000; Olivo Díaz López 2002; Ensor 2003). These projects and publications notwithstanding, a gender focus has yet to become a mainstream approach to research on disasters (Enarson 1998:156).

Gender and the Vulnerability Approach

Conditions of vulnerability are deeply embedded in everyday life and include gender differences in socioeconomic status, domestic responsibilities and power, and access to and control over such resources as income, health, education, and political representation. When women and men confront routine or catastrophic disasters, their responses tend to reflect their status and roles in society. In times of crisis—whether an acute shock, such as Hurricane Mitch, or a chronic stress, such as the pervasive economic crisis that affects most of the Honduran population—the already disadvantaged status of women is likely to be exacerbated and become more conspicuous. Disaster events can perpetuate the poverty trap for women and contribute to the "feminization of poverty."

The vulnerability approach to the study of disasters, described by Anthony Oliver-Smith in chapter 1, is concerned with the social processes of marginalization that produce unequal risks to hazards (Blaikie et al. 1994). Disenfranchised groups on the margins of survival—living with the "daily disaster" of poverty prior to, during, and after "natural" disasters and other crises—are especially vulnerable. When disasters strike, the poor and socially disadvantaged suffer the most and are least equipped to cope with the impact (UN/DAW and UN/ISDR 2001).

Acknowledging these facts, the vulnerability approach highlights the importance of adopting a gender perspective, one that can account for the differential impact of disasters on women and men and also for the different strategies adopted by women and men in their efforts to survive disaster.

As Blaikie et al. (1994:48) point out:

> Gender is a pervasive division affecting all societies, and it channels access to social and economic resources away from women and towards men. Women are often denied the vote, the right to inherit land, and generally have less control over income-generating opportunities and cash within their own households. Normally their access to resources is inferior to that of men. Since our argument is that less access to resources, in the absence of other compensations to provide safe conditions, leads to increased vulnerability, we contend that in general women are more vulnerable to hazards.

"Specifically engaging those groups most vulnerable to disasters is an essential part of building disaster-resilient communities" (Enarson 1998). Understanding women's and men's differential vulnerabilities facilitates the development of assistance programs that neither exacerbate social inequalities nor privilege men over women or households over individuals. Furthermore, drawing attention to gender differentials helps highlight some of the root causes of vulnerability, rather than focusing only on the consequences (Blaikie et al. 1994). Gender inequality is arguably one of the most serious obstacles to developing increased resilience to disasters and other crises, since it places half the population in a situation of heightened vulnerability. Thus, examining the structures of vulnerability is the first step toward creating meaningful and efficient measures for disaster mitigation. In turn, effectively addressing the specific vulnerabilities of both women and men requires disaster management interventions that acknowledge the link between mitigation and sustainable human development and that address the root causes of inequality (Miami Conference on Reaching Women and Children in Disasters 2000:2).

In light of the clearly disadvantaged situation of women in Honduran society (described in the next section), it can be assumed that Honduran women are generally more vulnerable to hazards, such as the disaster provoked by Hurricane Mitch, than their male counterparts.

General Overview

The increasing levels of poverty and vulnerability that Honduras was suffering during the 1990s were brought into sharp focus when Hurricane Mitch hit Central America in October 1998, provoking one of the worst catastrophes in recorded history. In Central America as a whole, the disaster affected almost 3.5 million people, with 18,000 dead and losses in the region estimated at over USD 6 billion (CEPAL 1999). A large part of the population lost their homes, land, and means of survival. The damages disproportionately affected the poorest sectors of the population, many of whom were living in inadequate housing located in vulnerable areas exposed to strong winds, flooding, and landslides. Hurricane Mitch set Honduras back by decades and increased the poverty of wide sections of the country's population. According to the Center for Women's Studies in Honduras, 80 percent of the population was living in poverty before the hurricane and there was already a tendency toward the feminization of poverty. With lower salaries and no direct access to land, poor women experienced the impact of the disaster more acutely, which in turn worsened already high rates of infant malnutrition and mortality (Kennedy 1999).

Data suggest that gender inequalities did indeed impair women's ability to recover from the impact of the disaster (Buvinic 1999; Delaney and Shrader 2000). However, more men than women died as a direct result of Hurricane Mitch. In Nicaragua, 54 percent of the casualties were male (see table 6.1). The majority of those who disappeared are also believed to be men who either perished in their homes or emigrated to other countries after the hurricane (Gomáriz 2000). Although statistical data are not available for Honduras, anecdotal information indicates a similar pattern. This difference in death rates by gender is attributed to (1) men's higher threshold of risk tolerance and (2) increased male involvement in high-risk activities, such as search and rescue operations, resulting from their ascribed role as protectors (Buvinic 1999:7; Delaney and Shrader 2000:22). Women's activities may have been less dangerous and typically included protecting children, tending the injured, setting up shelters, and preparing and distributing food. Their physical vulnerability can be viewed in terms of their restricted autonomy and their potentially reduced ability to escape the flood waters by, say, climbing onto rooftops or up into trees (Gomáriz 2000:13–14).

Table 6.1 The Human Toll of Hurricane Mitch

		Nicaragua			El Salvador		
	Honduras	Number	Percent	Guatemala	Number	Percent	Total
Deaths	5,657	3,045		268	240		9,210
Women			46			43	
Men			54			57	
In shelters	285,000	65,271		54,725	55,864		46,860
Women			50			49	
Men			50			51	
Affected	1,500,000	867,752		730,000	364,910		3,444,662
Women			49				
Men			51				
Percent affected	24	20		6	6		10

Source: ECLAC (1998), reported in Buvinic (1999).

On the other hand, surviving women in Honduras reported more health problems, both physical and psychological, than men. "Significantly more women than men reported and sought care for depression and other stress related illnesses, reflecting gender differences in the incidence of depressive disorders" (Buvinic 1999:10). Research also shows that a significant link can be established between emotional impact, property damage caused by Mitch, length of time spent in a shelter, and, above all, the death of a family member. "A total of 50 percent of households which reported the loss of one or more of their members indicated that one or more people suffered an emotional impact compared to 22 percent of households which had not lost any of their members" (Bradshaw 2004:31). Women also expressed a widespread feeling of insecurity in the streets and noted the increase of crimes, drug abuse, and teenage pregnancy—problems that can clearly be associated with the emotional and economic impact of the disaster. The patterns observed in Honduras, which are consistent with the literature on disasters worldwide, further highlight the importance of including gender considerations in all phases of disaster management, including ongoing mitigation and preparedness, immediate emergency response, and long-term reconstruction.

Gender-disaggregated data obtained through household interviews in Honduras (*Encuesta de Hogares*) administered in 1998 and 1999 provide interesting insights regarding the differential impact of Hurricane Mitch on the economic situation of women and men. Data show that the number of women in the labor force increased by 12 percent one year after Mitch, while the number of men increased by only 5.1 percent. However, this apparent measure of women's progress is deceptive. Analyses by the United Nations Development Programme (UNDP) show that the number of women classified as "non-remunerated relative" increased by 4 percent during the same period; this indicates that, although more women entered the labor force, they did so by contributing their efforts to the family industry and without receiving an individual salary for their work. Similarly, the number of women employed in the unstable informal sector increased while the number of women working in the formal sector decreased (UNDP 1999:32–33). Educational attainment was one area where the situation of women showed some real improvement at the national level. Only two Honduran departments, Yoro and Choluteca, had a school enrollment ratio lower for women than for men one year after the disaster (ibid.: 30).

Another significant impact of the hurricane was a considerable increase in the rates of female heads of households, which doubled by some accounts in both rural and urban settings. A year after the disaster, humanitarian workers in Honduras reported that half of the households still living in shelters were maintained solely by women. Similarly, in Nicaragua, 40 percent of sheltered households were female-supported (Delaney and Shrader 2000). High incidences of family abandonment and male out-migration are the most common causes. Gomáriz (2000) also suggests that part of the reported increase in female headship might have been due to the general perception of female-headed households receiving priority assistance and that some of the women in the shelters who registered as heads of household actually had a stable male partner. On the other hand, it may also be the case that most of these women were indeed their family's main breadwinner, the economic "head" of the family. Indeed, other studies show the proportion of families in which women are in this position to be significant in the region (Gammage 1998).

An important dimension of vulnerability, and one of the most problematic areas of Honduran society, is its endemic violence. In the 1990s, social violence and delinquency replaced the political violence that had plagued Central America years before. In Honduras, statistics show a 500 percent increase in delinquency reports between 1988 and 2000. Several factors have been proposed to explain these alarming figures, including the large number of weapons present in the country after the conflicts from the previous decade; the growth of organized crime, including the *maras* (street gangs; see Barrios, chapter 7 in this volume); and the deterioration of living conditions that followed the impact of Mitch. Women have often been the victims of this generalized violence.

In 1997, the Law Against Domestic Violence was created in Honduras to strengthen women's rights and to increase the penalties for crimes of domestic violence. In theory, this law would require the government to protect battered women through emergency measures, such as detaining aggressors or separating them temporarily from the victim's home (USDS 2004). However, violence against women has continued to be widespread in Honduras since the law was passed. In fact, the level of domestic and sexual violence against women and girls actually increased dramatically after Hurricane Mitch, with 54,270 cases reported in 2000 compared to 46,200 cases reported in 1998 (*Dirección Nacional de Investigación* 1998; *Dirección General de Investigación Criminal* 2000). A study carried out by the United Nations Population Fund in 2000 estimated that 8 of every 10 Honduran women suffered from domestic violence (Kennedy 1999). Research suggests that the levels of violence against women after Hurricane Mitch have also risen in Nicaragua (Bradshaw 2002:877). However, Bradshaw (2004:33, 42) argues that, although overall levels of violence (including violence against women) have clearly increased since Mitch, the trend may not be directly attributable to the disaster. Instead, she suggests that an exacerbation of previously existing tendencies, a generalized frustration leading to greater conflict in the households, and the lack of public safety in the hurricane's aftermath are the most likely causes. These reports are consistent with the disaster literature worldwide, which often reveals an increase in levels of domestic and sexual violence following disasters (Enarson 1998; McCarrher and Bailey 2000). For instance, research on the aftermath of Hurricane Andrew documented an initial decline in levels of domestic violence right after the hurricane hit the South Florida coast, in August of 1992, followed by a sharp increase in the subsequent months as disaster-related stress built up (Enarson and Hearn Morrow 1997).

Domestic violence is more than an extremely damaging form of female disempowerment; it also increases the risk of HIV infection, especially when it takes the form of sexual abuse. Furthermore, violence, or fear of violence, may act as a significant barrier to women negotiating condom use or requesting fidelity from their partners. The relationship between domestic violence and HIV may also be indirect. "Girls and boys who are victims [or witnesses] of physical and/or sexual abuse during childhood are more likely to exhibit high-risk sexual behavior later in life, lowered self-esteem, and decreased ability to negotiate safer sex" (Heise, Ellsberg, and Gottemoeller 1999). The differential socioeconomic status of women and men before, during, and after a disaster has a significant impact on their susceptibility to being infected by HIV/AIDS (Moraga 1999). For example, economically vulnerable women with little bargaining power may feel compelled to remain in abusive and potentially dangerous relationships out of fear of abandonment and destitution, or they may even resort to high-risk behaviors as a source of income.

The risk of HIV transmission, the demands placed on overburdened community and national infrastructures and health services, and women's productive and reproductive workloads are all increased in disaster situations. At the same time, the "tyranny of the urgent" that frequently prevails following a crisis often results in a lack of attention given to providing reproductive and sexual health services, which tend not to be seen as pressing concerns. The combination of these mutually related risk factors has had severe consequences in Honduras, which is currently one of the countries in Central America in which the HIV/AIDS epidemic has become both more virulent and increasingly feminized (see Ensor et al., chapter 8 in this volume).

In the late 1980s, the male:female ratio of AIDS cases was 2:1. By 2002, this gap had practically closed (see table 6.2). A report by the World Bank (2006:5) cites gender relations—including women's lack of autonomy and empowerment within and outside of marriage in addition to such socioeconomic factors as migration and increasing employment of women in factories and *maquilas*—as some of the many factors that may account for the increased vulnerability of Honduran women to HIV/AIDS in the post-Mitch period.

Delaney and Shrader (2000) have argued that a gender focus would contribute to ensuring that the impacts of "second generation

Table 6.2 Rates of HIV Infection among Women Aged 15 to 49 in Central America

Country	Infected adults	Infected women	Percent
Belize	2,200	1,000	45.5
Costa Rica	11,000	2,800	25.5
El Salvador	23,000	6,300	27.4
Guatemala	63,000	27,000	42.9
Honduras	54,000	27,000	50.0
Nicaragua	5,600	1,500	26.8
Panama	25,000	8,700	34.8

Source: PAHO (2002).

disasters"—such as the rape, unwanted pregnancies, and domestic violence that often accompany post-disaster settings—be prevented or mitigated. In the case of Honduras, the HIV/AIDS epidemic constitutes an additional and urgent reason for increased attention to gender issues, since gender is known to have a significant impact both on the transmission of HIV/AIDS and on the differential experiences of the infected, or affected,[1] women and men (Gupta 2002).

Despite the multipronged discrimination faced by women in Honduran society, their roles took on a new public dimension after the devastation caused by Hurricane Mitch. Women were, and continue to be, key protagonists in the post-disaster reconstruction process by negotiating support from the state and other institutions and by creating links with local nongovernmental organizations (NGOs), religious groups, international humanitarian agencies, and even the mass media (Kennedy 1999).

Post-Mitch Reconstruction in Honduras: A Gendered Process?

In spite of the human tragedy provoked by Hurricane Mitch—or perhaps because of it—civil society groups, humanitarian groups, and the Honduran government endorsed the idea of considering reconstruction as an opportunity for positive transformation. Hopes were high that new strategies for sustainable human development, focusing on vulnerable and marginalized sectors of society, would be put into effect. Clearly, reproducing the conditions that had prefigured the disaster was neither desirable nor advisable (Bradshaw 2004).

"Experts on gender and disaster believe that crisis situations provide a real opportunity for changing inequality in relationships between men and women" (Bradshaw 2004:20). The expectation that opportunities for transformation will emerge in the aftermath of a disaster stems from the likelihood that such an all-encompassing event may produce profound changes in the lives of the people involved (Byrne and Baden 1995). Furthermore, disasters tend to reveal existing inequalities in power relations, both at the household and broader levels, which can facilitate the identification of measures to address such problems (Enarson and Hearn Morrow 1998:2). In contrast, pre-existing conditions of vulnerability may be reestablished after a disaster, thus replicating the conditions for a repeat catastrophic event (Blaikie et al. 1994:210). Anderson and Woodrow (1998:2) are even more pessimistic in their assertion that disaster responses have often failed to promote long-term development and may actually have contributed to subverting or undermining it.

In effect, the way in which disaster response unfolds often creates another set of disasters; Fordham (2000:32) calls this "disastrogenesis," the negative consequences resulting from inadequate disaster management interventions (Miami Conference 2000). Similarly, Bradshaw (2004:47) has argued that ill-conceived reconstruction projects may have impacts as destructive as the disaster itself. An exclusive focus on material relief assistance leads to a disregard for gender concerns—including the need to provide reproductive and sexual health services—which are often overlooked or dismissed as being irrelevant, secondary, or impractical. As a result, opportunities for transformation toward gender equality and empowerment may be missed or compromised. "Donor fatigue" following protracted or repeated humanitarian crises often reduces the already limited funds available for gender-sensitive programming, and this phenomenon may result in the unwitting reconstruction of gender inequalities and other dimensions of social vulnerability. In this way, the post-disaster window of opportunity for positive social change may be missed (DAW and UN/ISDR 2001). Both negative patterns of disaster response—the tyranny of the urgent and donor fatigue—seem to have been pervasive in post-disaster interventions in Honduras, with important implications for the well-being of the affected women and men.

The Role of Humanitarian Assistance

An important dimension of humanitarian assistance is the distinction between "practical gender needs" (PGN) and "strategic gender needs" (SGN). This distinction arises because, since women and men have differing roles based on their gender, they likewise have differing gender needs. *Practical* gender needs derive from women's ascribed responsibility for household and child-rearing chores; they are practical in nature and often concern living conditions rendered inadequate by lack of nutrition, water, health care, and employment. Practical gender needs do not challenge—though they stem from—the gender division of labor and women's subordinate position in society. The common perception of women as the most efficient providers of services has been used to justify the emphasis usually placed on these practical gender needs. Yet, the inclusion of women's practical needs in relief and reconstruction projects after a disaster like Mitch does not, in itself, constitute a gender perspective. A comprehensive gender perspective must also incorporate *strategic* gender needs, which result from women's structural subordination in society. Such needs involve legal rights, protection from domestic violence, equal wages, and women's control over their bodies. Meeting strategic gender needs requires an examination of the roles and responsibilities of women and men and the interactions between them; it would also entail correcting the social, political, and economic disadvantages of women and include measures to correct power imbalances and to combat violence against women (Andersen 1992:172; Bradshaw 2004:19–20). The initial assistance provided to Honduran survivors addressed their most urgent practical needs, at least partially. Strategic needs, on the other hand, were ignored; women's and men's traditional roles were not questioned, and women's subordinated position in Honduran society remained unchallenged. Consequently, the emphasis on practical gender needs that characterized these initial interventions might actually have contributed to reestablishing the traditional, imbalanced gender relations, especially during the early emergency stages that followed the disaster.

An example of this pattern is revealed in a study of post-disaster measures in Morolica, Choluteca—the only Honduran town completely relocated after Mitch. All the relief and reconstruction interventions implemented in this community targeted women (Olivo Díaz López 2002); the only exception was the construction of new houses, a project in which mostly men and only a few widowed or single women participated (ibid.: 161). Most of the initial assistance received in Morolica came in the form of one-shot types of interventions, usually involving the donation of food, medicine, toys, school materials, and so forth. Even though the material resources provided by the donors potentially benefited all household members, they were perceived as being more directly related to women's traditional responsibilities for household caretaking. Subsequent projects—some of them designed to improve children's education and nutrition levels, others to increase household income generation—also targeted women, since the activities involved were perceived as extensions of women's socially-ascribed roles (ibid.: 150–51). These interventions exemplify the prevalent focus on practical gender needs arising from women's position within the division of labor, which frequently translates into an absence of recognition of women's triple role: reproductive work, productive work, and community work. In effect, Morolican women often complained that, although their workload had increased dramatically after the disaster, they received no recognition because they were not participating in the reconstruction of the community in the sense of physically building the houses on the site selected for relocation. And unlike the men, the women did not get a salary for their extra work (ibid.: 154).

Similarly, in a study of reconstruction practices in post-Mitch Nicaragua, Bradshaw (2002:875) reports that "while half the women interviewed in the communities perceive[d] that it [was] they who have participated most in the project for reconstruction, only a quarter felt that it [was] women who benefit[ed] from reconstruction projects. The majority stated that it was the family that benefited from their participation." Indeed, the inclusion of women in Central American post-disaster interventions—with projects tending to focus on women and children in terms of the distribution of products and services—has been widely documented (Buvinic 1999; Delaney and Shrader 2000; Bradsaw 2002; Ensor 2003). Nevertheless, though women were active participants in post-Mitch reconstruction activities and though their access to material resources was generally similar to that of men, gender differences in decision-making patterns were not considered; nor was there examination of the actual use made of those material resources (Bradshaw 2002).

In spite of their presence in post-disaster interventions (as illustrated by the studies cited), Honduran women did not fully participate in the reconstruction process. Nor can it be said that their strategic needs were adequately addressed, since the projects were not designed to overcome women's subordination or to eliminate institutionalized forms of discrimination. Although a large number of post-Mitch projects trumpeted a gender perspective, their design and implementation in many cases targeted women only as efficient service providers for the family. This pattern also suggests that reconstruction projects tended to reinforce stereotypical women's roles, falling short of their stated goal of encouraging transformation and diversification. As such, the programs implemented in Honduras are examples of female-centered approaches that are already considered outmoded by many development theorists—even as such approaches continue to be resisted by practitioners who still formulate and implement development programs without any reference to gender differentials at all.

The Role of Civil Society

The number of NGOs and civil society groups had dramatically increased in Honduras—and elsewhere in the region—during the last few decades before the disaster. Hurricane Mitch intensified this process and signaled the beginning of a new era in civil society organization, with INTERFOROS in Honduras (Fuentes, chapter 5 in this volume) and the Civil Coordination for Emergency and Reconstruction (CCER) in Nicaragua being the most active groups. Both coalitions sought to participate in the establishment of national disaster reconstruction plans and to monitor their implementation, and they generally managed at least to draw attention to the shortcomings of proposed reconstruction initiatives (Bradshaw 2002; Bradshaw and Linneker 2003, 2004; Fuentes, chapter 5 in this volume).

In Honduras, the reconstruction proposal drafted by INTERFOROS focused almost exclusively on economic growth and macroeconomic policy, marginalizing gender concerns. Furthermore, women were not invited to participate in the production of this proposal even though the women's movements, which had already been active in pre-Mitch Honduras, had maintained or intensified their efforts in the post-disaster period. Instead, the INTERFOROS proposal was initially drafted by a small group of people that did not include representatives from women's groups. When women's groups were finally consulted (after the first draft had already been produced), they were given just one day to study and then "engender" the proposal. Not surprisingly, the document ultimately presented by INTERFOROS lacked a true gender focus (Bradshaw 2004:38; Bradshaw and Linneker 2004:23). In effect, "in late 2000, INTERFOROS was considered to be problematic in gender terms, some going as far as to suggest that it actually represented another site in the battle against gender discrimination and sexist attitudes, rather than one of solidarity and shared agenda" (Bradshaw and Linneker 2004:23).

A similar pattern was found among the numerous international humanitarian agencies that poured into Honduras in the aftermath of Mitch. Many of them were committed through their mission statements to adopt a gender approach in any projects undertaken, and they sought venues for entering into dialogue with the women of the country. Unfortunately, the previously mentioned "tyranny of the urgent" that so often plagues post-disaster interventions manifested itself, and the fastest—but not necessarily the most efficient—way to include women's concerns was often adopted (Blaikie et al. 1994; Anderson and Woodrow 1998). Consulting "experts" on gender issues (and/or representatives of wider social movements) was perceived as the simplest approach. The actual implementation of gender-sensitive projects was further hindered by funding restrictions, particularly as time went by and donor fatigue set in. Donor organizations opted for financing larger, well-established NGOs—which may or may not have been sensitive to gender concerns—because this was perceived as being more cost-effective and straightforward than promoting the efforts of emerging women's movements. In an effort to respond to their marginalization from mainstream civil society activity, women's groups held their own meetings to discuss reconstruction in Honduras and produced a number of documents containing their own views and recommendations on the subject (CEM-H 1999, 2000; Convergencia de Mujeres 2000).

The strengthening of civil society organization that was evident in the post-disaster reconstruction period has been described as a process leading Honduras from an exclusionary and semi-authoritarian democracy to one that is more participatory and inclusive (Fuentes, 2003). However, the impact of "umbrella" or "one voice" civil society organizations such as INTERFOROS and CCER was not as straightforward as might have been expected. The Honduran case in particular suggests that civil society actors cannot automatically be assumed to be more sensitized to women's concerns, or more inclined to draft their proposals from a gender perspective, than the government or any other organization. For civil society initiatives to address gender concerns, the involvement of women at all stages of the process and at all decision-making levels is required. Ensuring a gender perspective in post-disaster reconstruction programs—as should any intervention that seeks to improve the well-being of those most affected—requires a change of focus so that both women and men are included at all levels. Furthermore, "participation must move beyond consultation to a genuine process of consensus reaching and joint development of policies" (Trócaire 2004:19).

As the policy focus shifted from post-disaster reconstruction to poverty alleviation, the processes involved in the formulation of poverty reduction strategies brought new challenges that contributed to a further deterioration in the relations between women's groups and other civil society organizations in Honduras. As a general proposition, women have not been sufficiently visible within these processes.

Gendered Reconstruction and Poverty Alleviation

Poverty alleviation lies at the heart of reconstruction and development discourse and practice. Poverty is a multidimensional condition with many causes and diverse manifestations. It has often been simplistically defined as the lack of income necessary to achieve a minimum standard of living, but poverty goes beyond an exclusively economic dimension. New conceptual understandings of poverty also examine the conditions that result in the "failure to satisfy a set of basic human needs, or the dearth of social opportunities open to groups suffering such conditions" (Government of the Republic of Honduras 2000:7). Nonmaterial factors such as self-esteem, respect, power, and resilience are also being recognized in more inclusionary conceptualizations (Chant 2003:9).

Poverty in Honduras has been characterized as the historical outcome of a combination of high population growth and low economic growth (Government of the Republic of Honduras 2000:34). It is also "the result of an exclusionary political, economic and social model, manifested in high levels of inequality in the distribution of income and wealth and in access to productive assets coupled with low levels of democratic participation by the poor" (Trócaire 2004:4). The Poverty Reduction Strategy Papers (PRSP) initiative described in chapter 2 has been heralded as marking a new policy era for International Financial

Institutions (IFIS) such as the World Bank and the International Monetary Fund. The PRSPS are becoming the overarching development planning instrument in many countries, determining national priorities as well as the allocation of domestic and external resources. In the case of heavily indebted poor countries (HIPCS) such as Honduras, poverty reduction strategies shape the speed of debt relief and the allocation of debt relief savings (Bjorkman 2002:1).

The Honduran PRSPS use four methods to measure poverty: percentage living below the poverty line, unsatisfied basic needs, prevalence of undernourishment among first-grade schoolchildren, and the Human Development Index calculated by the UNDP. Based on these indicators, the eighty poorest municipalities in the country have been identified. Data suggest that poverty is highest in rural areas (Trócaire 2004:4). Thus, Honduran PRSPS promote a model of rural and agricultural development that emphasizes economic growth, further liberalization of the market, and an increase in exports (ibid.: 6). Although it is evident that the Honduran PRSPS have been formulated within a neoliberal perspective that focuses on economic factors (ibid.: 4), social inequality is also recognized as an important determinant of poverty. The proposed measures do incorporate a gender perspective, but so far they have not adequately considered gender differentials in access to and control over income, resources, and services as a means of reducing poverty (ibid.: 2).

As noted by Kabeer (1997:1):

> Poverty has not always been analysed from a gender perspective. Prior to the feminist contributions to poverty analysis, the poor were either seen as composed entirely of men or else women's needs and interests were assumed to be identical to, and hence subsumable under, those of male household heads.

It has been almost forty years since Ester Boserup (1970) first brought world attention to the role of women in economic development. The first explicit acknowledgment of women's roles in the development process was included in a foreign policy act—the Percy Amendment the U.S. Foreign Assistance Act of 1973—occurred thirty-five years ago; the first World Conference on Women was held in Mexico in 1975; and the Beijing Platform for Action set the stage for promoting gender equality worldwide in 1995. In spite of these groundbreaking events, the progress made in acknowledging gender inequity as a core poverty issue has been limited. Even after four decades "of knowing that poverty affects men and women differently, that not understanding these differences results in women losing from the development process, and that focusing on just women and not the process itself doesn't address the issue" (Woodhouse 2003:1), mainstream approaches to poverty alleviation still attempt to make existing strategies more gender sensitive (often outside the main poverty reduction initiatives) rather than striving to incorporate both women's and men's concerns during all stages and at all levels. More recently, however, there has been a discernible trend for more holistic and gender-sensitive approaches to development and poverty alleviation. Gender perspectives have also made important conceptual contributions to the study of poverty, broadening its definition by recognizing its multidimensionality and heterogeneity.

Incorporating gender analysis into the assessment and conceptualization of poverty may significantly improve the outcome of poverty reduction strategies. The Beijing +5 Platform for Action (PFA) recommendations on goals and monitoring of women and poverty should be included in such strategies as a means to mainstream gender issues. In particular, the PFA recommends poverty reduction strategies that avoid directing women to low-wage labor markets and that prevent gender discrimination in salaries or access to credit (Castillo-Ruíz 2003:5). Investing in women reduces the continuance of poverty in the next generation, increases the level of family welfare, and promotes economic growth. Although gender forms part of the discourse in the Honduran PRSPs, women have merely become a new means to promote macroeconomic growth through increased "efficiency." In other words, current strategies attempt to promote the participation of women as a means of fostering economic growth rather than as a development objective in its own right (Bradshaw and Linneker 2004:4). As was the case with the structural adjustment policies implemented in the past (ibid.: 15), this strategy will likely harm rather than improve the situation of women in Honduras. Partially informed by the World Bank's (2001:xii) "Gender Mainstreaming Guidelines," the Honduran PRSP advocates equal educational access to increase women's human capital potential. However, only 4.4 percent of the Honduran PRSP budget for 2001 was intended to address women's education, labor potential, and health (Rossell 2001). The Honduran PRSP health initiative for women focuses on maternal mortality and reproductive health care. The expected outcome is national economic growth due to decreased fertility rates. Although social protection strategies target those living in conditions of extreme poverty as well as poor disabled people, children and adolescents, and senior citizens, the Honduran government does not target women as a group because, it claims, "important achievements" in the socioeconomic advancement of women make their inclusion unnecessary (Gobierno de Honduras 2001:87).

The Honduran PRSPs also include macroeconomic growth strategies that promote free trade zones and tourism, which employ large numbers of women (Bradshaw and Linneker 2004:30). Related proposed policies include developing women's labor skills and support for women's "micro enterprises" (Gobierno de Honduras 2001). The implicit assumption appears to be that women will gain from economic growth via "trickle down"—in spite of overwhelming evidence to the contrary—or through their direct employment in the labor force (Bradshaw and Linneker 2004:37).

Although women's groups have been active in all aspects of the post-Mitch reconstruction processes in Honduras (CEM-H 1999, 2000; Convergencia de Mujeres 2000), their participation in the Honduran PRSP process has been hampered by civil society groups' limited commitment to a gendered approach and by practices that exclude input by civil society groups to begin with. Initial efforts to include civil society organizations in the Honduran PRSP process included establishing the Commission for Civil Society Participation as a forum for discussions among NGOS, INTERFOROS, local government and business interests such as the Association of Municipalities of Honduras (AMHON), and the two main chambers of commerce (San Pedro Sula and Tegucigalpa). However, INTERFOROS and its partner organization, the Social Forum on External Debt and Development (FOSDEH), withdrew from the Commission for Civil Society Participation after citing a lack of influence in discussions on policies (Bradshaw and Linneker 2004:20). Although the government suggested that the PRSP was based on consultation with over 2,500 people, the document was criticized for incorporating few of the civil societies' recommendations. INTERFOROS/FOSDEH has refused to endorse the PRSP, which challenges the document's validity and chances of success (ibid.: 22).

Relations between government and civil society as well as gender relations within civil society groups may together determine the extent to which women become involved in development processes such as the PRSP initiatives. The Honduran PRSP document contains contradictory messages about women's roles, explicitly reinforcing their role as mothers and caretakers while implicitly relying on women to assume a role outside of the home and in the workplace (Bradshaw and Linneker 2004:5). The expectation that PRSPs would be "engendered" through bottom-up participatory processes remains unrealized.

Conclusions and Recommendations

The literature reflects a growing recognition that gender-sensitive interventions are more successful at empowering the vulnerable (Enarson and Hearn Morrow 1998). In practice, however, many disaster response institutions either ignore the specific needs of women or, in the urgency of the moment, put aside gender-based policies and practices. Women's representation at all levels of policy and decision making is still limited, and their participation in disaster management is largely related to responsibilities for caring and nurturing. Women's skills, roles, capabilities, and contributions need to be reexamined and addressed by disaster and reconstruction research and policy if the measures implemented are to be inclusive and effective.

On the positive side, post-disaster reconstruction may provide opportunities to challenge established discriminatory practices by creating new social and political alignments and by promoting the reorganization of access to resources. Women often have a prominent role in the control and distribution of food in most societies. It has been proposed that humanitarian efforts should channel food assistance primarily through women (rather than directing assistance to a presumed head of household), since this is more likely to result in an equitable distribution of food and other resources to children and others in need (FAO 2001). On the other hand, relegating women to activities that are an extension of their traditional household maintenance responsibilities—that is, retaining an exclusive focus on their practical gender needs—may hinder their participation in management and decision-making activities and may also prevent them from assuming larger community roles, such as disaster mitigation and disaster recovery operations. Thus, the leadership position of women in the reconstruction and national transformation processes needs to be strengthened. This is particularly crucial given that the integration and cohesiveness of communities have been found to increase their resilience to disasters (Berke, Kartez, and Wenger 1993). Women's and men's experience as community workers and informal neighborhood leaders equips them to respond more efficiently than the government to community crises, and this in turn could mitigate the impact of future disasters. In reexamining Glittenburg's (1982) study of post-disaster resettlement after the 1976 Guatemalan earthquake, Oliver-Smith (1991:20) concludes that "the high degree of participation in decision-making . . . conferred both a sense of competence and proprietorship on the people." The ultimate objective should be to meet women's strategic needs by enabling them to achieve greater equality and by changing discriminatory practices, thereby challenging their subordinate position. Encouraging female participation in decision making would not only bring about a needed sense of personal and political empowerment for women, it would also increase the resilience of the entire community by ensuring that everyone's needs are being adequately met.

Because of their subordinated position in many societies, it is undeniable that women are often more vulnerable to disasters than men. Nonetheless, it is crucial to start considering women as assets and not simply as victims. A policy is misguided and myopic if it focuses only on women's status as dependents and so excludes them from community or national decision making in post-disaster relief and reconstruction processes (Enarson and Hearn Morrow 1998:6–7). It is also important to acknowledge that not all women are equally vulnerable and that many factors influence women's position in society and thus their vulnerability to disasters. A better understanding of the gendered dimensions of post-disaster reconstruction is an important step toward the difficult work of rebuilding devastated communities and social relationships, and it is an essential part of "rising from the ashes" (Anderson and Woodrow 1998).

Although both Honduras and Nicaragua have made appreciable progress in the area of gender equity, significant challenges to the inclusion of gender-sensitive approaches were noted during the post-Mitch period. In her account of post-hurricane reconstruction in Honduras and Nicaragua, Delaney (2000:19) reports that "those organizations with technical expertise in short-term disaster relief and rehabilitation expressed the greatest resistance to the importance of gender." Furthermore, not only did most disaster evaluation efforts not examine gender issues, they often failed to disaggregate what data they had collected by sex, making gender analysis impossible. Gomáriz (2000) reports that neither Central American governments (with the exception of Nicaragua) nor NGOs gathered gender-disaggregated information during the emergency phase. "Most of the agencies interviewed indicated that they did not explicitly take gender into account and did not break down their data on the disaster by sex nor analyze their results from a gender perspective" (Delaney and Shrader 2000:14). Overall, relief efforts during this stage did not take into account gender differentials at all (i.e., shelters made no provisions for female needs such as menstruation or other reproductive health needs), and the involvement of women's groups was sporadic and ad hoc. It is essential to gather solid empirical evidence from both women and men on the impact of and responses to disasters as well as to increase the availability of funding for applied research that can lead from theory to practice (Miami Conference 2000:3–4). Castillo-Ruíz (2003:5) offers several specific recommendations for gender inclusion: (1) incorporating women's groups and experts on gender issues in project design; (2) avoiding the portrayal of women as passive recipients of aid and instead highlighting both women's and men's capabilities and potential contributions; (3) promoting gender-sensitive monitoring and evaluation mechanisms; (4) improving the quality of available data on gender differentials, including information on domestic violence and the impact of gender norms and stereotypes on women and men living with HIV/AIDS; (5) incorporating sexual and reproductive health services into disaster response plans so that disaster events do not worsen the spread of HIV and other sexually transmitted diseases; and (6) accumulating and disseminating knowledge about best practices and lessons learned.

As suggested by the evidence presented in this chapter, hopes that post-disaster reconstruction processes would create opportunities for positive change for the women and men of Honduras have not fully materialized. Although post-Mitch policies and projects appear to have been pro-women and attempted to meet their ascribed practical gender needs, the extent to which these interventions have been pro-gender—in the sense of addressing strategic gender needs and challenging imbalanced gender relations—is highly debatable. It is uncertain that women benefited personally from their participation in post-disaster interventions; it is even more questionable whether the factors underlying women's unequal access to resources, and thus their increased vulnerability to crises such as disasters and pandemics, have been ameliorated. On the other hand, the revitalization of women's movements in Honduran society and the increased participation of women in civil society activities, though problematic at times, have emerged as potentially positive trends. Although the promised improvements have yet to become evident, the definite gender focus of the Honduran PRSPs, and their specific (although small) budget allocated for gender equity, also provide cause for hope.

Note

1. Traditional gender norms in Honduras ascribe to women the caretaking of children, the elderly, and the sick. Thus, noninfected women may still be negatively affected in that often they must bear the burden of caring for household members infected with HIV.

References

Andersen, Cecilia. 1992. "Practical Guidelines." In *Gender and Development: A Practical Guide,* edited by Lise Ostergaard, 65–197. London: Routledge.

Anderson, Mary B., and Peter J. Woodrow. 1998. *Rising from the Ashes: Development Strategies in Times of Disasters.* London: IT Press.

Berke, Philip, Jack Kartez, and Dennis Wenger. 1993. "Recovery after Disaster: Achieving Sustainable Development, Mitigation and Equity." *Disasters* 17, no. 2: 76–99.

Bhatt, Mihir. 1995. *Gender and Disaster: Perspectives on Women as Victims of Disasters.* Gulbai Tekra, Ahmedabad, India: Disaster Mitigation Institute.

Bjorkman, Hakan. 2002. "HIV/AIDS and Poverty Reduction Strategies." Policy note, United Nations Development Programme, New York.

Blaikie, Piers, Terry Cannon, Ian Davis, and Ben Wisner. 1994. *At Risk: Natural Hazards, People's Vulnerability, and Disasters.* London: Routledge.

Boserup, Ester. 1970. *Woman's Role in Economic Development.* London: Allen & Unwin.

Bradshaw, Sarah. 2002. "Exploring the Gender Dimensions of Reconstruction Processes Post-Hurricane Mitch." *Journal of International Development* 14: 871–79.

———. 2004. *Socio-Economic Impacts of Natural Disasters: A Gender Analysis.* Santiago, Chile: United Nations.

Bradshaw, Sarah, and Brian Linneker. 2003. *Challenging Women's Poverty: Perspectives on Gender and Poverty Reduction Strategies from Nicaragua and Honduras.* London: Catholic Institute for International Relations.

———. 2004. *Gender and Poverty Reduction Strategies in Central America: Perspectives from Nicaragua and Honduras.* London: International Cooperation in Development and Catholic Institute for International Relations (ICD-CIIR).

Bryant, Raymond L., and Sinead Bailey. 1997. *Third World Political Ecology.* London: Routledge.

Buvinic, Mayra. 1999. *Hurricane Mitch: Women's Needs and Contributions.* Women in Development Program Unit, Inter-American Development Bank, New York.

Byrne, Bridget, and Sally Baden. 1995. "Gender, Emergencies, and Humanitarian Assistance." Briefings on Development and Gender BRIDGE Report (November).

Castillo-Ruíz, Paz. 2003. "Integrating Gender Analysis in Poverty Reduction Strategies." Poverty and Inequality Unit, Sustainable Development Department, Inter-American Development Bank, Washington, DC, vol. 4, no. 1 (June).

Centro de Estudios de la Mujer. Honduras (CEM-H). 1999. *Propuestas de las mujeres de Honduras: La equidad de género. Condición fundamental para la reconstrucción y transformación social.* Tegucigalpa, Honduras: CEM-H.

———. 2000. *Encuentro Centroamericano de las mujeres en la reconstrucción.* Tegucigalpa, Honduras: CEM-H.

Chant, Sylvia. 2003. *New Contributions to the Analysis of Poverty: Methodological and Conceptual Challenges to Understanding Poverty from a Gender Perspective.* Women and Development Unit, CEPAL, Santiago, Chile.

Comisión Económica Para América Latina (CEPAL). 1999. *Evaluación de los daños ocasionados por el Huracán Mitch, 1998: Sus implicaciones para el desarrollo económico, social y el medio ambiente.* Santiago, Chile: Naciones Unidas Centroamérica.

Convergencia de Mujeres. 2000. *Formulación de acciones e indicadores para el seguimiento de los compromisos y objetivos de la declaración de estocolmo.* Tegucigalpa, Honduras (March).

Delaney, Patricia. 2000. "Gender and Post-Disaster Reconstruction: The Case of Hurricane Mitch in Honduras and Nicaragua." Paper presented at Conference on Reaching Women and Children in Disasters, Florida International University, Miami (June 4–6).

Delaney, Patricia, and Elizabeth Shrader. 2000. "Gender and Post-Disaster Reconstruction: The Case of Hurricane Mitch in Honduras and Nicaragua." Decision review draft, LCSPG/LAC Gender Team, World Bank, Washington, DC.

Dirección General de Investigación Criminal 1992–2000. 2000. Tegucigalpa, Honduras: Gobierno de la República de Honduras.

Dirección Nacional de Investigación. 1998. Tegucigalpa, Honduras: Gobierno de la República de Honduras.

Economic Commission for Latin America and the Caribbean (ECLAC), Secretaría Nacional de la Familia. 1998. *Los effectos regionales del Mitch.* El Salvador: ECLAC.

Enarson, Elaine. 1998. *Surviving Domestic Violence and Disasters.* Vancouver, BC: Freda Center for Research on Violence against Women and Children.

———. 2000. "Gender and Natural Disasters." IPCRR working paper, International Labor Organization, http://www.ilo.org/public/english/employment/crisis/index.htm.

Enarson, Elaine, and Betty Hearn Morrow. 1997. "Gendered Perspective: The Voices of Women." In *Hurricane Andrew: Ethnicity, Gender, and the Sociology of Disasters,* edited by Walter Gillis Peacock, Betty Hearn Morrow, and Hugh Gladwin. London: Routledge.

———. 1998. "Why Gender, Why Women?" In *The Gendered Terrain of Disasters: Through Women's Eyes,* edited by E. Enarson and B. Morrow. London: Praeger.

Ensor, Marisa Olivo. 2003. "Disaster Evangelism: Religion as a Catalyst for Change in Post-Mitch Honduras." *International Journal of Mass Emergencies and Disasters* 21, no. 2: 31–49.

Food and Agriculture Organization (FAO). 2001. "Socio-Economic and Gender Analysis Programme: Intermediate Level Handbook." Prepared by Rosalie Norem in collaboration with the SEAGA Programme, Gender and Development Service, http://www.fao.org/sd/seaga/downloads/En/Intermediateen.pdf.

Fordham, Maureen. 2000. "Working across Barriers: How Are Disaster-Impacted Communities Divided and with What Effects on Women and Children? How Can Economic, Ethnic, Cultural, Generational, Religious and Other Barriers Be Bridged in Practice?" Paper presented at Conference on Reaching Women and Children in Disasters, Florida International University, Miami (June 4–6).

Fuentes, Vilma Elisa. 2003. "The Political Effects of Disaster and Foreign Aid: National and Subnational Governance in Honduras after Hurricane Mitch." PhD dissertation, Department of Anthropology, University of Florida, Gainesville.

Gammage, Sarah. 1998. "La dimensión de género en la pobreza, la desigualdad y la reforma macroeconómica en America Latina." In *Política macroeconómica y pobreza en América Latina y el Caribe,* edited by E. Ganuza, L. Taylor, and S. Morley. Comisión Económica para América Latina y el Caribe, UNDP, Madrid, Spain.

Glittenburg, Joan. 1982. "Reconstruction in Four Post-Disaster Settlements." In *Recovery, Change and Development: A Longitudinal Study of the 1976 Guatemalan Earthquake,* vol. 2, edited by F. L. Bates, 634–707. Athens: University of Georgia Press.

Gobierno de Honduras. 2001. *Poverty Reduction Strategy Paper.* Tegucigalpa, Honduras: Gobierno de Honduras. English version available at www.worldbank.org/poverty/.

Gomáriz, Enrique. 2000. "Género y desastres: Introducción conceptual y análisis de situación." In *La crisis del Huracán Mitch en Centroamérica.*

San José, Costa Rica: Fundación Género y Sociedad (GESO) y Banco Interamericano de Desarrollo (BID).

Government of the Republic of Honduras. 2000. *Interim Poverty Reduction Strategy Paper.* Tegucigalpa, Honduras (April 13).

Gupta, Rao G. 2002. "Vulnerability and Resilience: Gender and HIV/AIDS in Latin America and the Caribbean." Working paper, International Center for Research on Women, Washington, DC.

Heise, L., M. Ellsberg, and M. Gottemoeller. 1999. "Ending Violence against Women." *Population Reports* 27, no. 4, http://www.infoforhealth.org/pr/l11/violence.pdf.

Kabeer, Naila. 1997. "Tactics and Trade-Offs: Revisiting the Links between Gender and Poverty." *IDS Bulletin* 28, no. 3: 1–13.

Kennedy, Mirta. 1999. "Civic Participation of Women in the Reconstruction Process (CEM-H)." The Center for Women's Studies—Honduras.

McCarrher, D. R., and P. E. Bailey. 2000. *Evaluation of a Domestic Violence Mass-Media Campaign Targeted at Men.* Campaña Desastre, Nicaragua: Family Health International.

Miami Conference on Reaching Women and Children in Disasters. 2000. *Conference Proceedings.* Florida International University, Miami (June 4–6).

Moraga, E. 1999. "Género y desastres: Introducción conceptual y criterios operativos." In *La crisis del Huracán Mitch en Centroamérica.* San José, Costa Rica: Fundación Género y Sociedad.

Oliver-Smith, Anthony. 1991. "Successes and Failures in Post-Disaster Resettlement." *Disasters* 15, no. 1: 12–23.

Olivo Díaz López, María-Jesús. 2002. "Relocating Morolica: Vulnerability and Resilience in Post-Mitch Honduras." PhD dissertation, Department of Anthropology, University of Florida, Gainesville.

Pan-American Health Organization (PAHO). 2002. *The UNGASS, Gender and Women's Vulnerability to HIV/AIDS in Latin America and the Caribbean.* Report prepared by Hilary Anderson, Karen Marcovici, and Kathleen Taylor. Program on Women, Health and Development. Division of Health and Human Development with the Program on AIDS and Sexually Transmitted Infections. Regional Office of the World Health Organization. Washington, DC: Pan-American Health Organization.

Peacock, Walter Gillis, Betty Hearn Morrow, and Hugh Gladwin. 1997. *Hurricane Andrew: Ethnicity, Gender and the Sociology of Disasters.* London: Routledge.

Rossell, Z. M. 2001. "Demandas del movimiento social de mujeres y estrategias institucionales para erradicar la pobreza de Honduras." Working paper, Universidad Nacional Autónoma, Tegucigalpa, Honduras.

Spring, Anita. 1995. *Agricultural Development and Gender Issues in Malawi.* Lanham, MD: University Press of America.

Trócaire. 2004. "Combating Rural Poverty in Honduras and Nicaragua? Lessons for a New Generation of PRSPs." Policy briefing (August), Irish Catholic Agency for World Development (Trócaire), County Kildare, Ireland.

United Nations Development Programme (UNDP). 1999. *Informe sobre desarrollo humano Honduras 1999: El impacto de un huracán.* Tegucigalpa, Honduras: PNUD.

United Nations Division for the Advancement of Women (UN/DAW) and Inter-Agency Secretariat of the International Strategy for Disaster Reduction (UN/ISDR). 2001. "Environmental Management and the Mitigation of Natural Disasters: A Gender Perspective; Report of the Expert Group Meeting. Ankara, Turkey, 6–9 November 2001." New York: United Nations.

U.S. Department of State (USDS). 2004. *Country Reports on Human Rights Practices 2003.* Released by the Bureau of Democracy, Human Rights and Labor (February 25), Washington, DC.

Woodhouse, Mandy. 2003. *Gender Mainstreaming into Poverty Reduction Strategies: Reflections from Oxfam and Civil Society.* Siem Reap, Cambodia: Oxfam.

World Bank. 2001. *Gender Mainstreaming Strategy Paper,* http://www.worldbank.org/gender/overview/ssp/ssppaper.

———. 2006. *HIV/AIDS Vulnerability in Central America: Honduras—HIV/AIDS Situation and Response to the Epidemic.* Washington, DC: World Bank.

7
Tin Roofs, Cinder Blocks, and the Salvatrucha Gang
The Semiotic-Material Production of Crisis in Post–Hurricane Mitch Reconstruction

Roberto E. Barrios

Toward a Critical Approach to Disasters and Development

During Hurricane Mitch, the southern Honduran city of Choluteca suffered the destruction of 3,000 homes in the *barrios* (urban neighborhoods) and *colonias* (suburban subdivisions) that lined the city's major river (Municipalidad de Choluteca 2000). Those Cholutecans who lost their homes during the storm came to be known as *los damnificados*—the damaged. Approximately three months after the storm, 6,000 damnificados from Choluteca resettled in two communities, Limón de la Cerca and Marcelino Champagnat, on the outskirts of the city. Two years later, these communities demonstrated dramatically different reconstruction outcomes: strides toward disaster mitigation in Marcelino but conditions of social crisis in Limón. This chapter examines the relationships between discourse, expert knowledge, materiality, and subjectivity involved in the production of these different outcomes, and it calls attention to institutional practices that either impede or facilitate the transformation of aid resources into arrangements that make sense and are useful to disaster survivors in the reconstruction of their communities.

During the past two decades, multiple investigations have shown that the conceptualization of development as the attainment of a singular form of modernity is both unfeasible and a manifestation of colonialist politics whose associated impositions in terms of policy and resource distribution disrupt livelihoods and alternative ways of knowing (Escobar 1995, 1997; Esteva 1993; Zea 2001). Subsequent critical studies of development and modernization have added new levels of complexity to these observations by accounting for the processes through which the multiple practices collectively known as "development" are contested, subverted, and transformed into multiple modernities that do not fall neatly within a linear notion of progress (Gaonkar 2001). However, modernity's heterogeneity is not without problems, and several anthropologists have documented the exclusions, inequities, and multiple forms of violence that can accompany the formation of modern social orders (Ferguson 1999). There is a long history of addressing these issues in the anthropology of development, but their discussion has only begun in the anthropology of disasters (Bankoff 1999, 2004; Bankoff and Hilhorst 2004; Oliver-Smith 2001).

Critical examinations of development are relevant to the study of disasters because leading paradigms in the field were conceived using many of the premises of linear/singular imaginings of modernization (Berke, Kartez, and Wenger 1996; Blaikie et al. 1994; Cuny 1983; Lewis 1999). One of the foundational texts in the field, Frederick C. Cuny's *Disasters and Development,* proposes the development of vulnerable societies through a rigid application of technologies as the primary means of mitigating disasters. Cuny (1983:7) introduces the discussion of development to disaster studies with the following declaration:

> Some disaster specialists argue that any examination of disasters in the context of development automatically becomes political, that reducing vulnerability of the poor is a development question, and that such questions must be answered politically. I agree. But this should not deter us from examining disasters individually. For a society to develop, many obstacles must be overcome, and it is important that each be examined thoroughly in its own right. In this way, basic problems can be identified and alternatives reviewed. This is important in the field of disasters for even if all players have the best of intentions, current practice complicates—not complements—development.

Later in the text Cuny specifies what he means by *development* through his use of two images. The first is titled "Flooding and Its Causes" and is meant to represent "the poorer developing nations, which we call the Third World" (Cuny 1983:3). The image is a line drawing of a three-dimensional landscape where far-off mountains are labeled "poor farming techniques"; urban areas, "increased population prevents ground absorption of water"; and farmlands, "flood plains in rural areas attract farmers because of fertile land" (ibid.: 34). The second image, "Flood Plain Management," shows development in action. The faraway hills are now labeled "contouring of farmland"; the central city is labeled "dikes, walls, etc. help protect urban areas"; and farmlands are dissected by "channels leading to water reservoirs" (ibid.: 35).

Cuny's presentation is of interest because it assumes that a singular application of technologies will universally harness the constellation of nonhuman agencies we call nature. However, the assumption that such technological arrangements are universally applicable has been questioned in the science studies literature for quite some time (Latour 1988, 1993; Pickering 1995). Andrew Pickering has demonstrated that replication of experiments in laboratory settings by different researchers can be a difficult task that is complicated by the unexpected resistance of objects that do not always behave as researchers would like. In the world of disaster mitigation, where project managers are confronted by even greater and unspecified types of resistance to their goals of producing specific outcomes, the achievement of particular results through the application of allegedly universal technologies is an unrealistic objective.

Cuny's image of flood plain management presents disaster mitigation technologies as if operating upon a world of things in themselves, objects evacuated of meaning. Plains, mountains, rivers, terraces, and irrigation channels are rendered as if they exist and are experienced in the same capacity from one location to another, irrespective of the varying meaningful relationships people establish with their surrounding resources. The "Flood Plain Management" image is made powerful by its ample use of fetishes, which mask the histories of embodiment and accommodation to nature that are necessary for such arrangements to work in a particular way (Farquhar 2002; Latour 2004; Lock 2002). Thus, the desire of reconstruction program managers to give material form to such concepts as flood plain management carries the potential of ignoring subjectivities of the inhabitants (who are conspicuously absent from Cuny's image) and of disrupting their crucial relations with other humans and the resources that surround them (Escobar 1995).

Recognizing the social and material implications of rigidly conceptualized mitigation strategies like "Flood Plain Management," Greg Bankoff and Dorothea Hilhorst have proposed an approach to disaster mitigation in which "attempts to control the environment" are "replaced by approaches that emphasize ways of dealing with unexpected events and that stress flexibility, adaptability, resilience and capacity"

(Bankoff and Hilhorst 2004:4). But what do such practices look like in the context of disaster reconstruction? And to what extent are the lessons from the anthropology of development and vulnerability theory being applied in reconstruction practice? The ethnography of Choluteca's reconstruction reveals that rigidly conceived natures and modernities still abound in the practices of major international aid agencies. Such conceptions lend themselves to knowledge hierarchies that create critical disjunctures between disaster survivor community reconstruction priorities and aid policies. In contrast, there are reported cases of project managers reconstructing Choluteca in a manner that permitted the semiotic-material negotiation of aid programs, allowing for the distribution of assistance resources in patterns that made sense and were useful to community residents.

The Ethnography of Disaster Reconstruction

Disaster reconstruction is not a monolithic practice. International nongovernmental organizations (NGOs) vary to some degree in their operations and personnel and from one country's office to the next. Moreover, as in the case of NGOs (like CARE) in Honduras, staff members may have various national identifications, different life histories, and different ideas on how communities should be reconstructed after a disaster. These intraorganizational heterogeneities should warn anthropologists against the simple representation of reconstruction as following a singular method or of institutional actors as fitting within a neatly bounded group of Western, Northern, or bourgeois. Recognizing the complexity of reconstruction requires the application of ethnographic methodologies that illustrate why, at a particular moment, a collection of different technologies, systems of knowledge, and human actors work in conjunction to produce a specific outcome that creates new types of subjects and materialities and so enables a particular modality of power (Foucault 1980; Latour 1988).

Just as aid institutions and their workers cannot be fairly subsumed by a single category, the damnificados of Choluteca experience and understand their world from subjectivities that share constitutive histories but are not homogeneous (Bhabha 1994; Farquhar 2002). This diversity poses a methodological challenge that can be met by conceptualizing the reconstruction process as a network of multiple encounters, negotiations, and contestations among a collection of actors that includes aid workers, institutional knowledge systems and organizational structures, disaster survivors, neighborhood leaders, emerging organizations, local government officials, and the nonhuman agency of reconstruction resources. The network's actors engage one another from positions that differ both culturally and politically. This means that actors engage one another with particular, profoundly held and practiced notions of social nature. These different embodiments influence the actions that are considered necessary to reconstruct a community. Actor subjectivities are neither static nor monolithic, and they are often reconfigured through the reconstruction encounter. Nonetheless, the particular composition of these subjectivities at key moments of reconstruction has important implications for the types of practices and outcomes that become possible in this interactive network.

Anything that creates resistance in a network is considered to be an agent capable of influencing outcomes (Callon 1986; Latour 1988; Law 1992). Conceiving of human nature as being able to resist the desire of an aid program manager to follow a particular course of reconstruction is just as much an "agent" as a tin roof that cannot withstand the environmental stresses of a reconstruction site. Both are agents but they have different capacities and, depending on how they are mobilized, different effects on disaster mitigation. Furthermore, these agents can be transformed and organized into different arrangements through a negotiation between human intentions and the resistance of nature.

The network of disaster reconstruction has official and unofficial rules that allow certain actors, resources, and ideas to travel with greater facility than others. The rules can be changed, but this may be a difficult task. The rules are weighted with colonialist, racist, and gendered legacies, tropes of needy beneficiaries, state-building imperatives, and imaginings of modern futures (Anderson 1996; Crewe and Harrison 1998; Douglas 1992; Foucault 1980; Gronemeyer 1993). The objective of this chapter is to identify those operations in the actor-network of the reconstruction of southern Honduras that created conditions of social crisis in one resettlement community yet allowed for important strides toward recovery to be made in another.

This ethnography was conducted over a thirteen-month (July 2000 to August 2001) stay in Choluteca, Honduras. Research consisted of collecting institutional reports on reconstruction practices in Choluteca; completing 230 household nutritional surveys in two resettlement communities ($N = 160$) and eight hurricane-affected neighborhoods of

Choluteca ($N = 70$); recording and transcribing forty structured ethnographic interviews with resettlement community residents; and completing more than a hundred field-note entries (cited as "Field notes" in the subsequent text) from interviews conducted with aid workers, program managers, local government officials, and community residents and leaders. Additional ethnographic visits were also conducted for five weeks in July 1999 and for two weeks in July 2003.

The Politics of Community Resettlement in Southern Honduras

Before the hurricane, Limón's and Marcelino's residents lived in twenty-two different barrios and nine colonias of Choluteca. During the storm, survey respondents sought refuge in schools, churches, and private residences in nearby neighborhoods that were not affected by the river's flooding. The storm's widespread destruction challenged the logistical capacities of government agencies throughout the country (Fuentes 2003) and, two months later, many of Choluteca's displaced were still living in the town's schools and churches. With mounting pressure to vacate school facilities for January's start of the school year, and in the face of continued municipal delays in initiating a permanent resettlement process, neighborhood leaders and local church officials began to search for a reconstruction locality. They found one 7 km northeast of the city along a major highway: a semiarid plain known as Limón de la Cerca. The land was available for purchase at favorable prices from a national bank because various agricultural initiatives had proven unprofitable. The site was appealing to neighborhood leaders because low land prices allowed for the allotment of 400 m^2 land parcels to each family. This size was considered necessary because it provided sufficient separation between housing structures and latrines and allowed for small-scale animal husbandry, the planting of fruit trees and house gardens, and future house expansions.

In January of 1999, a group of damnificados vacated the city's shelters and settled in shanties at the edge of the bank's land along the sides of the Panamerican Highway. They hoped their presence at the site would expedite the municipality's execution of the purchase. Soon after the settlement, a traffic accident on the highway resulted in the death of a young resident; the municipality's delayed response to the catastrophe intensified the frustration of many damnificados. With the assistance of a religious official, neighborhood leaders organized a protest at the city's major landmark, the Choluteca River Bridge. This brought unwanted attention to the municipality's handling of the reconstruction, and the local police disbanded the protest.

After the protest, the municipality increased its involvement in the land purchase: it conducted closed-door negotiations with the owning bank, limited the dissemination of purchase information to damnificado leaders, reduced the land parcel size by half (to 200 m^2), and appointed members of a land commission that would oversee the distribution of house lots to affected families. Under the guise of maintaining equity and transparency, the land commission distributed land parcels by raffling them off among damnificados while ensuring that protest organizers were excluded from the process.

The damnificados who were excluded from the land raffle seceded from Limón de la Cerca in June 1999 and, accompanied by a group of sympathizing neighbors, took over some nearby land 200 m up the highway. The community named itself Marcelino Champagnat after the patron saint of the *Marista* religious brotherhood, whose members assisted leaders in their mobilization. In July of 2000, approximately 4,000 people lived in Limón de la Cerca in 904 households (Matus, Giacolleti, and Portillo 2000). In Marcelino Champagnat, population estimates ranged from 1,000 to 2,000 residents living in 330 households (CARITAS Española 2000). Women in both communities were primarily dedicated to their own housekeeping, but many worked also for wages by vending fast food and tortillas or by washing clothes for other households. Men were primarily employed in construction work, drove taxis and dump trucks, and worked as security guards and wage laborers in commercial agriculture.

The municipality's actions had profound impacts on the reconstruction process (Barrios 2000). The exclusion of community organizers from the land parcel raffle denied Limón de la Cerca its most proactive leaders. The random distribution of land parcels disintegrated important neighborhood constituencies that had provided assistance with child care, helped prevent delinquency, and created a sense of place for residents—what the damnificados called *hallarse*, to find oneself at ease. In July 2000, Limón de la Cerca was renowned in Choluteca as a place of rampant delinquency carried out primarily by street gangs known as *maras*. Mara graffiti adorned major community landmarks, including the principal NGO billboard welcoming visitors to the reconstruction

Figure 7.1 *Mara* graffiti painted on a donated house.

site as well as houses donated by international assistance agencies (see figure 7.1). The raffle distribution led to conditions of anonymity or limited familiarity among new neighbors, which reduced the likelihood of residents forming alliances to denounce or confront mara members. Delays in the installation of public lighting throughout the period of this ethnography—which resulted from the mayor's refusal, as retribution for perceived political misconduct on the part of Limón residents, to sign a tax waiver for the national electric company—compounded the mara problem during nighttime hours. According to the city mayor, mara membership increased from several dozen to nearly 500 recognized members after the hurricane (Field notes, 2001). In the interview transcription that follows, Limón resident Cecilia Ordoñez raises these issues while responding to a question about her acclimatization to the reconstruction site.

CECILIA ORDOÑEZ: No, we don't feel calm because we live with fear, we live with fear in the night, and sometimes one starts to think at what time will they come to bother you in the night? and one sometimes doesn't sleep, because in these *micros* [temporary shelters], they're not too safe, because these things, with one strike you can break them. It breaks, and one thinks of the children, that they are going to be hurt by the delinquents. Because now they don't respect, not even the children are respected now.

ROBERTO BARRIOS: But things were the same in Buenos Aires [Cecilia's prior barrio of residence in Choluteca]?

CO: No, you know, over there it was healthier, yes, it was healthier there.

RB: Why do you think things were healthier there?

CO: Because no, look, here we are all mixed, and sometimes we don't know the people, from what barrio they were, it's that of one to know somebody, of the same barrio, that we already knew each other from before . . . and now we're all mixed with people we don't know. Then, that's why one, one sometimes has fear. Because, like sometimes you don't have neighbors, you don't have neighbors, and one with the neighbor gets along well, and then that's why one is afraid, and me over there in my barrio I had my neighbors, me I wasn't afraid.

Because one has more trust with the neighbors, yes, yes, imagine, me over there [in barrio Buenos Aires], I would go to the market, and I left my children, they were younger, they were younger, and now that they are bigger, now they are more afraid, I am afraid because someone can do something to them.

Cecilia's responses show the material and social reverberations of specific practices in community reconstruction. As she indicates, limited access to assistance with childcare and increased delinquency restricted her capacity to leave her home and travel to the town where she and the majority of other Limón residents worked. The effects of the land parcel distribution indicate that social relations were shifting in Limón as a result of reconstruction practices. These shifts had transformative effects in terms of gender, subjectivity, and the relations between community residents and emerging organizations like the maras. Whereas mara graffiti was ubiquitous in Limón in 2000, it was entirely absent in Marcelino Champagnat—where Limón's exiled leaders, with the help of religious officials and CARITAS Spain volunteers, created a cohesive community structure. Although *mareros* did live in Marcelino, they did not enjoy the privileges of their counterparts in Limón. In Marcelino, mareros remained subordinate to community leaders and elders; were subjected to searches for weapons prior to entering community events like farewell parties for NGO volunteers; and were, on occasion, sought out for extrajudicial execution by an anonymous group of resident vigilantes. In the next interview excerpt, a 62-year-old resident of Limón speaks about a traumatizing event in which his 40-year-old daughter was assaulted by a group of mareros for allegedly denouncing them at a nearby police dispatch. Such actions were unthinkable in Marcelino at the time of this ethnography, but they were part of the social landscape materializing in Limón through the reconstruction.

CARLOS MARADIAGA: Look, because here, even this daughter of mine, she gets up, she wants to work, she wants to work, but she can't, she can't. She has to look for someone here in the house so they can go in the night, in the darkness to the mill. Alone she can't go, because they could come out. Because here, the maras hang out. You should see how they go, yes, there. Then, they can take the maize bucket, they can dump it and, well, they can hurt her, and she, by herself, she can't. Then those things one sees. There is, there is necessity.

Because look, one time, one of them, right here, they gave me this big story that she had gone to, that she had gone to report them, those that were in the mara. And she, and she wouldn't even go out because she was scared. Well, they came here. Look, some people, and such men, to question her. Then, [she] said "and what am I going to do? Getting involved, going, going to declare when I don't even know you!" They told her "but you are the one who went, since there is proof, look!" That is what happens.

Then they came and lashed her. Then that is how that is. One in his home, and you think you are safe, and they said, "if we knew [for certain] who that person was, we would burn her!"

The random distribution of 200 m^2 land parcels makes sense as an adequate reconstruction practice only if Limón residents are viewed as minimally worthy of investment (the small parcels) and as willingly alienated (the disintegrating effect of randomly distributed land parcels). Unfortunately, this view conflicted with damnificado subjectivities, given that community residents existed in meaningful relational networks with their neighbors and homes prior to the hurricane. This is not to suggest that conditions of neighborhood life were idyllic prior to the disaster; rather, through a particular process of reconstruction, the resulting arrangements of aid resources and disaster survivors created new agencies (or amplified old ones) that were testing the resiliency of Limón residents. Most importantly, these conditions were avoidable.

The distribution of land parcels, with its effects in Limón, is just one of multiple nodes in the actor-network of Choluteca's reconstruction. It demonstrates the intimate relationship—between various ontologies and materialities—that is critical in whether crises or mitigation follows a catastrophic event. The different semiotic-material relations that compose the realities of Limón residents and the members of the municipality's land commission, for example, reveal that human worldviews vary in composition and that attempts to favor one of them in reconstruction practice had detrimental effects for disaster survivors.

Flying Rooftops and Matchbox Houses

From June 1999 to July 2000, 1,200 houses were built in Limón de la Cerca by international donor agencies including Samaritan's Purse, Atlas Logistique, and various private charity groups. Houses were built with U.S. Agency for International Development (USAID) and private funds. Most of the structures were built following a similar design. Houses had a single-room 25 m^2 floor plan, cinder-block walls, no reinforcing columns at their corners, and tin roofs. Only 235 houses (built by the French transportation company Atlas Logistique) had internal divisions that allowed for multiple living spaces and ceramic tile roofs that provided better insulation from the hot Choluteca sun. During the course of this ethnographic study, over 300 homes remained vacant for a number of reasons. Because of mareros and violence in the community, some residents preferred to stay in Choluteca until public lighting was installed. Other residents tried living in Limón but then returned to Choluteca owing to complications with transportation. In other cases, houses were donated to people who had multiple properties in Choluteca and were not left homeless by the storm. Meanwhile, some families continued living in temporary shelters (the micros) because they were not eligible for any of the various home construction programs. Vacant houses were systematically dismantled by community residents and outsiders who used or sold the wooden doors and tin roofs.

In 2000, people were not the only agents depriving houses of their roofs. The strong winds of the semiarid plain periodically formed small funnels that ripped the roofs from houses, sometimes with fatal results. The small size of the living quarters, the small size of land parcels that limited the possibility of future expansions, the poorly attached, overheating, and sometimes dangerous tin roofs, and the limited structural soundness of the houses had the cumulative effect of challenging damnificados' (and others') capacity to perceive these houses as adequate reconstruction strategies. In the transcription excerpt that follows, Limón resident María Amado speaks about how she experiences her house and points to critical problems in the Samaritan's Purse housing reconstruction program. On this occasion, she was sitting outside her house with her neighbor because they were unable to tolerate the heat inside.

ROBERTO BARRIOS: I wanted to ask you about your house; you already told me that it is very hot inside.

MARÍA AMADO: Yes, sometimes I have to sit outside . . . look at the houses of Marcelino, how pretty, because there they do have [internal] divisions. They feel fresh when there is more space, and since here we have a lot of family, you know, with all the reduced space. . . . I see that my house is cracking, you know. I start to think that it's going to fall down. One thinks, how many winds will the roof be able to stand? Two houses went up.

NEIGHBOR: Where was it that a roof fell and killed two children?

MA: Over there, by colonia Samaritana [another subdivision of Limón]. Over there they killed two children because the roof was lifted [by the wind], there was some rain and the wall collapsed. It fell on top of the two children.

Twenty-seven percent of the adult men included in this ethnography's survey reported construction work as their primary occupation, which suggests that many of Limón's residents had substantial knowledge and experience in construction. Nevertheless, their repeated requests to housing program architects and foremen for different material arrangements (e.g., including columns to prevent the walls from cracking or securing tin roofs with welded pieces of rebar) were routinely declined on the basis of cost–benefit narratives. In the following field-note entry, Ramón Rosa—an experienced construction worker, neighborhood leader, and small-scale grocer—explains the shortcomings of housing programs in Limón.

> A well-constructed house has four columns, and the horizontal beam supports go on top of them. But not these houses. They only have a piece of rebar that goes through the cinder blocks on the corners. And I told the construction foreman of the [Samaritan's]

Purse, but he did not want to listen to me. . . . They don't like it if you make suggestions. (Field notes, 2000)

According to Don Ramón, it would have cost no more (in terms of materials) to build the houses with columns; the only cost increase would have been for labor, but this was provided primarily by the damnificados themselves. Don Ramón continued to point out further structural weaknesses in the roofs: "They should have put a piece of rebar connecting the [support] beams. How much does a piece of rebar cost? That way, the roof wouldn't go like this [makes a flexing gesture with his hands]." Here Don Ramón suggests that an inexpensive piece of rebar connecting the roof's tin sheets and support beams would prevent the flex that occurs in heavy winds and usually results in roofs being blown off houses. Once again, in Don Ramón's narration, Samaritan's Purse foremen did not accommodate the damnificados' suggestions. Consequently, Limón residents routinely refused to recognize single-room, 25 m^2 buildings as "houses," instead referring to them as "matchbox," "storage box," or "micro" structures. In the next interview transcription, another resident, Jose Luis, questions the "intelligibility" of distributed aid among damnificados, by which he means inhabitants' subsequent capacity for hallarse (finding themselves at ease) at the reconstruction site. This criterion was hardly satisfied in the early months of 2001, given the land parcel size, housing dimensions, and housing policies followed in the reconstruction.

JOSÉ LUIS: We lived better in Choluteca. We had our house there. That's where we were born and raised. In barrio La Cruz, where we lived, but because we came to seek shelter here, without wanting to. Look, that bandit hurricane, isn't it that it took the house and left us in the street? And well, and here, it's that here I don't find myself (*poco me hallo*). But what is one to do, you have to stay.

ROBERTO BARRIOS: Why do you not "find yourself" here? Do you not get along with your neighbors?

JL: Yes, yes, we always get along with the rest of the neighbors. The thing is that it's not enough [the land parcel]. We're between two empty lots, and they don't want to sell us another lot. They say no, that you can't have two lots, and I say, what they want is the money. These little lots, they're very little. Look, from that post to the other post . . . small. The ones they gave out in Marcelino are larger. It's that, over there, they are very large, in that colonia, they have progressed. Look, there's light over there, and even potable water and everything, look!

RB: And who said you could not buy another parcel?

JL: Yes, we can buy it, we want to buy it, but, because they say we can't buy it. They say you can only have one. And it's the [neighborhood] president, the woman that came. We've told her we want to buy another lot, and she says that no, that you can't have another lot, that you can only have one. Look at that one [another resident] in the Panamericana [another subdivision of Limón], she has three lots, look at the big parcel she has. Better yet, she's building another house there.

I wish I could buy another one, to make this parcel bigger. Imagine, that one day I may have money and I want to build a small room to rent. Where am I going to build it if nothing fits here? Here you can't fit another room if you want to build it.

Jose Luis' responses tie together the issues of home construction and land distribution. The 200 m^2 land parcel, when combined with a single-room, 25 m^2 housing structure, is not readily intelligible to him as an adequate strategy for community reconstruction. He wishes to buy an additional land parcel, something that will allow him to expand his house and thus help create the sentiment of hallarse in Limón de la Cerca. His desire, however, is resisted by another *damnificada,* the neighborhood president, who mobilizes the narrative of minimal investments and alienated subjects. In this case, a narrative of undifferentiated subjects is allied with neighborhood politics to create a powerful resistance that limits the capacity of Jose Luis to "make his everyday existence readable, if not give it actual meaning" (Mbembe 2001:144; Pottier 1996).

Budgets, Markets, and Integrated Solutions: Contested Concepts

The Choluteca municipality's 1998/1999 *Informe de Gobierno Municipal* (Municipal Government Report) devotes three of twenty-two pages to Limón de la Cerca. The first of these three pages (see figure 7.2) bears the title *Participación para la Reconstrucción* (Participation toward Reconstruction) and showcases photographic images of neatly aligned, single-room, tin-roofed houses as a sign that post-Mitch reconstruction is proceeding successfully in Choluteca (Municipalidad de Choluteca

Participación para la Reconstrucción

En 1998 todo era esperanzador en Choluteca, la economía crecía y la capital de la agro industria visualizaba un futuro promisorio. Pero todo este potencial económico, fue reducido por el fenómeno nacional MITCH. La ciudad fue afectada en un 18 por ciento, equivalente a nueve barrios totalmente destruidos y ocho en forma parcial.

Informes estadísticos reportaron tres mil viviendas afectadas, 167 muertos y 500 millones de lempiras en pérdidas en activos de viviendas, a esto se suma el cementerio que quedó totalmente destruido.

La industria camaronera fue afectada en un 100 por ciento, la melonera en un 40, la azucarera en un 70, las vías de comunicación en un 60. También fue afectada los granos básicos y ganadería. La inundación provocó una evacuación de 39,200 personas, los cuales se ubicaron en 202 albergues provisionales: escuelas e iglesias y municipalidad.

La Corporación de Choluteca se convirtió en un ente facilitador através de Compra y gestión de terrenos donde se construyeron las viviendas a los ciudadanos reubicados.

En la ciudad nueva se compraron 114 manzanas de terreno por valor 3,573,000.00 millones de lempiras, don-

En la reubicación Colonias Unidas, se asentaron 1500 familias, donde ya se han construido 120 casas por parte de la iglesia evangélica.

Vista panorámica de Ciudad Nueva donde han sido beneficiadas más de mil familias.

P. 18 INFORME DE GOBIERNO 98/99

Figure 7.2 From the Choluteca Municipality 1998/1999 Annual Report.

2000). Not visible in the pictures are the spray-painted logos of the *Mara Salvatrucha* that were an ever-present reminder of the social fragmentation occurring in Limón during the period of this ethnography. Partially destroyed housing structures are also absent from the report, as are the damnificados' denunciations of the so-called participatory reconstruction practices. The photographs use selective framing and "the sympathetic law of contagion" (Taussig 1993) in order to convince viewers that they depict what really *is*. In their supposedly neutral role as a descriptive resource, photographs carry out an act of ontological politics (Castañeda 2003). Here, the reader is prompted to recognize the single-room structures as houses and to view their orderly arrangement as an indicator of effective reconstruction management by local government and aid agencies.

The report's photographs of Limón, especially the pentagonal overhead architectural diagram of the community (see figure 7.3), reflects the government's desire to constitute a social body of damnificados that follows bourgeois conventions of uniformity, restraint, individual autonomy, and care of the self (Stoler 1995). This social body is to emerge from a disciplinary regime embodied in the construction of the resettlement site, where damnificados are individualized in their cell-like living quarters aligned in neat rows, allowing for ease of access and visibility (Foucault 1995). However, architectural forms constructed to embody specific discourses of social body formations do not always realize their explicitly stated objectives (DeCunzo 2001; Foucault 1995; McNay 1993). The proliferation of maras, the refusal of some damnificados to live in the community, the dismantling of abandoned housing structures, and the destruction of houses under the environmental stresses of the site: all this I read as conscious and unconscious resistance to the discursive concepts of aid program managers and municipality officials.

The ethnography of resettlement in Limón de la Cerca raises a number of issues concerning (1) program evaluations to assess the local relevance of reconstruction practices and (2) the incorporation of learned lessons into future programs. I engage the discussion of these issues with an image derived from a USAID report (see figure 7.4). The figure shows a budget forwarded to me by USAID public relations personnel in response to a request for information concerning the activities and evaluation of this agency in the reconstruction of Choluteca. The budget (which was not accompanied by a narrative text), like the Choluteca municipality's *Informe de Gobierno Municipal,* is yet another form of abstracting from Honduras' reconstruction. In this case, fiscal accounting becomes the system of representation through which reconstruction is best conceptualized and articulated. The proper movement of mathematical figures through the budget's grid is taken to indicate that the

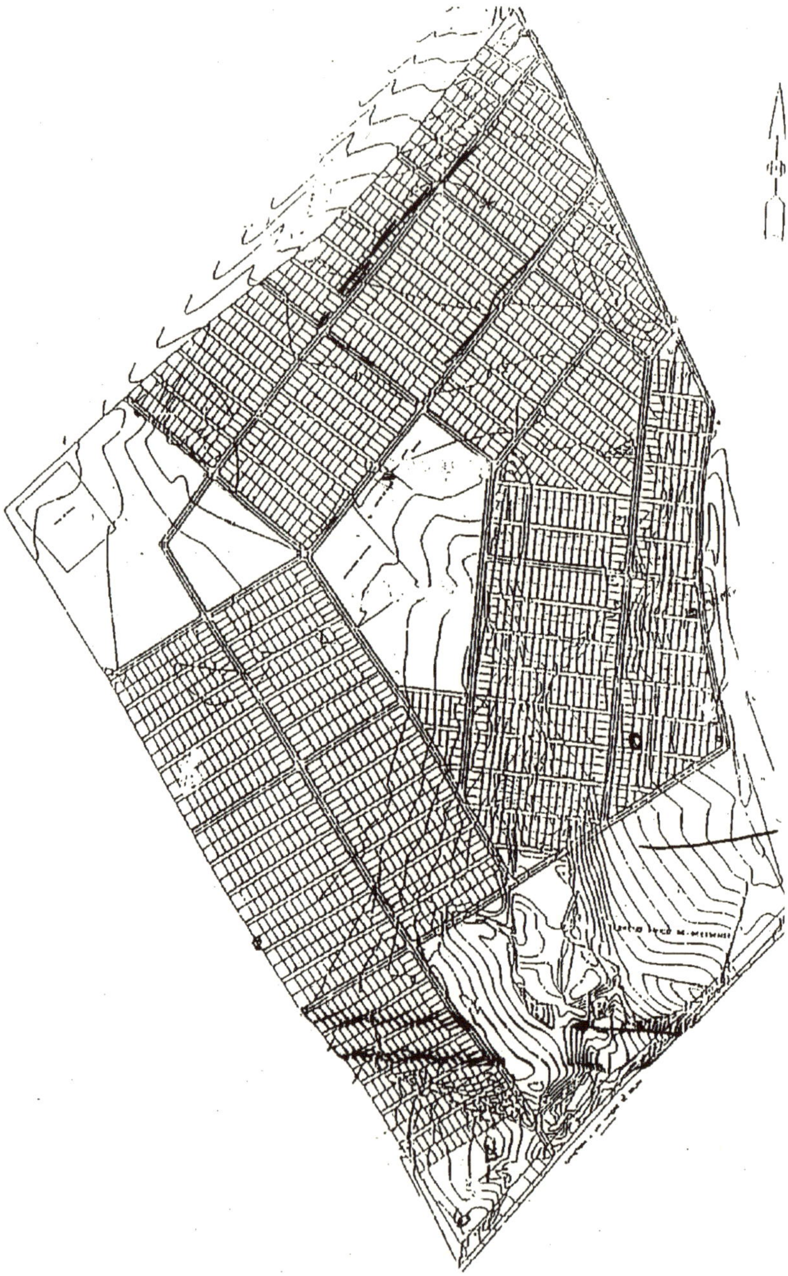

Figure 7.3 Overhead diagram of Limón de la Cerca.

USAID/HONDURAS
HURRICANE RECONSTRUCTION PROGRAM (HRP)
QUARTERLY FINANCIAL INFORMATION
(US$ 000)

Component Number	Program Description	Obligations	Cumulative Commitments as of 03/31/01
	SUPPLEMENTAL ASSISTANCE	293,100	286,779
410.00	Road and Bridge Reconstruction (RECAP)	48,100	48,000
	FHIS/RECAP Budget CY2000		48,000
	Activity Management		0
	USPS Contracts		0
	Evaluation and Audits		0
	Uncommitted Balance		100
410.01	React of the Econ through Agr. Cred. & Tech. (REACT)	56,000	55,594
	Agricultural Credit and Technologies		51,880
	Credit-Fonaprovi/MOF/P.Banks		14,986
	Barents/Carana Design		1,832
	Facach		6,000
	ACDI/Finacoop		5,000
	Fundacion Covelo		7,139
	Katalysis/Fama		861
	FHIA		3,160
	Escuela Agricola Panamericana (EPA)		5,902
	Land O'Lakes		3,000
	FINTRAC		4,000
	Policy		2,999
	Chemonics Intl. Inc.		2,999
	Project Management/Other		715
	Uncommitted Balance		406
410.02	Environmental and Disaster Mitigation	9,385	9,050

Figure 7.4 USAID Budget Expenditures Report.

reconstruction of southern Honduras is proceeding as expected (Foucault 1994). Requests of damnificados for alternative distributions of reconstruction resources—and their calls for considering the ontological stakes of community resettlement—are not deemed to be relevant objects within this system of evaluating reconstruction projects. The budget is just a caricature of reconstruction but claims to capture its essence, assuming a magical power over what it represents (Taussig 1996).

Beyond the production of budgets and government reports, the responses of assistance agency managers to questions about the cultural relevance of assistance programs indicate that institutional knowledge systems did not place these issues in the foreground when conceptualizing the reconstruction. In the next field-note excerpt, AID's National Chief of Housing in Honduras responds to questions concerning the stipulations of AID grants to NGOs like Samaritan's Purse for the consideration of community needs and cultural nuances in post-Mitch housing programs. In his response, the AID manager shifts the discussion from one group of concerns (the small size of houses, the absence of supporting columns, the destruction of roofs by strong winds, the disintegration of neighborhood constituencies, the proliferation of maras) to those of the institution he represents (fiscal accounting, transparency, housing markets). In response to a question about specific stipulations for cultural sensitivity and relevance, the AID manager replies as follows:

> Housing projects were required to be permanent solutions, with an emphasis on what we called integrated solutions. The "integrated" part refers to the integration of the home within its spatial conditions. Homes were meant to be more than just a housing structure. Constructed homes were required to be accompanied by potable water [which is not present in Limón], access to public ways, latrines and sewage [also not present, although funds have been disbursed for these] and that the area of reconstruction not be in a zone of high risk.
>
> Specific requirements for the actual homes were not made as a way to open it up to the creativity on the part of NGOs. We were not interested in establishing a specific design or location. In the whole country, AID is financing the construction of 6,000 housing units, for a value of 18 million dollars. There are 55 reconstruction zones around the country, in 25 of which AID is participating.

> With regards to housing, the major challenge was that in Honduras there is no real functional housing market. That was one of the greatest problems in structural terms. Instead of channeling money for the reconstruction through the existing mechanisms, we had to create a market. We created a parallel housing market, which will disappear when our funding ends. (Field notes, 2001)

In this excerpt, AID's National Chief of Housing shows how his concept of reconstruction—as something to be managed through the discourse of integrated solutions—delimits the objects that can be thought of, spoken about, and acted upon in the resettlement of communities (Butler 1993; Daston 1988). The advocated *integrated solutions* approach claims to understand that a house exists not only as an object unto itself but also as an object in relation to other resources (paved roads, sewage systems, potable water); nonetheless, it omits critically important elements of community reconstruction in Choluteca: the relational networks of disaster survivors, the meaningful relations they enjoy with objects such as houses and land parcels, and the recommendations they may have about construction of the houses they receive. Such semiotic slippage is not simply characteristic of development discourses, it is also one of the key reasons they are so powerful (Brosius 1999; Taussig 1987). As Peter Brosius (1999) has aptly indicated, rhetorical catchphrases like "sustainable development," "participatory development," and "integrated solutions" may conjure up visions of harmonious global orders that are at odds with the technocratic practices (and results) to which they refer.

The AID manager's response also highlights the priority given to the housing market as a system, akin to modernist views of nature, that transcends cultures and must be attended to before considering any other domains of the reconstruction process. In this case, "housing markets" refer to specific relationships between people, commodities, and value that were not extant in Choluteca prior to the hurricane. Home construction in the hurricane-affected neighborhoods of Choluteca did not follow patterns and relationships that are customary in North America. The designation of subdivision areas, the allotment of construction contracts, and the retail sale of constructed houses was not the system of value and exchange through which homes were constructed in most hurricane-affected neighborhoods. Instead, homes were built piecemeal, usually by their owners with the assistance of hired labor, with materials that were locally produced (e.g., sand extracted from the Choluteca river) or imported from other localities (e.g., electrical appliances) and sold at family-owned or chain hardware stores. Hence, the AID manager's allusion to the absence of a functional housing market should not be interpreted as a claim that homes were not constructed in Honduras prior to Mitch; rather, the system of value and exchange through which homes were produced was not readily intelligible as a market to AID staff in their culturally located terms.

The language of integrated solutions and functional housing markets is problematic because it shifts the focus of community reconstruction away from those issues that are directly relevant to people like the residents of Limón de la Cerca. Instead, such language imposes a collection of "objects of concern" that is privileged in policy and practice; this created conditions that enhanced the capacities of agents (Choluteca's mayor, Samaritan's Purse architects and foremen, maras) whose actions presented substantial resistance to disaster survivors' attempts to reconstruct their communities. It could be said that the systems of population management and bureaucratization of the reconstruction process mobilized a modality of representation (budgets, markets, integrated solutions) that silenced the voicing of pressing problems, objections, and alternative practices in Limón de la Cerca (Brosius 1999; Mbembe 2001).

Marcelino Champagnat: Alternatives in Reconstruction Practice

In Marcelino Champagnat, 330 homes were constructed by various international donors including CARE, CARITAS Española, the Marista Catholic brotherhood, and the Spanish/European Union's Cooperación Europea. The majority (250) of these homes had 48 m^2 floor plans with internal divisions that allowed for the separation of sleeping quarters and cooking/dining areas. The structures featured supporting columns in their main corners and external clothes-washing basins (*pilas*). The remaining 80 houses, which were constructed by CARE, differed only in their overall size (35 m^2). Although the dimensions, structural qualities, and internal space distribution of the houses in Marcelino were regarded by their owners and Limón residents as more adequate than the housing construction in Limón de la Cerca, they were not necessarily the structures that some aid institutions intended to build. Instead, the specific dimensions and properties of these houses were negotiated between program managers and damnificado leaders.

In Marcelino Champagnat, CARE approached damnificado leaders with the intention of building more than a hundred housing structures. The program was intended to hire highly qualified construction workers from the community and the urban area of Choluteca who would assist the damnificados with the building of new houses. CARE would provide materials and highly skilled personnel such as foremen and architects, while the recipients of the houses would provide the necessary labor. According to community leaders, CARE's proposed housing design for Marcelino residents was similar to that of the houses in Limón: a single-room structure with no internal divisions and a 25 m^2 floor plan. Marcelino's leadership was faced with a difficult decision. To accept such a minimal investment would set the tone for the long-term welfare of the community. In early 1999, for example, Marcelino damnificados chose not to accept the donation of temporary shelters from the International Migration Organization (IMO) because they suspected that these would become the permanent place of residence for those families that did not benefit from housing reconstruction programs. Their intuition served them well. In 2001, multiple families remained living in dismal conditions in the micros of Limón, as they had not benefited from any of the housing reconstruction programs. Realizing that long-term consequences would result from accepting a housing package that suited neither their aesthetic sensibilities nor their logistical necessities, Marcelino leaders decided to resist the desire of CARE staff to distribute as many minimal housing units as possible. At the time of this ethnography, the meeting where Marcelino leaders voiced their objections was retold as a proud moment in the oral history of the community:

> We told them we did not want their matchbox houses, and that we would rather stay living in the *conos* [donated tents]. And two weeks later, they came back with plans for larger houses and with four rooms! (Field notes, 2001)

In the following field-note transcript, Hernán Martinez, the CARE housing program manager, describes in more detail the process through which reconstruction resources were transformed.

> I participated in those meetings. Especially, the meeting where the damnificados asked that the houses be made bigger. You know how those meetings are, sometimes people get excited. The people said that they did not like the design. They said they were used to sleeping more than one to a room, and that the small size of the houses was not suitable.
>
> The houses were not originally of a single room, but the rooms were smaller than the ones that were constructed. The plan was brought in from the project at Renacer Marcovia [a nearby reconstruction site], where there was a plan and design. We did not hire a civil engineer in this case [Marcelino Champagnat], to control the costs.
>
> The design was for Marcovia. There were two designs, one for Renacer Marcovia and one for Marcelino. It was a matter of cost and benefit. The problem was that in Marcovia, costs were higher. There was an engineer, a manager, and architects, a civil engineer, and a foreman. All of this increased our costs.
>
> With CARE we eliminated the manager, the architect and we hired five foremen and one senior construction worker per house. The construction assistants were the damnificados, and, that way, the houses came out more affordable.
>
> We had planned to build houses with two rooms and a dining area, and to have a pila outside. The beneficiaries wanted houses with rooms that were 36 m^2 in size. Originally, the rooms were 14 m^2 in size, but they ended up with 20 m^2 rooms. (Field notes, 2003)

Hernán's recounting of the housing project's transformation in Marcelino Champagnat reveals the complexity of this reconstruction encounter's actor-network nodes. In this instance, CARE staff and Marcelino residents came together with the intention of reconstructing a community. Each of these actors engaged the other with subjectivities shaped by a complex of cultivated desires, internalized discourses, personal experiences, social visions, and performative realities. The CARE staff had every intention of providing damnificados with adequate housing, approaching them with a plan that was devised for another reconstruction location (Renacer Marcovia) in Choluteca. This technology, however, did not work as intended "out of the box," demonstrating the limitations of its assumed universal efficacy (Latour 1993; Pickering 1995). Marcelino residents thought the dimensions of the houses were too small and rejected the plan.

Faced with significant resistance from the damnificados' vision of their community and the types of houses they desired, CARE staff decided to reevaluate their proposed project. The staff's desire to provide damnificados with a housing structure that was considered adequate and intelligible by both institutional and damnificado standards (i.e., to produce commensurable reconstruction outcomes) was itself confronted by yet another form of resistance: an internalized cost–benefit narrative. Hernán and his staff accommodated this resistance by reconfiguring their administrative costs, eliminating nonessential personnel, and building fewer but more suitable houses.

Discussion

The case of housing reconstruction in Marcelino contributes to anthropological literature on the social production of commensurability (Maskrey 1995; Pigg 2001). Hernán's story demonstrates the relationships between discourse and materiality that are at stake in disaster recovery (Maskrey 1995) as well as the possibility that such relationships may be transformed in order to yield forms of community reconstruction that are intelligible to program managers and project beneficiaries alike. Whereas this malleability is evident in Marcelino, Limón's reconstruction demonstrates how prioritized narratives of cost–benefit analysis, housing markets, integrated solutions, and monolithic subjects engendered powerful resistance and challenged the cognitive and logistical capacities of project managers like Hernán.

The mediation of resistance and accommodation that was central to elaborating a housing program that met the criteria of adequate reconstruction for multiple actors in Marcelino became possible only under the particular context of establishing the nature of the differences between damnificados and aid program managers. In the case of CARE's home construction program in Marcelino, the project manager did not mobilize expert knowledge and a cost–benefit narrative for the purpose of creating inflexible resistance to the desires and subjectivities of community residents and leaders. Conversely (and no less important), damnificado resistance to the project manager's intentions and desires was not interpreted as a dangerous transgression of conventional cliches of disaster survivors as needy, docile, unknowledgeable subjects (Crewe and Harrison 1998; Douglas 1992; Gronemeyer 1993).

This mediation contrasts sharply with circumstances in Limón, where expert knowledge on housing markets, integrated solutions, fiscal transparency, home construction, and equity were continually mobilized to create a *cordon sanitaire* that rigidly distinguished project managers from community residents and that denied the validity of damnificado recommendations for different reconstruction practices. Most importantly, the particular ways in which Limón residents were marginalized—as unqualified, dependent, needy, and/or delinquent—by program managers and workers led to a hierarchical view of knowledge that produced crises, in both semiotic and material terms, in this locality.

References

Anderson, Warwick. 1996. "Immunities of Empire: Race, Disease and the New Tropical Medicine, 1900–1920." *Bulletin of the History of Medicine* 70, no. 1: 94–115.

Bankoff, Gregory. 1999. "Rendering the World Unsafe: 'Vulnerability' as Western Discourse." *Disasters* 25, no. 1: 19–35.

———. 2004. "The Historical Geography of Disaster: 'Vulnerability' and 'Local Knowledge' in Western Discourse." In *Mapping Vulnerability: Disasters, Development, and People,* edited by Greg Bankoff, Georg Frerks, and Dorothea Hilhorst, 25–36. London: Earthscan.

Bankoff, Gregory, and Dorothea Hilhorst. 2004. "Introduction: Mapping Vulnerability." In *Mapping Vulnerability,* edited by Greg Bankoff and Dorothea Hilhorst, 1–9. London: Earthscan.

Barrios, Roberto E. 2000. "Reconstruyendo la marginalidad: La economía política de la reubicación después del Huracán Mitch en el sur de Honduras." *Yaxkín* 19: 5–13.

Berke, Philip, Jack Kartez, and Dennis Wenger. 1996. "Recovery after Disaster: Achieving Sustainable Development, Mitigation and Equity." *Disasters* 17, no. 2: 93–109.

Bhabha, Homi K. 1994. *The Location of Culture.* London: Routledge.

Blaikie, Piers M., with Terry Cannon, Ian Davis, and Ben Wisner. 1994. *At Risk: Natural Hazards, People's Vulnerability, and Disasters.* New York: Routledge.

Brosius, Peter. 1999. "Green Dots, Pink Hearts: Displacing Politics from the Malaysian Rain Forest." *American Anthropologist* 101, no. 1: 36–57.

Butler, Judith. 1993. *Bodies That Matter: On the Discursive Limits of "Sex."* New York: Routledge.

Callon, Michel. 1986. "Some Elements of Sociology of Translation: Domestication of the Scallops and the Fishermen of Saint Brieuc Bay." In *Power, Ac-*

tion and Belief: A New Sociology of Knowledge? edited by John Law, 196–233. London: Routledge & Kegan Paul.

CARITAS Española. 2000. *A dios rogando y con la Barra Luchando.* Choluteca, Honduras: CARITAS Española.

Castañeda, Claudia. 2003. *Figurations: Child, Bodies, Worlds.* Durham, NC: Duke University Press.

Crewe, Emma, and Elizabeth Harrison. 1998. *Whose Development? An Ethnography of Aid.* New York: Zed Books.

Cuny, Frederick C. 1983. *Disasters and Development.* New York: Oxford University Press.

Daston, Lorraine. 1988. *Classical Probability in the Enlightenment.* Princeton, NJ: Princeton University Press.

DeCunzo, Lu Ann. 2001. "On Reforming the 'Fallen' and Beyond: Transforming Continuity at the Magdalen Society of Philadelphia, 1845–1916." *International Journal of Historical Archaeology* 5, no. 1: 19–43.

Douglas, Mary. 1992. *Risk and Blame: Essays in Cultural Theory.* New York: Routledge.

Escobar, Arturo. 1995. *Encountering Development: The Making and Unmaking of the Third World.* Princeton, NJ: Princeton University Press.

———. 1997. "Anthropology and Development." *International Social Science Journal* 49, no. 4: 497–513.

Esteva, Gustavo. 1993. "Development." In *The Development Dictionary: A Guide to Knowledge as Power,* edited by Wolfgang Sachs, 6–25. London: Zed Books.

Farquhar, Judith. 2002. *Appetites: Food and Sex in Post-Socialist China.* Durham, NC: Duke University Press.

Ferguson, James. 1999. *Expectations of Modernity: Myths and Meanings of Urban Life in the Zambian Copperbelt.* Berkeley: University of California Press.

Foucault, Michel. 1980. *Power/Knowledge: Selected Interviews and Other Writings 1972–1977,* edited by Colin Gordon. New York: Pantheon.

———. 1994 [1970]. *The Order of Things: An Archaeology of the Human Sciences.* New York: Vintage.

———. 1995 [1975]. *Discipline and Punish: The Birth of the Prison,* translated by Alan Sheridan. New York: Vintage.

Fuentes, Vilma Elisa. 2003. "The Political Effects of Disaster and Foreign Aid: National and Subnational Governance in Honduras after Hurricane Mitch." PhD dissertation, Department of Anthropology, University of Florida, Gainesville.

Gaonkar, Dilip Parameshwar. 2001. "On Alternative Modernities." In *Alternative Modernities,* 1–25. Raleigh, NC: Duke University Press.

Gronemeyer, Marianne. 1993. "Helping." In *The Development Dictionary: A*

Guide to Knowledge as Power, edited by Wolfgang Sachs, 53–69. London: Zed Books.

Latour, Bruno. 1988. *The Pasteurization of France*, translated by Alan Sheridan and John Law. Cambridge, MA: Harvard University Press.

———. 1993. *We Have Never Been Modern*, translated by Catherine Porter. Cambridge, MA: Harvard University Press.

———. 2004. "Why Has Critique Run Out of Steam? From Matters of Fact to Matters of Concern." *Critical Inquiry* 30, no. 2: 225–48.

Law, John. 1992. "Notes on the Theory of the Actor-Network: Ordering, Strategy and Heterogeneity." *Systems Practice* 5, no. 179: 393.

Lewis, James. 1999. *Development in Disaster-Prone Places: Studies of Vulnerability*. London: Intermediate Technology.

Lock, Margaret. 2002. *Twice Dead: Organ Transplants and the Reinvention of Death*. Berkeley: University of California Press.

Maskrey, Andrew. 1995. "The Semiotics of Technological Innovation." In *Developing Building for Safety Programs: Guidelines for Organizing Safe Building Improvement Programs in Disaster-Prone Areas*, edited by Aysan Yasmin. London: Intermediate Technology.

Matus, Marta, with Carlos Giacolleti and Myrna Portillo. 2000. *Censo de población de la Ciudad Nueva de Choluteca*. Choluteca, Honduras: Centro de Salud del Limón de la Cerca.

Mbembe, Achille. 2001. *On the Postcolony*. Berkeley: University of California Press.

McNay, Lois. 1993. *Foucault and Feminism: Power, Gender and the Self*. Boston: Northeastern University Press.

Municipalidad de Choluteca. 2000. *Informe del Gobierno Municipal 1998/1999*. Choluteca, Honduras: Municipalidad de Choluteca.

Oliver-Smith, Anthony. 2001. "Theorizing Disasters: Nature, Power and Culture." In *Catastrophe and Culture: The Anthropology of Disaster*, edited by Anthony Oliver-Smith and Susanna Hoffman, 23–47. Santa Fe, NM: School of American Research Press.

Pickering, Andrew. 1995. *The Mangle of Practice: Time, Agency, and Science*. Chicago: University of Chicago Press.

Pigg, Stacey Leigh. 2001. "Languages of Sex and AIDS in Nepal: Notes on the Social Production of Commensurability." *Cultural Anthropology* 16, no. 4: 481–541.

Pottier, Johan. 1996. "Why Aid Agencies Need Better Understanding of the Communities They Assist: The Experience of Food Aid in Rwandan Refugee Camps." *Disasters* 20, no. 4: 324–37.

Stoler, Ann Laura. 1995. *Race and the Education of Desire: Foucault's History of Sexuality in the Colonial Order of Things*. Durham, NC: Duke University Press.

Taussig, Michael. 1987. *Shamanism, Colonialism and the Wild Man: A Study in Terror and Healing.* Chicago: University of Chicago Press.

———. 1993. *Mimesis and Alterity.* New York: Routledge.

———. 1996. *The Magic of the State.* New York: Routledge.

Zea, Leopoldo. 2001. "Latin America and the Problem of Modernity." In *Latin America and Postmodernity: A Contemporary Reader,* edited by Pedro Lange-Churión and Eduardo Mendieta, 73–92. New York: Humanity Books.

8
The Legacy of Mitch
Conclusions for the New Millennium

Marisa Olivo Ensor, Bradley E. Ensor, Vilma Elisa Fuentes, and Roberto E. Barrios

As the twenty-first century gets underway, the situation in Honduras is characterized by a number of conflicting trends. On the positive side, the devastation caused by Hurricane Mitch pushed international donors to pay more attention to the high levels of social and environmental vulnerability of the region. In Honduras, in particular, reconstruction has been greatly facilitated by the major infusion of resources from the international community, totaling USD 3–4 billion. There is also evidence of national political transformation, with a positive trend toward increased transparency. Civil society groups, including women's groups, emerged in the immediate aftermath of Mitch and have remained active in the subsequent periods of reconstruction and poverty reduction. However, their ability to influence national processes remains questionable. The implementation of the Poverty Reduction Strategy Papers, the Millennium Challenge Account, and the Central American Trade Agreement—although still too recent to have made a significant impact—are also likely to have long-term consequences for the Honduran population's well-being. Overall, some minor progress in poverty alleviation has been made, primarily at the institutional level. On the negative side, the importance attached to environmental practices has actually declined, and the commitment initially made to improved disaster management has not materialized. And though the increasing role played in the aftermath of Mitch by remittances, *maquilas,* and tourism has helped lift some Honduran families above extreme poverty, it is also exacerbating dependency, imposing exploitative conditions for workers, and causing additional environmental degradation. Health concerns are dominated by the HIV/AIDS epidemic—with half of all AIDS cases in the region located in Honduras (CDC 2004; UNAIDS 2004; World Bank 2006)—and by food insecurity. An examination of these trends can improve our understanding of the seldom explored reconstruction stages that directly follow a disaster's aftermath and can also help identify guidelines and inform better practice in the areas of disaster management and policy. Given the increasing incidence and intensity of disasters in recent decades all over the world, improving strategies for post-disaster reconstruction has become a profoundly important concern of the global community.

From Post-Disaster Reconstruction to Poverty Reduction

While reconstruction planning was taking place in Honduras, there was increasing pressure on the World Bank and International Monetary Fund (IMF) to rethink their structural adjustment policies (SAPS), which had had devastating effects on poor countries. In 1999, SAPS were replaced by "poverty reduction strategies" whereby nations would present Poverty Reduction Strategy Papers (PRSPS), prepared under the guidance and approval of the World Bank and the IMF, to receive financing or debt relief. The development and implementation of PRSPS have since become requirements for governments seeking international financing for development (Fuentes, chapter 5 in this volume). Great development policy significance is attached to the PRSPS, as they usually provide a framework for HPIC II: the enhanced debt relief initiative for highly indebted poor countries (Rodenberg 2004:1). The original HIPC initiative was itself conceived in response to the failure of earlier structural adjustment programs to contribute to the human development of the world's poorest nations (Sachs 2005:342).

The PRSPS have been promoted as country-owned, participatory interventions that take a holistic approach to poverty alleviation. However, concerns have been expressed about whether these strategies have led to any real change in policy focus. "Questions were also raised about the extent to which the initiative would produce pro-poor policies and policies to promote gender equality" (Bradshaw and Linneker 2003:4). The Millennium Challenge Account and the Central America Free Trade Agreement are other recent initiatives that also aim to reduce poverty in the region but have yet to make a positive impact. In the meantime, the post-Mitch Honduran economy relies increasingly on migration-related remittances, *maquilas,* and tourism as sources of labor and revenues. The effects of these strategies on the population's well-being and their vulnerability or resilience to disasters are likely to be significant.

Poverty Reduction and the Millennium Development Goals

In September 2000, the United Nations Millennium Assembly brought together 147 heads of state and government in what was the largest gathering of world leaders in history. The Millennium Declaration adopted by the assembled leaders set forth a series of eight goals, known as the Millennium Development Goals[1] (MDGs), intended to reduce extreme poverty, disease, and deprivation on a global scale (Sachs 2005:210–11). The MDGs constitute an important turning point in the global debate on development and poverty alleviation policy (Rodenberg 2004:iii). They are unique in that they represent the first global agreement between the heads of state of developed and developing countries in partnership with the United Nations system, the World Bank, and the International Monetary Fund. In connection with the Millennium Development Goals, low-income countries are expected to adopt a poverty reduction strategy, culminating in the development of a Poverty Reduction Strategy Paper, in order to organize and give more coherence to their efforts against poverty. In general, PRSPs "are often ingenious, but are all chronically under-funded compared with what is needed to achieve the Millennium Development Goals" (Sachs 2005:270).

Implicit in the MDGs is an acknowledgment that poverty is a complex, multidimensional condition. Indeed, poverty is not simply characterized by low income but is also framed by multiple and interrelated factors such as exclusion from education, chronic hunger and undernutrition, lack of access to such basic resources as clean water and sanitation, vulnerability to disease, and environmental degradation (Sachs 2005:213). The most important determinants of poverty in Honduras include: few sources of employment; inadequate access to support services (infrastructure, credit, technical assistance, etc.); poor access to and low quality of social services (education, health, water, sanitation, housing, etc.); limited access to land and insecurity in land tenure; environmental degradation; low level of democratic participation; and social and gender inequality (Trócaire 2004:4). These interrelated factors affect the capacity of the women and men of Honduras to lift themselves out of poverty and also affect their vulnerability to disasters like that provoked by Hurricane Mitch.

Poverty Reduction Strategies in Honduras

After the post-disaster reconstruction phase was officially declared finalized on the third anniversary of Hurricane Mitch, the emphasis of national and international policy in Honduras shifted from reconstruction to poverty reduction. This approach places poverty alleviation at the heart of disaster mitigation, post-disaster reconstruction, and development discourse and practice.

The content of the Honduran PRSP—conceived as an effort to address the low economic growth, high national debt, extensive poverty, and vulnerability to disasters that characterize the country—was influenced to a large extent by the Master Plan for National Reconstruction and Transformation (MPNRT) implemented in the aftermath of Mitch (Benítez Ramos, Barrance, and Stewart 2005:9). Honduras produced its Poverty Reduction Strategy Paper under the government of the Liberal Party President Carlos Flores Facussé. It was approved by the World Bank and the IMF in 2001 and was first implemented in 2002 during the Maduro administration. Ricardo Maduro, from the National Party, was sworn in during January 2002 after defeating the former ruling Liberal Party contender Rafael Piñeda in presidential elections. However, 2002 and 2003—known as the two "lost years" in terms of the Honduran PRSP process—were also characterized by difficult negotiations with the IMF as the Maduro administration distanced itself from these reforms (Hunt 2004:3). In March 2003, the Honduran government produced a Progress Report (Government of the Republic of Honduras 2003) that underwent numerous later revisions before being approved by the International Financial Institutions (IFIs) in February 2004 (Trócaire 2004:3). By 2004, the presidential campaigns for the 2005 elections once again redirected public attention away from the PRSPs, at least for the moment (Hunt 2004).

The six pillars of the current Honduran PRSP are: accelerating equitable and sustainable growth; reducing rural poverty; reducing urban poverty; raising investment in human capital; strengthening social protection for vulnerable groups; and ensuring the strategy's durability by improving governance and environmental management (Trócaire 2004:3). The existing PRSP and donor strategies for Honduras have adopted a familiar liberal economic approach to poverty reduction. For example, the Inter-American Development Bank emphasizes poverty reduction as a by-product of economic growth. In this view, "human capital" is considered only in terms of improving economic productivity and competitiveness; similarly, the participation of civil society is promoted only if it leads to increased efficiency in state functions. The links between poverty, insecurity, and violence are disregarded, and the informal economy—which represents 49 percent of the gross domestic product (World Bank 2002)—is ignored altogether (Hunt 2004). Essentially, these strategies differ little from the previous structural adjustment policies, so they are likely to lead to the same economic and ecological vulnerabilities that characterized the pre-Mitch period.

A fundamental weakness of the Honduran PRSP is that the proposal was initially conceived as a strategy for absorbing debt relief funds. Implementing the proposed strategies was seriously compromised by the absence of these funds, which was due to Honduras' off-track status with the IMF. The level of implementation has been low, with only 54.5 and 42.2 percent (respectively) of the total budget for 2001 and 2002 implemented (Government of the Republic of Honduras 2003:11). Another serious limitation of the Honduran PRSP is that, despite its stated commitment to improved environmental and disaster management policies and practices, in the nearly ten years since Hurricane Mitch this commitment has not been translated into action and, moreover, the importance attached to improved environmental practices has actually declined. A sign of this neglect is that, of the funds allocated to this sector, only 12.9 percent and 35.2 percent were spent in 2001 and 2002, respectively (ibid.: 19). Furthermore, government policy has tended to interpret environmental management in terms of technical approaches that seek to maximize the potential of natural resources, with far less consideration for measures to address the links between inequality, poverty, and environmental destruction (Benítez Ramos, Barrance, and Stewart 2005:4).

A positive aspect of the implementation of PRSPs in Honduras is the adoption of gender-sensitive perspectives on poverty alleviation, at least on paper. With poverty reduction recognized by the Millennium Development Goals as an overarching development objective, the fact that women are disproportionately affected by extreme poverty has gained renewed urgency in the eyes of the international donor community. Adopting approaches to promote gender equality is acknowledged to be a task required for successfully meeting any of the eight development goals set forth in the Millennium Declaration (Rodenberg 2004:foreword-1). In Honduras, some progress has been made at the institutional level with a basis for mainstreaming gender across government policies set out in the National Policy for Women, the Plan for Equality of Opportunities (2002–2007). Similarly, the Strategy for Gender Equity in Honduran Agriculture is intended to improve the condition of women in the rural sector. Gender-disaggregated indicators are also being developed (Trócaire 2004:12). On the other hand, the extent to which the Honduran PRSPs reflect women's actual interests—rather than merely using women's participation as a means of promoting economic growth—is debated (see Ensor, chapter 6 in this volume).

At the completion of this volume, Honduras was in its fifth year of implementing its PRSP. The effectiveness of the Honduran PRSP in reducing poverty has been rather disappointing to date. Although poverty is slowly declining, it still remains above the pre-Mitch level. The growth in gross domestic product of 2.5 percent in 2001, 2.6 percent in 2002, and 3.2 in 2003 has been too sluggish to propel a more powerful advance against poverty (UNDP 2006). Overall, the most significant consequence of the PRSP process in Honduras so far is the creation of institutional structures and processes to support the prioritization, coordination, and funding of poverty reduction measures. These structures provide for improved coordination and tripartite dialogue between government, civil society groups, and donors (Trócaire 2004:13). A related initiative, the Millennium Challenge Account for Honduras, is being hailed as an innovative approach to promoting development, encouraging economic growth, and reducing poverty levels in the country.

The Millennium Challenge Account for Honduras

President George W. Bush unveiled the Millennium Challenge Account (MCA) initiative on March 14, 2002. Advertised as a "bold departure from past aid mechanisms" (Fox and Rieffel 2005:4), the MCA proposal focuses solely on low-income countries (Radelet 2003:1) that (1) are judged to be implementing sound economic development and poverty reduction strategies and (2) are, in the words of the president, "ruling justly, investing in their people, and encouraging economic freedom."[2] By the end of June 2005, MCA agreements—known as "compacts"—had been signed with four countries: Honduras, Nicaragua, Cape Verde, and Madagascar (Fox and Rieffel 2005:9).

In general, U.S. foreign assistance has been described as motivated by six broad purposes: promoting security; promoting development; providing humanitarian relief; supporting political and economic transitions; building democracies; and addressing transnational problems (Lancaster 2000). The MCA, however, is exclusively aimed at encouraging poverty reduction through economic growth and not at other foreign policy objectives (Radelet 2003:4). A problematic feature of the MCA initiative is its process for country selection, conceived as rewarding only a select group of low-income countries that are pursuing sensible approaches to economic growth (ibid.: 21). Economic freedom, ruling justly, and investing in people are the standards originally chosen for evaluating performance; natural resource management was also suggested as an additional indicator. However, selecting "objective and quantitative indicators" to measure country performance, as directed by the Millennium Challenge Act, has proven to be difficult. The credibility of the selection process has been further undermined by a failure to provide explanations for why some countries that met the selected performance standards were excluded while others that did not meet the standards were included (Fox and Rieffel 2005:32).

One of the alleged advantages of the MCA initiative is its ability to go from proposal to contract in record time: about 6 months, compared with the typical 18–24 months it takes for most bilateral and multilateral programs. Unfortunately, expediency is achieved by eliminating some of the most essential components of a sound assistance program—such as assessing the program's economic, environmental, and cultural impacts as well as its consequences for women, minorities, and other vulnerable groups (Fox and Rieffel 2005:12)—with potentially serious negative consequences.

The Honduras Compact, signed on June 13, 2005, focuses on infrastructure and rural development and is based on a proposed investment of USD 125 million over five years[3] (Fox and Rieffel 2005:10). The much-trumpeted high degree of country ownership and public participation in the discussions leading up to the compact's drafting reflects only that Honduras—just like the three other countries already approved—had previously completed Poverty Reduction Strategy Papers. The preparation of PRSPs is merely assumed to involve consultations with national nongovernmental organizations (NGOs) and other elements of civil society (ibid.: 14), since the extent to which the government has actually taken such outside recommendations into account is not assessed by the MCA initiative. As discussed by Ensor and Ensor (chapter 2 in this volume), civil society groups and women's groups (Ensor, chapter 6 in this volume) have questioned the degree to which the priorities of women, the poor, and other marginalized groups were actually incorporated into the PRSP proposals. And like the three compacts previously approved, the Honduras Compact does not provide any funding for social sectors such as health, education, or technology. The only exception is agricultural technology, yet the emphasis is not on new research or innovation but rather on disseminating current knowledge. Thus, once again the focus is on the promotion of economic growth (Fox and Rieffel 2005). Overall, the Honduras Compact is too narrowly focused on infrastructure and "too modest to be transformational" (ibid.: 17).

The Central America Free Trade Agreement

Another recent development that is likely to affect the vulnerability of the Honduran population is the Central America Free Trade Agreement (CAFTA). After the U.S. Congress approved a "Fast Track" bill in 2003, granting the White House authority to negotiate trade agreements without congressional input, the Bush administration hastily formulated CAFTA (Hunt 2004; WOLA 2005); little, if any, civil society input was solicited (WOLA 2005). The U.S. Congress approved the CAFTA agreement in July 2005, and President George W. Bush signed it into law on August 2, 2005, with January 1, 2006, the date set to begin implementation. On March 3, 2005, Honduras became the second country to ratify CAFTA, following in the footsteps of El Salvador. The legislature convened suddenly for a vote in both countries in an effort to minimize public opposition and discussion (Bilaterals 2005). In addition to Honduras and El Salvador, CAFTA has been approved by the legislatures in Guatemala and the Dominican Republic. On December 12, 2006, the International Affairs Committee of the Costa Rican Legislative Assembly approved the treaty by a close margin; after being revised by the Constitutional Room of the Supreme Court, it will be either ratified or rejected by the legislature. The insistence of the United States on significant constitutional reforms in the CAFTA countries caused considerable delays in implementing the agreement. Nevertheless, on April 1, 2006, Honduras and Nicaragua joined El Salvador as countries that have fully implemented CAFTA.

The agreement emphasizes market liberalization for goods and services in Central America in return for U.S. market access for some sectors such as textiles and agriculture, including increased sugar quotas. A problematic aspect of the agreement is that, although countries are expected to uphold their own labor laws (which may or may not be consistent with international standards), no effective enforcement mechanism is provided for even that limited commitment. Also troubling is that women—and other groups that have historically faced abuse in the workplace—are afforded no protection from discrimination. In fact, under CAFTA as currently drafted, parties have practically no incentive to strengthen deficient labor laws, improve mechanisms for enforcing labor laws, ensure adequate remedies for abuses of workers' rights, or protect female workers from discrimination. Although the impact of CAFTA cannot be predicted with certainty, analyses of experience with the similarly drafted North American Free Trade Agreement (NAFTA) suggest that CAFTA will probably not eliminate conditions of unequal development in the region (WOLA 2005).

Furthermore, the CAFTA agreement has the potential of exacerbating the current economic and ecological vulnerabilities in Honduras and of increasing the nation's reliance on foreign corporate interests in development schemes and national governance. The productivity level of Honduran poor small farmers is very low, as is their capacity to take advantage of any opportunities presented by the opening of the markets. The lack of strategies offered to mitigate CAFTA's anticipated negative effects, or to ensure that small producers are well positioned to take advantage of the agreement's potential benefits, is cause for concern. Vulnerable small producers and female workers, in particular, need support to help them mitigate the threats and avail themselves of the opportunities presented by CAFTA (Trócaire 2004:10). As the impacts of CAFTA, the PRSPs, and the MCA Compact unfold in Honduras, the immediate and long-term implications of these interventions for the population must be carefully examined. Ultimately, only measures that successfully reduce existing vulnerabilities and increase the inhabitants' well-being will ensure that Honduras has the social capacity to respond, decisively and efficiently, to future crises and catastrophic events.

Other Socioeconomic Trends

Current socioeconomic trends in Honduras have been shaped, to a large extent, by the impact of Hurricane Mitch and the subsequent post-disaster reconstruction and poverty reduction measures implemented in its aftermath. However, some of these trends—migration and the increasing role played by remittances as well as the growth of maquilas and the tourism industry—were already prevalent before Mitch and have intensified in its wake. More than twice as much money is now being sent as remittances (by Hondurans in the United States to households in Honduras) as before Mitch. Maquilas, which have flourished since the late 1980s, are playing an ever-larger role in Honduras' export economy. The tourism industry has also experienced a significant resurgence since Mitch. Yet the growth of these industries does not seem likely to reduce the vulnerability of Honduras' poor (Bair and Dussel Peters 2006).

An increasingly common feature of post-Mitch Honduras is for households with the means to support migration to send their members with the highest wage-earning potential to the United States in hopes that they will be able to send surplus earnings home. The granting of Temporary Protection Status (TPS) to migrant Honduran workers in the United States has played an important role in the increasing number of Hondurans migrating north. TPS visas are granted by the Secretary of Homeland Security to eligible nationals of designated countries suffering the effects of an environmental disaster, ongoing armed conflict, or extraordinary and temporary conditions within that country. TPS beneficiaries may remain in the United States and obtain work authorization during the period for which their country has been designated under the TPS program (USDOJ 2006). After Hurricane Mitch, approximately 82,000 undocumented Hondurans living in the United States received TPS visas protecting them from deportation. Although TPS status was initially set to expire in July 2000, it was later extended until July 2005 in response to the continued difficulties experienced by Mitch-affected countries (CRS 2005:5). On March 31, 2006, the U.S. Bureau of Citizenship and Immigration Services formally announced an additional twelve-month extension of the TPS designation for Honduras and Nicaragua. That extension was set to expire on July 5, 2007 (USDOJ 2006).

TPS status was granted in recognition that Honduras, like other countries impacted by disasters and conflicts, would not be able to cope with the sudden return of its large migrant population. TPS visas allow Hondurans and other eligible migrants to work legally in the United States, increasing the flow of remittances to their respective countries and providing an additional source of income that, it was assumed, could temporarily decrease the vulnerability of receiving households. Sending remittances from the United States to Latin America has been facilitated by the establishment of the International Remittance Network by credit unions in Central America (Agunias 2006:5). Data from the Central Bank of Honduras indicate that the annual rise in remittances over the last five years has been about 30–34 percent. During 2005, a total of USD 1.765 billion was sent from the United States, an increase of USD 628 million from 2004. For 2006, officials estimated another 30 percent rise, which would take the year-end total over the USD 2 billion mark (Latin America Monitor 2006).

The contribution of remittances to economic development is currently a topic of debate. Some analysts view remittances as a potentially dangerous source of dependency (Agunias 2006:3). Nevertheless, there are clear indications that households have benefited from this source of income, at least in terms of meeting their most basic needs. The World Bank, for instance, estimates that 77 percent of remittances to Honduras are spent on immediate needs. In contrast, a study in Guatemala (Adams 2006) suggests that households receiving remittances spend less on consumption, possibly because remittances are viewed as temporary. The study by Adams (cited in Agunias 2006:3) does suggest that extreme poverty may be reduced by remittances, at least under certain circumstances. This finding is echoed in an Economic Commission for Latin America and Caribbean report analyzing data from household surveys, which indicate that 28 percent of receiving households in Honduras were lifted out of extreme poverty in 2002 (ibid.: 4). In view of the rather contradictory data available, the role that remittances play in reducing vulnerability in post-Mitch Honduras remains uncertain.

Another important element in the post-Mitch Honduran economy is the growing role played by maquilas. Textiles/garment maquilas and other export-oriented industries have already absorbed many Honduran workers as wage laborers. The United States–Caribbean Basin Trade Partnership Act of 2000 (CBTPA) and the Central America Free Trade Agreement are expected to increase this trend (CRS 2005). Concentrated in the north coast of the nation, foreign-owned and domestic elite maquilas have contributed to making Honduras the fifth-largest garment exporter to the United States. Maquila production currently constitutes one of the fastest-growing market shares in Honduras, accounting for 69 percent of the country's total exports to the United States in 2004

(Bair and Dussel Peters 2006:205, 211). Originally scheduled for expiration on September 30, 2008, the provisions of the CBTPA have been extended until September 30, 2010. The 2005 WTO Agreement on Textiles and Clothing, which phases out quotas to North America and Western Europe and the eventual expiration of CBTPA benefits, may jeopardize the Honduran industries unless new agreements are made.

According to Bair and Dussel Peters (2006:211), in 2003 an estimated 52.7 percent of Honduran maquilas were U.S.-owned while 15.1 percent were Korean-owned; only 17.4 percent of plants were Honduran-owned (or Honduran subsidiaries of multinationals). The long-term impact of foreign-owned enterprises on national industries is a source of concern because high-capital multinationals compete for labor with local producers that could otherwise hire more employees and that are more likely to service the national economy. As with maquilas elsewhere, most of the profits created by these industries do not result in the host nation's markets becoming more developed. For example, most of the textiles and garment maquilas in Honduras import yarns rather than purchase them from Honduran producers; this practice is actually encouraged under CAFTA in order to increase U.S. textile exports (ibid.: 212, 216). Furthermore, the maquila industries in Honduras have a poor record on labor conditions in general, which includes blacklisting for employee union activities and some child labor cases (CRS 2005)—not an encouraging prospect for employees' empowerment or resilience.

A third significant socioeconomic strategy in post-Mitch Honduras is the promotion of the tourism industry as a source of jobs and revenues. The Instituto Hondureño de Turismo (Honduran Tourism Office) established its tourism objectives for the country in 1999, shortly after Mitch. These goals include improving the national image, reinforcing the nation's reputation as a tourist destination, strengthening relations with U.S. and European tourism companies, reinforcing national promotion of tourism, increasing tourism expenditures, and promoting sustainable development (Lumsdon and Swift 2001:78). Also, the World Bank has invested in interest-free USD 5 million and 12 million grants for the sustainable development of Honduras' northern coast and Copán Valley, respectively. These efforts led to marked growth in multinational tourist industries in the country, including ecotourism and culture tourism. In fact, tourism is now ranked first in generating foreign exchange earnings for Honduras (Stonich 2003:125). But as with the maquilas, multinational corporations appear to be the primary beneficiaries. There is little apparent economic benefit to the poor and other vulnerable groups when tourism industries are based on the prevailing models of "Third World" tourism implemented in most Caribbean Basin nations. Many observers note that the recent expansion in this type of tourism is more likely to benefit multinational corporations and the local wealthy than the region's poor and that it is increasingly associated with negative effects on the regional economies, peoples, and environments where it is located (Mullings 2004). These problems arise primarily because of the greater use of international markets for cheap resources—massive amounts of food, beverages, and supplies—rather than using the local or national markets of the destination country. In many cases, licensing schemes prohibit all but the elite businesses from servicing hotel and resort visitors with guided tours, recreational activities, and souvenir shopping. Labor is commonly imported, leaving only the lowest-paid job categories available for nationals. Mass tourism industries serving visitors from developed nations also have a tendency to replace existing landscapes, cultures, and economies to create a false North American and European image of "laid-back" exotic paradises (ibid.).

Unregulated or poorly regulated coastal resorts and associated tourist activities on the Bay Islands (off the north coast of Honduras) are principally responsible for the destruction of mangroves and beach shorelines, overfishing, contaminating waters, preventing local populations from accessing natural resources they once relied upon, and insufficient employment opportunities for local people in the tourist sector (Stonich 2003). Despite promoting an image of community tourism projects at archaeological and environmental sites, Honduras' corporation-dominated ecotourism industry has been criticized as a top-down development scheme with little benefit to the peoples whose cultures are being used to attract visitors (Weaver 1998:102–3; Weaver and Schlüter 2001:180). An example of this strategy is the "Mundo Maya Project," an initiative funded by the Inter-American Development Bank in Honduras, Guatemala, El Salvador, Belize, and the Mexican states of Campeche, Chiapas, Quintana Roo, Tabasco, and Yucatán. Promoted as a strategy to preserve the historical, environmental, and cultural heritage of the "Maya world," this project's promise to provide alternative sources of income for the poor inhabitants of the region has not yet materialized.

Overall, the large-scale bilateral investments in the Honduran economy that have contributed to recent growth in the maquila and tourism industries are mostly benefiting multinational corporations and wealthy nationals. In both cases, investors' interests appear to outweigh public interests in the same way that the Honduran PRSP reflects a donor strategy that bypasses civil society organizations (Dijkstra 2005:450–51; Fuentes, chapter 5 in this volume). It should be noted that current trends of increased reliance on remittances associated with emigration result partly from the lack of resources and employment opportunities in Honduras. Although remittances may be helping to lift some families above extreme poverty, they may also be creating family dependency on temporary and unreliable sources of income. Essentially, these strategies constitute a continuation of the structural policies that have historically reproduced poverty, dependency, and vulnerability in Honduras. An examination of the impact of various trends that characterize post-Mitch Honduras suggests that some positive changes are already evident, including some minor progress in poverty alleviation. Nevertheless, significant transformation has not taken place. Without broader and more profound changes in the political, socioeconomic, and environmental conditions in Honduras, the long-term vulnerability of its citizens will remain high.

Health Issues in the Post-Mitch Era

Conditions of chronic disease are a common feature of the social and environmental vulnerability that frequently frames disasters like the one provoked by Hurricane Mitch. In addition to the immediate consequences, disasters may also have significant secondary public health repercussions resulting from relocation into overcrowded and unsanitary shelters and resettlement schemes, widespread flooding and exposure to stagnant waters, and the destruction of crops and other food sources (Barrios et al. 2000:381). Lapses in food security in the aftermath of a disaster are at the heart of nutrition and other public health problems. "Although casualty rates may stabilize during the postdisaster phase, undernutrition is most likely to develop over the long term among affected populations" (ibid.). Yet it remains an open question whether, in any given crisis situation, diminished food security is the result of decreased food availability, a failure of entitlements, or a combination of these factors (Blaikie et al. 1994). Generalized food shortages may be the result of crop losses and the destruction of agricultural land. And even when household supplies appear to be adequate, women, children, the elderly, and other marginalized groups may face an increased risk of food deficiencies or deprivation if there are discriminatory practices of food distribution and consumption. Furthermore, preexisting regional vulnerabilities and differences in the culture of response to the disaster, including the ability to focus and sustain local and international assistance, are likely to play a role in the pace of recovery in terms of public health indicators.

Although Honduras was one of the first countries in Latin America to develop a national Epidemiological Control System—the National AIDS Commission was merged with the Sexually Transmitted Infections program in 1994 (World Bank 2006:7)—the majority of HIV/AIDS-related policies in the country have been established in the post-Mitch era. In 1999, the Ministry of Health devised the first National Strategic Plan to Fight against HIV/AIDS, PENSIDA I (Plan Estratégico Nacional contra el SIDA) for the 1999–2002 period. In September 1999, the Honduran government approved the Special Law Regarding HIV/AIDS—Decree No. 147-99, with additional guidelines approved in May 2003 (World Bank 2006:7–8).

The National AIDS Forum (Foro Nacional del SIDA) was established in 2001. This forum comprises twelve regional chapters in the central and southern regions of the country and in San Pedro Sula, Gracias a Dios, and the Bahía Islands (World Bank 2006:10). At the beginning of 2002, the National Human Rights Commission (Comisión Nacional de Derechos Humanos, or CONADEH) initiated actions combining HIV/AIDS and human rights in collaboration with the International Institute for Human Rights and other related organizations and institutions. A conference was organized that same year, which led to the implementation of the Program for HIV/AIDS Human Rights in 2003 (ibid.: 14). A follow-up to the initial National Strategic Plan to Fight against HIV/AIDS, known as PENSIDA II, was devised for the 2003–2007 period (ibid.: 20). In spite of these institutional provisions, half of all AIDS cases in the region are found in Honduras.[4] Data from the Honduran health authorities show that a total of 21,617 HIV-positive cases were reported between 1985 and 2005 (Ministry of Health 2005). However, the Honduran Association of People Living with HIV/AIDS, ASONAPVISIDAH (Asociación Nacional de Personas Viviendo con SIDA), cautions that there is considerable underreporting of cases, especially those diagnosed by private laboratories.

Gender differentials, discussed by Ensor (chapter 6 in this volume), help explain the growing feminization of HIV/AIDS in Honduras. Factors that account for the increase in absolute numbers of both infected females and males include migration (a common post-Mitch livelihood strategy) and proximity to the Caribbean. While in transit, migrants may engage in high-risk sexual behavior, increasing the odds of infection with HIV and other sexually transmitted diseases. Their sexual partners are then exposed to these infections, both at the place of destination and back home when the migrants return. The prevalence rates for HIV have been found (World Bank 2006:xi) to be higher in San Pedro Sula (a large urban center located some 60 km south of Puerto Cortés on the Caribbean Sea) and among the Garifuna population (an Afro-Caribbean group from the Atlantic Coast of Honduras), suggesting a link between Honduras and the Caribbean—the two most severely affected areas of the Americas.

It is known that the increase in adult deaths from AIDS has led to a rising number of orphans and vulnerable youth being left without homes, food, health care, and education, but there is insufficient information on the situation of minors who have lost their parents to AIDS. One of the few studies, carried out by UNICEF in 2002, estimated that 14,000 Honduran children have become orphans due to the epidemic (UNICEF 2002). Unquestionably, the HIV/AIDS epidemic is having serious repercussions for individuals, households, and country health systems as well as for the economy (World Bank 2006:x).

The case of Honduras underscores the need to pay closer attention to the context-specific nature of public health in post-disaster situations. The increased risk of food insecurity and malnutrition, and the diminished ability of overburdened health care systems to provide for or even reach the most vulnerable groups (such as those affected by HIV/AIDS), should be concerns of the highest priority. Attending to place—and to the processes by which aid is administered and reconstruction is implemented—contributes to more accurate predictions concerning the health consequences of disasters, thus increasing the potential for more effective recovery and reconstruction.

The Legacy of Mitch: Challenges and Opportunities Ten Years after the Disaster

Around the world, vulnerability is on the rise. The incidence and intensity of disasters have increased in recent decades, with lives being shattered and resources being destroyed across broad geographic regions each year. Consequently, improving strategies for post-disaster reconstruction has become a concern of increasing importance for the global community. The impact of disasters poses enormous challenges both to developed and developing countries. However, a disaster's impact on poorer regions is often more severe because of their diminished capacity and limited resources to cope with the attendant losses. Although the most immediate causes of disasters such as Hurricane Mitch are natural phenomena, their consequences are not. Rather, their impact is the result of human agency framed by (among other factors) social conditions such as poverty, unsustainable resource use, and social inequalities.

Indeed, as the case of Honduras illustrates, vulnerability is a multifaceted condition and has been associated with various interrelated factors including poverty, powerlessness, lack of access to necessary resources (Delica-Willison and Willison 2004:145), and unresolved development problems (Frerks and Bender 2004:195). It has also been argued that vulnerability is generated in the making and remaking of (under)development (Escobar 1995; Hilhorst and Bankoff 2004:7); these authors caution against development policies that create conditions that foster vulnerability. Although it is recognized that vulnerability is not always equated to poverty (Cardona 2004:48), current understandings consider vulnerability and poverty as social conditions that mutually reinforce each other. "This correlation assumes that the alleviation of poverty would result in a significant reduction of vulnerability" (Delica-Willison and Willison 2004:146). It is obvious that the poor are least equipped to cope with the impact of disasters and other crises, but an exclusive focus on providing material resources has already proven inadequate in both development and disaster management arenas. Modern formulations—such as the one espoused by the Millennium Development Goals—have moved beyond simplistic definitions that equate poverty with lack or shortage of income and instead advocate a much broader and comprehensive approach. Although some positive signs are already evident, especially at the rhetorical and institutional levels, actual implementation to date is far from having reached the ambitious goals set in country Poverty Reduction Strategy Papers. As previously mentioned, most PRSPs worldwide are severely underfunded (Sachs 2005:270). Given the more pressing shorter-term demands on limited public resources, disaster management is rarely given a high priority, and issues of risk and vulnerability are frequently ignored in development planning (Benson 2004:170). The unintended adverse effect of this neglect is a diminished ability to cope with the impact of disasters. This is an alarming situation when one considers that the number of people affected by catastrophes worldwide tripled to 2 billion during the past decade and that those considered to be at risk have been increasing by 70–80 million per year (ISDR 2002; cited in FAO 2003).

Blaikie et al. (1994:3) caution against considering disasters as unusual circumstances or as events detached from people's daily lives. The material presented in this volume illustrates the importance of adopting an approach to disaster research and practice that places the "natural" event, which constitutes the most immediate cause of disasters, within its political, cultural, and socioeconomic context. Environmental degradation—a common factor in disaster vulnerability—is often a product of political and socioeconomic factors in combination with environmental conditions. Promoting the unsustainable exploitation of resources in the name of economic growth and modernization, as is being done in Honduras, can only lead to long-term high levels of poverty and food insecurity while forcing disenfranchised populations to seek livelihoods and residential locations in unsuitable, environmentally sensitive locations such as hillsides and mountainsides. This practice, in turn, exacerbates deforestation and increases the risks of landslides and mudslides, resulting in heightened conditions of vulnerability for the affected population.

As Maskrey (1989:25) notes:

> When daily survival itself is fragile, people are forced to adopt settlement patterns, housing solutions and economic activities which make them vulnerable to hazards. Vulnerability to hazard may be chosen as a lesser evil, because the hazard is infrequent, compared to the more pressing day to day problems of homelessness, lack of income or inaccessibility. Poor people are vulnerable to hazard as a result of processes that have deprived them of any power to affect their own physical, social or economic environment.

Thus, post-disaster reconstruction must be a developmental activity that focuses on addressing the underlying causes of vulnerability, identifying and integrating actors involved in decision making at all levels. Paradigms that view disasters like Hurricane Mitch exclusively as climatological phenomena tend to focus on reactive, ad hoc responses and technocratic reconstruction programs, often replicating the conditions that prefigured the catastrophe. Conversely, environmental and social vulnerability can be reduced through the application of targeted systematic methods of data analysis, such as indices of environmental and social vulnerability, that can help identify high-risk areas and populations and so close the gap between research and action. Developing reliable indicators of risk has been recognized by the United Nations International Strategy for Disaster Reduction (UN/ISDR 2005) as a crucial component of disaster preparedness. As Winograd (chapter 3 in this volume) illustrates, such data can be used to create and compare cost–benefit models that can assist in increasing resource accessibility, identifying the most resilient environmental management strategies, and determining the most sustainable land-use options. When applying this methodology to Honduras, it is found that 60 percent of the nation's used lands are now at risk of landslides or droughts and that 50 percent of used lands are vulnerable to flooding; furthermore, people's access to markets and services has decreased considerably after Mitch. Also significant is that fewer than 10 percent of post-Mitch reconstruction and mitigation projects have been carried out in highly vulnerable municipalities. It is safe to conclude that much smaller investments, when coupled with more adequately targeted mitigation efforts, would have decreased vulnerability more efficiently and would have also prevented USD 3.5 billion in losses to the nation (ibid.). These conclusions highlight the advantages of gathering and applying systematic vulnerability data, and underscore the need to improve collaboration between researchers, grassroots organizations, program directors, policy makers, and other stakeholders involved in disaster mitigation and vulnerability reduction.

The aftermath of a massive disaster like Hurricane Mitch often poses a monumental challenge to the national institutions and the population of the affected country in terms of emergency relief and reconstruction. On the other hand, an examination of the relation between disaster assistance and long-term development points to the important conclusion that disasters often open opportunities for positive transformation and long-term development, by encouraging increased material and social investment in disaster-prone areas. Effectively strengthening the resilience of the population as a whole—while focusing on vulnerable groups such as the poor, women and children, and other disenfranchised minorities—requires a comprehensive disaster management strategy that is tied to mitigation and sustainable development and that addresses the underlying causes of exclusion and inequality. Interventions should ensure that physical reconstruction is integrated with other aspects of human development, such as access to employment, health care, and education. Proper consideration must be given to differences (in age, ethnicity, gender, and any other relevant variables that affect people's position in society) in a context of meaningful consultation and participation of communities at all stages of the process.

Current policies in Honduras still contain an almost exclusive focus on macroeconomic policy and so are seemingly based on the continued belief that macroeconomic growth will somehow "trickle down" to the poorest and most marginalized sectors of society. Gender issues, an important consideration of humanitarian and development interventions, are traditionally excluded from macroeconomics, which is conceived as a gender-neutral—or, some would say, gender-blind—approach. However, it is now well documented that the impacts of macroeconomic policies are deeply gendered and far from neutral (Elson 1998; Bradshaw 2004; Ensor, chapter 6 in this volume). As revealed by Ensor's analysis of the role of gender in post-disaster interventions in Honduras, it is essential to avoid strategies that either disregard gender differentials or focus exclusively on women's practical needs. Instead, interventions that address imbalanced gender relations, as well as unequal access to resources and decision-making power, should be implemented if both women and men are to derive sustained benefits from participation in post-disaster reconstruction processes. As Fordham notes, "*active intervention* is necessary if women are to be not just visible but empowered" (2004:182; emphasis in the original). Starting at the early stages of disaster response, it is crucial to adopt a gender-sensitive framework—one that examines gender relations, not just the position of women (ibid.), and one that advocates the collection of gender-disaggregated data and the allocation of specific budgets for gender equity.

Post-disaster reconstruction interventions can also encourage a more equitable balance between society and state by providing new venues for improving political institutions and energizing civil society. These objectives are facilitated by highlighting the often closed or inefficient manner in which political decisions are made by the state and by providing strong justification for people to mobilize. Disaster victims may initially organize simply to survive and to rescue others from precarious situations. Such organizations may persist beyond the disaster period and evolve into more permanent civic groups. The greatest level of political organization and mobilization, however, is most likely to come from those not directly affected by a disaster and thus not preoccupied with immediate survival strategies. Citizens who can observe their government's response to a disaster from a distance and who are not constrained by a lack of housing or basic necessities seem to be better able to organize and detect flaws in the political decision-making process. Such organizations are most likely to mobilize in order to demand political reforms, and not just to request emergency or reconstruction assistance; this was the case in post-Mitch Honduras.

In Honduras, the Maduro government initially tried to manage the disaster of Hurricane Mitch by centralizing power and excluding civic groups and municipal governments from the decision-making process. Despite such measures, the state proved unable to manage the situation on its own and was forced to depend on foreign donors, as well as churches and other religious groups, during the emergency phase of the disaster. Unfortunately, many NGOs acted more as channels of funding than as direct implementers of projects (Fuentes, chapter 5 in this volume). Some international organizations had little or no experience in the region or with the type of assistance being delivered. Some arrived with staff unable to speak Spanish, and many involved in housing reconstruction reported that this was their first experience with that activity (Telford et al. 2004:iv–v). Such lack of preparedness resulted in substandard work and in the failure to assess socioeconomic and environmental impacts. Furthermore, the sectarian methods of certain religious NGOs operating in Honduras were noted by a number of observers, and concern was expressed that these NGOs used their reconstruction activities as an excuse to engage in religious proselytizing (Olivo Díaz López 2002; Ensor 2003; Telford et al. 2004:24).

Had the government been able to manage the post-disaster emergency period more efficiently, it might have further legitimized its rule and discouraged civic groups from organizing or demanding participation in government, as occurred in Argentina after the 1944 earthquake (Healy 2000). Conversely, as the case of Honduras suggests, government mismanagement or ineptitude during a post-disaster period may raise citizen discontent and demands for political change. The Honduran government's inability to confront the immediate aftermath of Hurricane Mitch encouraged civic groups in the country to unite and discuss how they could contribute to the planning and implementation of reconstruction. As a result, civic groups not only increased their cooperation compared with the pre-disaster period, they also experienced significant increases in membership. The government's exclusionary and often authoritarian style of management during this period eventually led organized groups in the country to more than simply requesting participation in the reconstruction process: they also demanded broader institutional and governance changes. In particular, the INTERFOROS coalition was created post-Mitch to conduct social audits of the actions of local mayors; although it experienced the internal tensions typical of NGO coordination, INTERFOROS was bolstered by the challenges of, and the resources made available during, the reconstruction phase (Fuentes, chapter 5 in this volume).

In general, civil society groups, including women's groups, have either emerged or been strengthened during the post-Mitch era. The increasing involvement of civil society, initially in response to the central government's inadequate management and later as a result of subsequent structural changes, has been a crucial aspect of the reconstruction phase. Municipal-level political coordination was also more efficiently conducted through key actors such as mayors and other community leaders. A celebrated example that illustrates how local authorities can effectively lead recovery efforts is the mayor of Morolica, who became a local hero after walking for 40 hours to summon help for his devastated town—successfully mobilizing national and international assistance, together with self-help, to rebuild what eventually became Nueva Morolica (Olivo Díaz López 2002; Ensor 2003; Ensor, chapter 6 in this volume).

It is unclear whether any political reforms would have been implemented in Honduras had international donors not supported them. It is possible that domestic civic groups alone can prompt significant political reforms in post-disaster situations. However, analysis of the situation in Honduras reveals that foreign donors play a significant if not determining role in promoting political change. Crisis events clearly heighten donor influence on developing countries by augmenting citizen demands on the state while dramatically increasing foreign aid to a country. Foreign donors can further increase their leverage or degree of influence over states during these periods by conditioning reconstruction assistance on a particular set of reforms and by working closely with other donors to demand a government's compliance with them. This international pressure alone may be enough to encourage domestic politicians to make key political concessions. Even so, the case of

Honduras clearly shows that political transformations in the aftermath of a disaster are more likely to occur if a state faces both international *and* domestic pressures for change. Indeed, the 1999 Stockholm conference that developed guidelines for post-disaster interventions (see Ensor and Ensor, chapter 2 in this volume) set *transformation,* not just reconstruction, as the objective for post-Mitch interventions.

Although top-down approaches have been vigorously criticized since the 1980s, disaster management remains notorious for favoring hierarchical planning and responses (Hewitt 1983). This despite the fact that more participatory, community-based disaster management interventions have proven to be more effective and more readily accepted by the population. Examples from Honduras indicate that mobilization of "expert knowledge" to mollify or dismiss requests for different arrangements of reconstruction resources can have severe consequences in disaster reconstruction and can lead to conditions of social crisis. Institutional or "expert" knowledge systems enact a form of ontological politics—a struggle over definitions and what constitutes the nature of problems—that must be critically reexamined from one project to the next by program designers and project evaluators, especially in cases involving socially and economically marginalized populations. Thus, the link between this expert knowledge, discourse, and subjectivity must be analyzed, bearing in mind that post-disaster reconstruction involves more than the mere transfer of material aid from donors to disaster victims. It is also an encounter between multiple human actors who make sense of, and act in, the reconstruction process from different subjective positions. These positions reflect different life experiences as well as exposure to different discourses on human and social nature that are manifested as particular forms of practice and are conducive to the establishment of diverse meaningful relationships with the resources that surround reconstruction actors (Barrios, chapter 7 in this volume). Resistance must also be taken seriously as a primary component in the devising of culturally relevant reconstruction programs. In effect, it has been argued that "real change is not going to happen without the consistent pressure of local resistance and social movements against policies and practices that make people more vulnerable" (Hilhorst and Bankoff 2004:9).

As emphasized by Oliver-Smith (chapter 1 in this volume), ethnographic narratives and detailed observation of local-level responses to disaster provide useful insights that enable a more thorough understanding of disaster management strategies and recovery processes from the viewpoint of the affected population. Loker (chapter 4 in this volume) illustrates this premise through the ethnographic analysis of his own experiences as a Hurricane Mitch survivor. Specifically, the narratives presented in his chapter reveal the responses and coping strategies developed in the face of disaster by those who struggle with poverty on a routine basis; hence they facilitate the identification of more effective context-specific strategies for reducing vulnerability. Data gathered through his narrative approach further support the position that governmental agencies and aid organizations must make available resources and mechanisms to enhance people's own ability to cope with disasters, instead of creating dependency on the assistance provided.

The aftermath of Hurricane Mitch in Honduras has witnessed the emergence of new institutional economic strategies—including the implementation of PRSPs, the MCA, and CAFTA—as well as the reinforcement of some of the patterns that already characterized this country before the disaster: reliance on migration, maquilas, and tourism as key economic strategies. Honduras' vulnerability or resilience to future disasters will be framed by the interrelations of these factors and by the degree to which they successfully meet the needs of the population. The material presented in this volume indicates that the political and economic context responsible for the population's vulnerability to Mitch has not been corrected, with the shift in aid policy from debt relief and reconstruction to poverty reduction remaining highly problematic. The World Bank maintains that economic growth is the "single most important factor influencing poverty" and that the stability of macroeconomic indicators must be "a key component of any poverty reduction strategy" (World Bank 2001). At the same time, "poverty continues to be conceived of in economic terms rather than wider conceptualizations of well being and resource access, and thus policies are designed to reduce income poverty via economic growth" (Bradshaw and Linneker 2004:13). It is questionable whether this emphasis on economic dimensions has resulted in a measurable reduction in poverty in the developing world. Indeed, the PRSP for Honduras includes many of the same strategies that led to the high poverty levels, food insecurity, and environmental degradation that characterized Honduras prior to Mitch. The consequences of some of the other strategies being implemented are also cause for concern, since they may foster dependency, environmental destruction, and the further marginalization of the country's poor. Although certain indicators (such as price stability and output growth) have shown a measure of success, the promised reductions in poverty and inequality have rarely materialized for the poor in general or for poor women in particular (Dollar and Kray 2000). Clearly, attention to the actual impact of the implemented strategies on the population—rather than an exclusive focus on their effect on macroeconomic indicators—is essential if a real, sustainable improvement in women's and men's socioeconomic conditions are to be achieved.

A further dimension of foreign assistance is the issue of conditionality (Fuentes, chapter 5 in this volume). Aid conditions have been described as "the tools with which the IMF and World Bank act as gatekeepers for bilateral aid channels based on an assessment of compliance to their policy prescriptions" (Tomlinson 2005:8). Ending the overwhelming policy influence that donors exercise over the governments of the poorest countries is essential. Otherwise it is likely that developing country partners will experience PRSPs as another set of top-down policy directives. Humanitarian aid and debt relief have long been used as a strong incentive for the poorest countries to adopt policy prescriptions imposed by donors. These prescriptions, commonly referred to as the "Washington consensus," have limited and privatized government services, often to the detriment of the poor. Donor-imposed Washington consensus policies, however, remain at the heart of Poverty Reduction Strategy Papers. Civil society organizations in Honduras have challenged the policy prescriptions that lie behind PRSPs and have questioned the degree to which there is any "ownership" by poor and marginalized people for the priorities expressed in them. It is essential for country "ownership" to be centered on societal, economic, and political choices that are framed as much by people living in poverty, and other marginalized groups, as by their government (Tomlinson 2005:7).

The material presented in this volume illustrates the premise that "disasters do not just happen" (Oliver-Smith and Hoffman 2002:3). Rather, disasters reflect a society's historically produced pattern of vulnerability, which is embedded in both natural and social systems. Thus, a thorough examination of the root causes that prefigure disasters, as well as a longitudinal analysis of their long-term consequences, becomes indispensable if the complex pattern of events and processes that constitute a disaster is to be fully understood. At the same time, the multidimensional expression of disasters challenges experts to come to grips with the theoretical and practical problems that disasters present (ibid.:

5). Our study is an effort to meet that challenge. In particular, this volume adds to our understanding of the little-explored reconstruction stages that follow the immediate aftermath of a disaster. We caution against homogenizing, "blueprint" approaches that disregard local contexts and local voices, acknowledging instead that disaster vulnerability reflects "the interplay between local and global processes" (Hilhorst and Bankoff 2004:1). Furthermore, although based on research carried out primarily in Honduras, the issues examined—the social character of "natural" disasters; the need for developing effective methods for determining areas of vulnerability and for identifying reconstruction and mitigation options for possible future events; the role of foreign aid and national civil society; the importance of gender differentials in reconstruction processes; the link between disaster vulnerability and health issues; the contribution of participatory community-based strategies; and the significance of examining local perceptions of risk—all have a broader applicability. By way of a final concluding thought, we express the hope that the lessons learned in our study of post-disaster reconstruction processes in Honduras will help develop models of good practice and encourage those involved in disaster policy and management to implement effective measures worldwide, thus contributing to the increased resilience and well-being of all disaster survivors.

Notes

1. There are eight Millennium Development Goals: (1) eradicate extreme poverty and hunger; (2) achieve universal primary education; (3) promote gender equality and empower women; (4) reduce child mortality; (5) improve maternal health; (5) combat HIV/AIDS, malaria, and other diseases; (7) ensure environmental sustainability; and (8) develop a global partnership for development.

2. George W. Bush's speech is available at www.whitehouse.gov/news/releases/2002/03/20020314-7.html.

3. The four components of the Honduras compact are *highway construction* (USD 96 million), which intends to improve a portion of the principal artery connecting large parts of Honduras, El Salvador, and Nicaragua; *rural road construction* (USD 42.9 million), which will build secondary and farm-to-market roads; *rural business development* (USD 51 million), which will improve access to credit and also provide technical assistance that encourages farmers to shift to cash crops of higher value; and *highway weight control* (USD 4.7 million), which is intended to prevent overweight vehicles from damaging the main arteries (Fox and Rieffel 2005:10).

4. According to the World Bank (2006:x), Honduras has the highest adult prevalence of AIDS in the region (1.6 percent); it is followed by Guatemala (1 percent), Panama (0.9 percent), Costa Rica (0.6 percent), El Salvador (0.5 percent), and Nicaragua (0.2 percent).

References

Adams, Richard. 2006. "Remittances, Poverty and Investment in Guatemala." In *International Migration, Remittances, and the Brain Drain,* edited by Caglar Ozden and Maurice Schiff. Washington, DC: World Bank.

Agunias, Dovelyn. 2006. *Remittance Trends in Central America.* Migration Information Source, http://www.migrationinformation.org/Feature/display.cfm?id=393.

Bair, Jennifer, and Enrique Dussel Peters. 2006. "Global Commodity Chains and Endogenous Growth: Export Dynamism and Development in Mexico and Honduras." *World Development* 34: 203–21.

Barrios, Roberto E., James P. Stansbury, Rosa Palencia, and Marco T. Medina. 2000. "Nutritional Status of Children under 5 Years of Age in Three Hurricane-Affected Areas of Honduras." *Revista Panamericana de Salud Pública* 8, no. 6: 380–84.

Benítez Ramos, R. F., A. Barrance, and H. Stewart. 2005. *Have the Lessons of Mitch Been Forgotten?: The Critical Role of Sustainable Natural Resource Management for Poverty Reduction in Honduras.* Study initiated under the Poverty and Environment Partnership (PEP) and jointly funded and managed by CIDA, DFID, and GTZ.

Benson, Charlotte. 2004. "Macro-Economic Concepts of Vulnerability: Dynamics, Complexity and Public Policy." In *Mapping Vulnerability: Disasters, Development and People,* edited by Greg Bankoff, Georg Frerks, and Dorothea Hilhorst, 159–73. London: Earthscan.

Bilaterals. 2005. "Honduras Ratifies CAFTA." http://www.bilaterals.org/article-print.php3?id_article=1398.

Blaikie, Piers, Terry Cannon, Ian Davis, and Ben Wisner. 1994. *At Risk: Natural Hazards, People's Vulnerability, and Disasters.* London: Routledge.

Bradshaw, Sarah. 2004. *Socio-Economic Impacts of Natural Disasters: A Gender Analysis.* Women and Development Unit, United Nations. Santiago, Chile: Economic Commission for Latin America and the Caribbean (ECLAC).

Bradshaw, Sarah, and Brian Linneker. 2003. *Challenging Women's Poverty: Perspectives on Gender and Poverty Reduction Strategies from Nicaragua and Honduras.* London: Catholic Institute for International Relations.

———. 2004. *Gender and Poverty Reduction Strategies in Central America: Perspectives from Nicaragua and Honduras.* London: International Cooperation in Development and Catholic Institute for International Relations (ICD-CIIR).

Cardona, Omar D. 2004. "The Need for Rethinking the Concepts of Vulnerability and Risk from a Holistic Perspective: A Necessary Review and Criticism for Effective Risk Management." In *Mapping Vulnerability: Disasters, Development and People,* edited by Greg Bankoff, Georg Frerks, and Dorothea Hilhorst, 37–51. London: Earthscan.

Centers for Disease Control (CDC). 2004. "Global AIDS Program for Central America." Program profile. Atlanta, GA: CDC.

Congressional Research Service (CRS). 2005. *Honduras: Political and Economic Situation and U.S. Relations.* Washington, DC: Library of Congress.

Delica-Willison, Zenaida, and Robin Willison. 2004. "Vulnerability Reduction: A Task of the Vulnerable People Themselves." In *Mapping Vulnerability: Disasters, Development and People,* edited by Greg Bankoff, Georg Frerks, and Dorothea Hilhorst, 145–58. London: Earthscan.

Dijkstra, Geske. 2005. "The PRSP Approach and the Illusion of Improved Aid Effectiveness: Lessons from Bolivia, Honduras, and Nicaragua." *Development Policy Review* 23: 443–64.

Dollar, David, and Aart Kray. 2000. "Growth Is Good for the Poor." Preliminary paper, Development Research Group, World Bank, Washington, DC.

Elson, Diane. 1998. "Talking to the Boys: Gender and Economic Growth Models." In *Feminist Visions of Development: Gender Analysis and Policy,* edited by Cecile Jackson and Ruth Pearson, 155–70. London: Routledge.

Ensor, Marisa Olivo. 2003. "Disaster Evangelism: Religion as a Catalyst for Change in Post-Mitch Honduras." *International Journal of Mass Emergencies and Disasters* 21, no. 2: 31–49.

Escobar, Arturo. 1995. *Encountering Development: The Making and Unmaking of the Third World.* Princeton, NJ: Princeton University Press.

Food and Agriculture Organization (FAO). 2003. "The Impact of Disasters on Long-Term Food Security and Poverty Alleviation—Policy Implication." Rome.

Fordham, Maureen. 2004. "Gendering Vulnerability Analysis: Towards a More Nuanced Approach." In *Mapping Vulnerability: Disasters, Development and People,* edited by Greg Bankoff, Georg Frerks, and Dorothea Hilhorst, 174–82. London: Earthscan.

Fox, James W., and Lex Rieffel. 2005. *The Millennium Challenge Account: Moving toward Smarter Aid.* Washington, DC: Brookings Institution.

Frerks, Georg, and Stephen Bender. 2004. "Conclusion: Vulnerability Analysis as a Means of Strengthening Policy Formulation and Policy Practice." In *Mapping Vulnerability: Disasters, Development and People,* edited by Greg Bankoff, Georg Frerks, and Dorothea Hilhorst, 194–205. London: Earthscan.

Government of the Republic of Honduras. 2003. *Honduras Poverty Reduction Strategy: Progress Report.* Tegucigalpa, Honduras.

Healy, Mark Allen. 2003. "Ruins of the New Argentina: Peronism, Architecture and the Remaking of San Juan after the 1944 Earthquake." PhD dissertation, Duke University, Durham, NC.

Hewitt, Kenneth. 1983. "The Idea of Calamity in a Technocratic Age." In *Interpretations of Calamity from the Viewpoint of Human Ecology,* edited by Kenneth Hewitt. London: Allen & Unwin.

Hilhorst, Dorothea, and Greg Bankoff. 2004. "Introduction: Mapping Vulnerability." In *Mapping Vulnerability: Disasters, Development and People,* edited by Greg Bankoff, Georg Frerks, and Dorothea Hilhorst, 1–9. London: Earthscan.

Hunt, Sarah. 2004. *Honduras Update.* Tegucigalpa, Honduras: Trócaire (May).

International Strategy for Disaster Reduction (ISDR). 2002. *Living with Risk—A Global Review of Disaster Reduction.* Interagency Secretariat of the International Strategy for Disaster Reduction. New York: United Nations.

Lancaster, Carol. 2000. *Transforming Foreign Aid: United States Assistance in the 21st Century.* Washington, DC: Institute for International Economics.

Latin America Monitor. 2006. "Rapid Rise in Remittances." Economic analysis, www.latinamericamonitor.com/file/30640/rapid-rise-in-remittances.html.

Lumsdon, Les, and Jonathan Swift. 2001. *Tourism in Latin America.* London: Continuum.

Maskrey, Andrew. 1989. *Disaster Mitigation: A Community Based Approach.* Oxford, UK: Oxfam.

Ministry of Health. 2005. *Epidemiological Data on HIV/AIDS.* Honduran Department of HIV/AIDS and Sexually Transmitted Infections. Tegucigalpa, Honduras: Ministry of Health.

Mullings, Beverley. 2004. "Caribbean Tourism: Trouble in Paradise?" In *Introduction to the Pan-Caribbean,* edited by Tracey Skelton, 97–117. London: Arnold.

Oliver-Smith, Anthony, and Susanna Hoffman. 2002. "Introduction: Why Anthropologists Should Study Disasters." In *Catastrophe and Culture: The Anthropology of Disaster,* edited by Anthony Oliver-Smith and Susanna Hoffman, 3–22. Santa Fe, NM: School of American Research.

Olivo Díaz López, María-Jesús. 2002. "Relocating Morolica: Vulnerability and Resilience in Post-Mitch Honduras." PhD dissertation, Department of Anthropology, University of Florida, Gainesville.

Radelet, Steven. 2003. *Challenging Foreign Aid: A Policymaker's Guide to the Millennium Challenge Account.* Washington, DC: Center for Global Development.

Rodenberg, Birte. 2004. *Gender and Poverty Reduction. New Conceptual Approaches in International Development Cooperation.* Bonn: German Development Institute.

Sachs, Jeffrey. 2005. *The End of Poverty: Economic Possibilities for Our Time.* New York: Penguin.

Stonich, Susan. 2003. "The Political Ecology of Marine Protected Areas: The Case of the Bay Islands." In *Tourism and Development in Tropical Islands: Political Ecology Perspectives,* edited by Stefan Gössling, 121–47. Cheltenham, UK: Edward Elgar.

Telford, John, Margaret Arnold, and Alberto Harth, with ASONOG (Asociación de Organismos No Gubernamentales de Honduras). 2004. *Learning Lessons from Disaster Recovery: The Case of Honduras.* Washington, DC: World Bank.

Tomlinson, Brian. 2005. "Politics of the Millennium Development Goals: Contributing to Strategies for Ending Poverty? A Summary of the Main Arguments and Conclusions." www.ccic.ca/e/docs/002_aid_2005-05_politics_of_mdgs_summary.pdf.

Trócaire. 2004. "Are PRSPs Combating Rural Poverty in Honduras and Nicaragua? Lessons for a New Generation of PRSPs." County Kildare, Ireland: Trócaire (Irish Catholic Agency for World Development).

UNICEF. 2002. "Niñez huérfana afectada o conviviendo con HIV/AIDS in Honduras." Tegucigalpa, Honduras: UNICEF.

United Nations Development Programme (UNDP). 2006. "Country Evaluations: Assessment of Development Results—Honduras." UNDP Evaluation Office. Available at http://www.undp.org/eo/documents/ARD/ARD_Reports/ARD_Honduras.pdf.

United Nations International Strategy for Disaster Reduction (UN/ISDR). 2005. *Strategic Directions for the ISDR System to Assist the Implementation of the Hyogo Framework for Action 2005–2015. Building the Resilience of Nations and Communities to Disasters.* Inter-Agency Task Force on Disaster Reduction, Geneva. Available at http://www.unisdr.org/eng/task%20force/tf-meeting-11th-eng.htm.

United Nations Joint Programme on HIV/AIDS (UNAIDS). 2004. *Honduras: Country Situation Analysis.* Available at http://www.unaids.org/en/geographical+area/by+country/honduras.asp#.

United States Department of Justice (USDOJ). 2006. *Extension of Work Authorization for TPS Recipients from Burundi, Sudan, Honduras, Nicaragua, El Salvador, Liberia, and Somalia.* Office of Special Counsel for Immigration-Related Unfair Employment Practices, Civil Rights Division, U.S. Department of Justice, Washington, DC. Available at http://www.usdoj.gov/crt/osc/htm/work_extension.html.

Washington Office on Latin America (WOLA). 2005. *United States–Central America Free Trade Agreement.* Available at http://www.wola.org/index.php?&option=com_content&task=blogsection&id=6&Itemid=&topic=Honduras.

Weaver, David B. 1998. *Ecotourism in the Less Developed World.* Wallingford, UK: CAB International.

Weaver, David B., and Regina Schlüter. 2001. "Latin America and the Caribbean." In *The Encyclopedia of Ecotourism,* edited by David B. Weaver, 173–91. Wallingford, UK: CAB International.

World Bank. 2001. *Gender Mainstreaming Strategy Paper.* http://www.worldbank.org/gender/overview/ssp/ssppaper.

———. 2002. *Governance and Anti-Corruption in Honduras: An Input for Action.* Washington, DC: World Bank.

———. 2006. *HIV/AIDS Vulnerability in Central America: Honduras—HIV/AIDS Situation and Response to the Epidemic.* Washington, DC: World Bank.

About the Contributors

Roberto E. Barrios is assistant professor of anthropology at Southern Illinois University, Carbondale. He has conducted research among displaced populations in Mexico and Central America. His work examines how refugees and those displaced by disasters interact with assistance agencies as they re-create their communities in new locations. He is currently conducting research on government–community relations in the reconstruction of New Orleans after Hurricane Katrina.

Bradley E. Ensor is associate professor of anthropology at Eastern Michigan University. He conducts research on prehistoric and ethnohistoric political economy and political ecology, on disaster vulnerability, and on issues related to forced migration. He has worked in Mesoamerica, North America, and Albania.

Marisa Olivo Ensor, the editor of this volume, is assistant professor of anthropology at the American University in Cairo. She has researched and published on disaster-, conflict-, and development-induced displacement in Latin America, North Africa, Spain, and the United States. She recently completed a study of the impact of Katrina on Honduran migrant children in New Orleans and is currently conducting research on intergenerational relations, nation building, and survival among Sudanese families in Egypt and South Sudan displaced by conflict and environmental problems.

Vilma Elisa Fuentes is associate professor of political science at Santa Fe College. A political scientist, she conducts research on Central American politics and governance, exploring how both are affected by foreign aid and other exogenous factors.

William M. Loker is professor of anthropology at California State University, Chico. He has conducted research in Central and South America with a particular emphasis on Honduras. His primary research interests include human ecology and the causes and consequences of environmental change. He edited a collection entitled *Globalization and the Rural Poor in Latin America* (2001) and is the author of *Changing Places: Environment, Development and Social Change in Rural Honduras* (2004).

Anthony Oliver-Smith is professor emeritus of anthropology at the University of Florida and was Munich Re Foundation Chair of Social Vulnerability at the Institute for Environment and Human Security at the United Nations University in Bonn during 2007/2008. A leading expert on the social science of disasters and resettlement, his books include *The Martyred City: Death and Rebirth in the Andes* (1992); he has co-edited *The Angry Earth: Disaster in Anthropological Perspective* (1999) and *Catastrophe and Culture* (2002), both with Susanna M. Hoffman. He has most recently edited *Development and Dispossession: The Crisis of Forced Displacement and Resettlement* (2009).

Manuel Winograd is an advisor on socioecological dynamics in the Natural Resources and Vulnerability Programme at the European Environment Agency, Copenhagen, Denmark, a former visiting scientist at CIRAD (*Centre de Coopération Internationale en Recherche Agronomique pour le Développement,* Montpellier, France), and a senior fellow at CIAT (International Center for Tropical Agriculture, Cali, Colombia). An environmental scientist, he works on the production of sustainability and vulnerability indicators as well as decision-making and information tools. His research examines the assessment of climate variability and of adaptation to climate change, land-use models and scenarios, and the strengthening of institutional capacity.

Index